AND YET THEY PERSISTED

AND YET THEY PERSISTED

HOW AMERICAN WOMEN WON THE RIGHT TO VOTE

Johanna Neuman

WILEY Blackwell

Registered Office
John Wiley & Sons, Inc., 111 River Street, Hoboken, NJ 07030, USA

Editorial Office
111 River Street, Hoboken, NJ 07030, USA

For details of our global editorial offices, customer services, and more information about Wiley products visit us at www.wiley.com.

Wiley also publishes its books in a variety of electronic formats and by print-on-demand. Some content that appears in standard print versions of this book may not be available in other formats.

Parts of this book first appeared in *Gilded Suffragists: The New York Suffragists Who Fought for Women's Right to Vote* (NYU Press, 2017) and in the *Journal of Gilded Age and Progressive Era*, July 2017, "Who Won Women's Suffrage? A Case for 'Mere Men'" (2016). They are reprinted here with the permission of New York University Press and of Cambridge University Press, respectfully.

Library of Congress Cataloging-in-Publication Data
Names: Neuman, Johanna, author.
Title: And yet they persisted : how American women won the right to vote / Johanna Neuman.
Description: Hoboken, NJ : Wiley-Blackwell, 2020. | Includes bibliographical references and index.
Identifiers: LCCN 2019030156 (print) | LCCN 2019030157 (ebook) | ISBN 9781119530831 (paperback) | ISBN 9781119530855 (adobe pdf) | ISBN 9781119530794 (epub)
Subjects: LCSH: Women–Suffrage–United States–History.
Classification: LCC JK1896 .N48 2020 (print) | LCC JK1896 (ebook) | DDC 324.6/230973–dc23
LC record available at https://lccn.loc.gov/2019030156
LC ebook record available at https://lccn.loc.gov/2019030157

Cover Design: Wiley
Cover Images: © Everett Historical/Shutterstock; "Men's League for Women Suffrage March in 1915 Parade" Bryn Mawr College Library, Special Collections; African American Photographs Assembled for 1900 Paris Exposition/Library of Congress

Set in 10.5/12 pt New Baskerville by SPi Global, Pondicherry, India

Printed in the United States of America

V10015276_110119

To the generation of my past:
Ruth Gribin, Dorothy Leeb, Evelyn Neuman, Roz Steinhauser

And to the generation of my future:
Maeve Burke, Amy and Rebecca Dersh, Lily and Hazel Francois,
Lane Garnett, Katherine and Alexandra Hughey, Arden Johnson,
Penelope Lopez, Ella Lyddan, Pearl Nessen, Saafi and Ndeji
Omekongo, Lauren and Rachel Thompson

Contents

Preface

The Mississippi Delta, sometimes called "the most southern place on earth," resonates with the racial history of cotton, slavery, and the blues. In 1962, it became known for something more. Deep in Sunflower County, a 44-year-old African American woman in ill health and with little education went to the county courthouse in Indianola to register to vote. For asserting this right, Fannie Lou Hamer, a poor sharecropper who made her living off the soil, was forced out of her home, fired from her job, menaced by drive-by shooters, and beaten by white jailers in a sexualized attack so severely that she was in pain for the rest of her life.

Had she done little else with her life, Fannie Lou Hamer might have been little remembered today, a statistic of a life lived in hardship. But like generations of women before her and since, she rose up like a lion, demanding her right to vote. Her defiance fueled a grassroots movement in Mississippi in 1964, when young college students moved by the persistent scourge of racism risked their own lives to help those, like Hamer, who had been turned away at the courthouse door. Resistance from white segregationists was fierce. Both sides understood that the vote could unlock other reforms, that it was a tool of empowerment. Often, after dangerous encounters with the white male political establishment, she became the singing voice of her corner of the campaign, calming young activists with her rendition of "This Little Light of Mine." Her testimony and her raw courage made her a memorable figure. When W. D. Marlow, owner of the plantation where she worked as time and record manager for sharecroppers, first heard she'd gone to the courthouse, he said menacingly, "We're not ready for that in Mississippi, now." To which Fannie Lou Hamer replied, "Mr. Marlow, I didn't go down there to register for you. I went down to register for myself."

For two centuries, American women of all races "went down to register" for themselves. From before the nation's founding in 1776 until the ratification of the Nineteenth Amendment in 1920, they sought the vote, sometimes individually, often in groups, sometimes alone, often with men at their side. In the 1950s and 1960s, African American women fought again, battling Jim Crow laws in the South that barred black Americans from quality education and public accommodations – and kept them from the ballot box. Obstacles in their path included literacy tests, poll taxes, and residency requirements, all meant to protect white supremacy. And later still other women of color – Asian Americans, Hispanic Americans, and Native Americans – were empowered by new minority language ballots to participate fully in the promise of the nation's elections. Today American women are still fighting to protect their votes. Then, as now, their motives differed. Some thought the vote would confer equal citizenship. Others hoped it would deliver the political muscle needed for their causes, from temperance to education, from abolitionism to civil rights, from social justice to pay equity. For all of them, the vote was their entry into public life.

What made the journey so compelling, made the stakes so enormous, is that female activists were asking men to share political power. In the recorded history of politics, no concept is more enduring than power. And in the pursuit of power, no quality is more essential than self-interest. As Niccolò Machiavelli explained in his 1513 philosophical tract *The Prince*, "A wise ruler ought never to keep faith, when by doing so it would be against his interests."

That is why the Revolution – with its rhetoric of no taxation without representation and its themes of life, liberty, and the pursuit of happiness – did not liberate American women from the cords of patriarchy that had restricted them since ancient civilizations. It is why the Civil War, which outlawed the cruel institution of slavery, did not banish racism. And it is why the Nineteenth Amendment, enacted in 1920 to guarantee women the right to vote, did not open all glass ceilings. Power guards its gates zealously, and no gates once locked open easily.

Because those in power never offer concessions to those without power unless they perceive that it would benefit them politically, female activists set out by the early twentieth century to convince men that the advent of women voting – or at least some women voting – would be in their interests. They organized one of the broadest class coalitions in history, a mass movement that before it finished in 1920 attracted working-class and elite women, professionals and educators, actresses and librarians, housewives and factory workers.

In building this mass movement, in appealing to both male and, in the West beginning in the 1890s, female voters, suffrage leaders assured those in power that enfranchising women would not change the electorate's racial composition. Playing the white race card, as Elizabeth Cady Stanton and Susan B. Anthony had done decades before, both moderates and militants in the twentieth-century movement limited their cause to expanding the voting population, not committing it to social change. They invited speakers from Colorado – which enfranchised women in 1893 – to lecture on how little had changed in the state's voting profile since. In public advertising campaigns and private buttonholing of legislators, they made clear they were fighting not for universal suffrage, but for educated suffrage, code for white entitlement. In their parades and their picketing of the White House, they rarely invited women of color to share the stage. The image, like the message, was Anglo-Saxon.

It might seem as if the right to vote is one of those "inalienable rights" promised to every citizen by the Declaration of Independence. But the U.S. Constitution does not describe voting as a right of citizenship. In fact the original document, enacted at the Constitutional Convention of 1787, made no mention at all of voting by the public. In a compromise crafted by the founding fathers as the price of uniting the colonies into a republic, the nation's foundational document left it to the states to develop their own qualifications for voting. At first, most states extended the vote only to white property owners, often also requiring a period of residency to prove fidelity to the state's interests. During the nineteenth century, some states extended the franchise to foreigners or to women, in hopes this offer of privilege would encourage more migration to their sparsely populated communities.

To readers interested in political reform, this long history of the Votes for Women campaign offers some lessons about the power of grassroots activism, and some cautionary tales about the speed of social change in the face of patriarchy, racism, and sexism – all weapons in the fight to maintain power. And to those seeking to add women back into history, or to put human faces to political events, it offers the narrative virtues of a group biography.

One mission of this book is to reinsert the story of women's struggle for equal rights into the meta-narrative of U.S. history. For too long, the cause has been studied as a separate story, untethered to its times. Suffrage leaders may have thought they could set sail alone, and often, they tried. In fact, their course was greatly swayed by other events in U.S. history – from the Revolution to the Civil War, from World War I to the Civil Rights Movement.

Most historians begin the story in 1848, at a women's rights convention in Seneca Falls, NY when Elizabeth Cady Stanton first stood in public and demanded the right to vote, and end it in 1920, when Tennessee became the 36th state to ratify the Nineteenth Amendment. This book seeks to extend the boundaries of that history, positioning its origins with the revolutionary fervor in the 1770s and its final triumph two centuries later, when the Justice Department won new tools to enforce the country's constitutional amendments. In widening the lens, it becomes clear that men would not voluntarily surrender power until women were powerful enough to demand it. At every marker of change – from the movement to give women the right to vote in school board elections in the 1880s to debates about whether to enfranchise illegal immigrants in the 2010s – politicians saw it in their interests to defuse demands for social change by opening the tent ever so slightly to those on the outside.

The other mindful contribution of this narrative is to return women of color to its telling. Black women have always treated the vote as a sacred trust, understanding its power to transform lives and, as suffragist Josephine St. Pierre Ruffin put it, to "lift as we climb." That white suffrage leaders shunned involvement of Asian Americans, African Americans, Hispanic Americans, and Native Americans in an effort to curry white male support has been much documented. The contributions and persistence of these suffragists of color in the face of abject discrimination is among the subplots that gives this story its poignancy.

Beyond broadening the movement's timeline, rejoining it to the arc of its times, and reinserting women too long silenced, this project seeks to equip readers about the tools to make their own history, in the shadows of this one. As voters and lawmakers now wrestle with issues such as the disenfranchising nature of gerrymandering, immigrant voting, and the drive to restore voting rights to felons, the nation's evolution from dedication to the common good to protection of individual rights here claims a place on the shelves.

Before we begin the story, a few words of explanation about language. Most American activists who participated in the movement shunned the words "suffragette," which had been applied to British activists. British journalist Charles Hands first coined the term in 1906 to mock female agitators who used militant tactics – arson, bombs, and destruction of public property – to draw attention to the cause. He meant to belittle the "-ettes" as less serious and respectable than the constitutional "suffragists." Mainstream leaders such as Millicent Fawcett, head of the National Union of Women's Suffrage Societies, relied on lobbying and public parades. Emmeline Pankhurst and members of her Women's Social and Political Union, who initiated militancy, embraced the suffragette slur as a badge of honor.

To American suffrage leaders, association with British movement violence was not calculated to win favor with the very male voters whose support they coveted. They called themselves suffragists – which had the further advantage of being a gender neutral term – and I have honored their choice by referring to them in that way as well. Likewise the term feminist was rarely used before the twentieth century, so I have avoided it as much as possible. As to the term suffrage, it derives from the Latin word *suffragium,* and the Old French word *suffrage,* and originally referred to "prayers or pleas on behalf of others." Its modern definition as the right to vote evolved in the United States.

A few words are in order too about organizational titles. In the nineteenth century, at the birth of many reform causes, it was the common expression to seek "a woman's right to vote," rather than "women's right to vote." That is why groups seeking rights for women are often styled in the singular, as in National American Woman's Suffrage Association (NAWSA). I have preserved that preference. Likewise, for African American advocates in the late nineteenth and early twentieth centuries, it was accepted style to use the word "colored" in titles. Examples include the National Association of Colored Women (NACW), and the National Association for the Advancement of Colored People (NAACP). Those titles are used here not to offend modern sensibilities, but to honor history.

Finally, wherever possible I have avoided the formulation that men "granted" women suffrage. As you will see in the pages that follow, there was nothing passive in the effort by American women to fight for their right to the ballot. For two centuries, in petitions and parades, with warring tactics and diverse motives, they fought for access to the ballot. It was the women who launched petitions in the 1830s, attended suffrage conventions in the 1850s, and strategized to win victories in the states in the 1870s and beyond. It was the women who studied politics and embraced tactical innovations that finally convinced Congress in 1919, and then the states in 1920, to enfranchise women. Both white and black activists gained suffrage by redefining male political self-interest. Expediency is the *lingua franca,* the common language, of politics. Male lawmakers voted for women's suffrage only after women were powerful enough politically to challenge the male hegemony. That was why the early victories in Wyoming, Colorado, Utah, Nevada, Washington, and California from 1890 to 1911 were so telling. By 1912, 1.2 million American women could vote for president. By 1918, Woodrow Wilson – a southerner and longtime opponent of women's suffrage – joined their cause. His stated public reason was that women had aided the win in World War I and deserved the vote as their reward. "We have made partners of the women in this war," he reminded a foot-dragging Senate. "Shall we admit them only to a partnership of suffering and sacrifice and toil and not to a partnership of privilege and right?" His private motive was more prosaic – he understood that without their votes he would not have been re-elected, that without female votes, no president would ever win again.

Political capital, like financial capital, atrophies if it lies dormant, shriveling from the missed opportunities of leveraging power. For two centuries, eight generations of American women learned to harness their aspirations to the self-interests of men with power. It was never a linear path, more often a history strewn with obstacles. And this demonstration of tenacity and grit began, as most things American, in the Revolutionary War.

About the Companion Website

This book is accompanied by a companion website:

www.wiley.com/go/Neuman

The website includes the following supplementary materials:

- Primary Sources
- Questions for Discussion
- For Further Reading

1

The Dawn of Republican Motherhood

Lydia Chapin Taft no doubt wore black on October 30, 1756 when she attended a town meeting in Uxbridge, Massachusetts. Both her 18-year-old son Caleb and her husband Josiah had died the previous month. During their twenty-five-year marriage, Josiah had worked his way through the ranks of the esteemed – becoming a captain in the militia, serving on the local Board of Selectmen, often chosen to represent their town in the Massachusetts General Court. His astute purchases and sales of property made him a wealthy landowner, and left Lydia, with three minor children still at home, the town's largest taxpayer. Property assured male patriarchy, and conferred status on landed families. So civic leaders in Uxbridge, not far from the Quaker stronghold of Worcester, where women were invited to speak at meeting, asked Lydia to cast a vote in her husband's place. Her affirmative vote on funding the local militia was the first of three she would cast as a widow. Two years later, in 1758, she voted on tax issues. And in 1765, she again appeared at a town meeting, this time to weigh in on school districts. Before Massachusetts or the other original Thirteen Colonies declared their independence from the British, she became America's first recorded female voter.

Central to scholars of women's history is why the American Revolution – with its rhetoric of no taxation without representation and its themes of life, liberty, and the pursuit of happiness – did not liberate American women. After the war, revolutionary leaders encouraged

And Yet They Persisted: How American Women Won the Right to Vote, First Edition. Johanna Neuman.
© 2020 John Wiley & Sons, Inc. Published 2020 by John Wiley & Sons, Inc.
Companion website: www.wiley.com/go/Neuman

women to act as keepers of civic virtue, teaching young Americans the perils of monarchies, instilling a quality of democracy in the next generation of patriots. Historian Linda K. Kerber, who coined the phrase "the Republican Motherhood," noted that this new function restricted women to the domestic arena, while giving them new standing in the polity. Others have countered that this post-revolutionary era saw more of a turn toward a Republican Womanhood, tethered less to a woman's role as a mother than to her place as a citizen in the new republic, with influence not only on children but also on suitors, husbands, and brothers. By whatever name, the emphasis on women's role in America's new democracy unleashed a surge of interest in female education and public participation. That is why it is important to begin this account of women's suffrage not in the 1840s, when women's rights activists began to call conventions, but in the 1790s, when they began to participate in the nation's political life. It was here, early in the Republic's history, that women joined the public sphere, learning "to stand and speak." This controversial first step toward activism would have lasting effects on the fight for the vote over the next two centuries.

Antecedents of Republican Motherhood

Like other linguistic constructs of history, patriarchy was a concept designed by men, to favor men. In Biblical story, Eve lured Adam to sin, casting both of them from the Garden of Eden. In ancient Greece, Aristotle excluded women from the polis, which he regarded as the highest calling in life, arguing that those who did not participate in the political life of the state were little better than idiots. The main function of wives in ancient Greece was to produce male heirs – girl infants could be killed at their father's discretion. Part of the patriarchal code required dividing the female population into respectable and non-respectable women, rewarding women who showed their obedience to men through sexual subordination, allowing men to roam the sexual field with slaves, lower-class women or young men. Men would fight wars, oversee property, participate in the nation's public life, and dictate the rules for women and children at home. Women would obey or find themselves further degraded as prostitutes or impoverished servants.

By the time of British kings, men had devised a new construct of power. The concept of coverture was embedded into Common Law, ensuring that a woman, on marriage, would cede all legal rights to her husband. She had no right to own property or keep income, no parental rights over her children, no standing in the law to make contracts or petition for divorce. Though they flew the British flag, the colonies survived in a land of natives, immigrants, and territorial ambition. Soon some laws of patriarchy loosened. Wives of German and Dutch immigrants, not bound by English laws, had more control over their own property, and could write wills. Once talk of rebellion began, with its rhetoric of "unhappy families" and "tyrannical rulers," colonies such as Massachusetts and Connecticut liberalized divorce laws, allowing women to divorce on grounds of adultery, bigamy or impotence. And by the 1750s, opportunities for both girls and boys to obtain a formal education increased, as academies in New York and Philadelphia advertised in newspapers.

In 1792, amid the French Revolution, English author and philosopher Mary Wollstonecraft further stoked the debate over education by publishing a tract, *A Vindication of the Rights of Woman*, pondering the injustices of male privileges and the meaning of women's rights. If women were assumed to have natural rights, conferred by God, then it was up to the state to validate them, she argued. The book, which sparked debate on both sides of the Atlantic, contested the male view of women as superficial. If women lacked the language of politics, she argued, it was only for lack of adequate education. Dismissing the idea of teaching women "ladylike" demeanor, she advocated co-educational institutions where women would be schooled for their minds, not their manners. "I do not want them to have power over men but over themselves," she wrote. "Their first duty is to themselves as rational creatures." With the sure knowledge that her idea might "excite laughter" among men, she also suggested "women ought to have representatives, instead of being arbitrarily governed without having any direct share allowed them in the deliberations of government."

The title of Wollstonecraft's book paid homage to the manifesto of the French Revolution, the Declaration of the Rights of Man and of the Citizen. But even before its publication, men and women in the colonies had pondered the roles of male and female citizens in a new republic. After the Revolution, American women would instill civic virtue in the next generation, while men attended to the dirtier call of politics. This gendering of America – much like the effort by Europeans to impose gender-based divisions of labor on native peoples – reassured men such as John Adams that "power always follows property." But on some level, Republican Motherhood was thus the price patriarchy paid for its survival. It was also the vehicle women would use to wrest new rights from a stubborn male polity.

Winning the War, and the Peace

Before the 1760s, many women were limited by their obligations in the home. The work was difficult and exhausting – described as backbreaking duties in the fields, repeated childbirths, taxing meal preparation and daily, and daylong, efforts to keep dust and dirt from invading primitive homes. Indentured servants, black and white, suffered from broken bones and pulled muscles from lugging 20-gallon containers of water from well to home, for bathing and cooking. For the African Americans who were enslaved, one fifth of the nation, duties were exhausting, tinged with the threat of whippings and separation from loved ones on the auction block. Women who expressed interest in politics were rare, as it was considered unnatural. Exceptions were made for some upper-class women, such as Mercy Otis Warren, who during the war years published plays and poems under the pseudonym, "A Columbian Patriot." But once appeals for resistance spread through the colonies, women for the first time joined debates, wrote missives, and asked their husbands to send them updates on military developments. "Nothing else is talked of," Sarah Franklin wrote to her father Benjamin Franklin. "The Dutch talk of the stomp tack, the Negroes of the tamp, in short everyone has something to say." Traveling from Cambridge to Boston, one writer reported seeing "at every house Woman & Children making Cartridges, running Bullets, making Wallets, baking Biscuit, crying & bemoaning & at the same time animating their Husbands & Sons to fight for their Liberties, tho' not knowing whether they should ever see them again."

As her husband John Adams set off for the Second Continental Congress in Philadelphia in 1776, Abigail Adams wrote him a letter. Hungry for details of the war effort, she begged him to write often, with details on "what sort of Defence Virginia can make against our common Enemy? Whether it is so situated as to make an able Defence?" In joining a governing body that would lead the Thirteen Colonies during the Revolution, she urged him to "Remember the Ladies," warning that women would foment a rebellion "if attention is not paid" to their interests, that they would "not hold ourselves bound by any laws in which we have no voice or representation." She was not the first woman to seek a voice in politics. In 1648, Margaret Brent, an unmarried property owner, went before the Maryland Assembly requesting "a vote … and a voyce" for herself, and for Cecil Calvert, Lord Baltimore, as she held his power of attorney. The governor of Maryland denied both requests. In 1733, a few property-owning women wrote the New York *Journal* protesting their disenfranchisement. There is no record of a response. Half a century later, as the colonies were on the cusp of revolution, there came a male rejoinder. It was filled with contempt and disdain. "To your extraordinary Code of Laws, I cannot but laugh," John Adams replied to his wife's warning of a female rebellion. "Depend upon it, we know better than to repeal our Masculine systems." (Fig. 1.1.)

Figure 1.1 As John Adams left for Philadelphia to attend the Third Continental Congress in Philadelphia in 1776, his wife Abigail Adams wrote urging him to "remember the ladies," or risk their "rebellion" from any laws "in which we have no voice or representation." To this early, private plea for female empowerment, John Adams replied, "We know better than to repeal our Masculine systems." *Source:* Getty Images. Time Life Pictures.

Soon after, James Sullivan, a member of the Massachusetts General Court and a colleague, likewise wrote John Adams suggesting that the vote be extended to disenfranchised citizens, such as women and men without property. One of the Revolution's legacies had been a loss of deference, where shoemakers stood next to their elite customers as both threw tea into the Boston Harbor. Sullivan's plea for universal suffrage was part of this new egalitarianism. The reply from John Adams was less flippant than that he offered his wife, but no less dismissive, reflecting his elitist views. Warning against altering voter qualifications, Adams predicted, "There will be no end of it. New claims will arise; women will demand a vote; lads from twelve to twenty-one will think their rights not enough attended to; and every man who has not a farthing [one-fourth of a penny in British coin], will demand an equal voice with any other, in all acts of state. It tends to confound and destroy all distinctions, and prostrate all ranks to one common level." Adams believed that granting a vote to citizens without a permanent stake in the community – without property, without residency – was dangerous, much as Greek philosopher Aristotle had suggested centuries before. But Adams also understood the implications of revolutionary rhetoric, the logical extension of its arguments. His comment, "there will be no end of it," was prescient. More than any other revolutionary leader, he feared and may have foreseen the waves of changes in the country's electorate, as succeeding classes of residents gained access to the ballot. For now, he and other founding fathers were busy leading a rebellion against the status quo. And in one of the revolution's unintended consequences, women heard its call. Once shielded from politics, occupied with backbreaking duties in "the domestic sphere," they became its great champions.

All over the colonies, effective boycotts against British products had required a buy-in from women. And buy in they did. Women founded anti-tea leagues, meeting to brew concoctions of raspberry, sage, and birch to substitute their herbal mixes for well-regarded English teas. Wives and daughters engaged in "public spirited measures" – growing their own food and weaving their own clothes. Called Daughters of Liberty, women would convene at the home of a local minister, sharing camaraderie as well as material, with as many as 100 weavers. Hundreds of spectators came to watch. Young women especially resonated to the task, feeling they were making a contribution to the nation's future. One girl who participated in spinning parties wrote that she "felt Nationaly," part of "a fighting army of amazones … armed with spinning wheels." Calling the phenomenon a display of female patriotism, an editor at the Boston *Evening Post* wrote, "The industry and frugality of American ladies must exalt their character in the Eyes of the World and serve to show how greatly they are contributing to bringing about the political salvation of a whole Continent."

Not all observers were so enamored. Both before and after the war, some newspapers complained that American women had undercut the boycott by their excessive spending on British imports. This was perhaps an assertion made by men who feared crediting any female contribution might lead to their emancipation. Accustomed to the insults, some women said they expected little from their participation. "You know that our Sex are doomed to be obedient in every stage of life," wrote Mary Stevens Livingston, whose husband Robert was named by George Washington as one of the committee of five that drafted the Declaration of Independence (the others were Thomas Jefferson, Benjamin Franklin, John Adams, and Roger Sherman). "So we shant be great gainers by this [revolutionary] contest." But there is little question that the boycotts politicized the household economy, and the domestic conversation. As John Adams put it, "Was not every fireside, indeed, a theatre of politics?"

Revolutionary excitement was evident throughout the colonies. Eliza Wilkinson, living in South Carolina's Sea Islands, said that by the time the British Army invaded her state in 1780, no greater politicos existed than "the several knots of ladies, who met together," looking for all the world like "perfect statesmen." After Charleston fell to the British on May 12, morale plummeted in the Continental Army. Poorly fed and rarely paid, they became the very definition of a rag tag army. Local officials and merchants in Philadelphia solicited funds to pay them. Women signed up for "public spirited measures" such as cleaning. And Esther DeBerdt Reed, wife of the governor of Pennsylvania, took to the newspaper to plead for female patriots to do more. In "Sentiments of American Woman," she urged women in Philadelphia to form an organization to raise funds for the American rebel troops.

"Animated by the purest patriotism," she wrote, "the time is arrived to display the same sentiments which animated us at the beginning of the Revolution, when we renounced the use of teas, however agreeable to our taste, rather than receive them from our persecutors." With Sarah Franklin Bache, she organized a Ladies Association, much imitated throughout the colonies. The Philadelphia chapter raised enough money – from Quaker homes and alehouses alike – to give each soldier $2, which Reed advocated. Fearing soldiers would use the money for alcohol, General Washington vetoed the idea, insisting the money be spent to sew shirts for them. Patriarchal to the women as well as his troops, Washington kept both in line. Commentators may have snickered at "General Washington's sewing circle," but the general ceded no ground. In the end, the Ladies Association of Philadelphia sent 2,220 shirts to the beleaguered Continental Army, while the New Jersey chapter sent 380 pairs of socks.

Other female patriots, less affluent, showed their support by cooking and cleaning for the troops, often seeking food in return. In an affidavit she filed to demonstrate her entitlement to a pension, Sarah Osborn testified that during the war, she did "washing, mending and cooking for the soldiers." Once while she was carrying provisions, she ran into General George Washington, who was exasperated by the presence of the so-called "camp followers," once describing them as "a clog upon every movement." He asked Osborn if she were "not afraid of the cannonballs." She replied that she was not. "The bullets would not cheat the gallows," she said. "It would not do for the men to fight and starve too."

Beyond demonstrating their patriotism in these gendered, acceptably feminine endeavors, other women, if only a few, actually engaged the enemy. Mary Hays McCauley was a camp follower who carried water to the troops, often under fire from British troops. When her husband William Hays was carried off field at the Battle of Monmouth in New Jersey in 1778, she kept his cannon loaded. Said to be the inspiration for the legendary "Molly Pitcher," Mary later received a pension "for services rendered in the revolutionary war" from the state of Pennsylvania. More directly, Deborah Sampson took up arms in men's clothing. Enlisting as Robert Shurtleff in the Fourth Massachusetts Regiment, she served for eighteen months in 1782–1783. Wounded twice, she was discharged after the second injury disclosed her gender. Kate, a slave on Stephen Heard's Plantation in Georgia, infiltrated a British war camp at Fort Cornwallis where Heard was being held. After a few days of earning the trust of British guards by doing their laundry, she advised them she wanted to give the prisoner clean clothes. Admitted to his cell, the six-foot-tall Kate picked up Heard, a small man, and placed him inside her basket, leaving the prison with the basket on her head. Arriving in Augusta, where she had hidden two of his Arabian horses, the two rode off. It is said that Heard offered Kate her freedom. Of pure African descent, claiming to be the daughter of a powerful king, she declined, perhaps understanding that she would always be rewarded for her loyalty as she and her husband Jack, a gardener, continued to work for the Heard family until their deaths.

As Britain had offered to free any slaves who joined the cause, black slave women often sought rescue from the Redcoats. In the South, an estimated 55,000 slaves escaped during the Revolution, one third of them women. After the British captured the estate of Mary Willing Byrd in Virginia, forty-nine of her slaves went with them. In later years of the war, as the British military sailed for home from Savannah and Charleston, an estimated 10,000 slaves from each port, male and female, accompanied them. Others resonated to the themes of the American cause. Phillis Wheatley, taught to read and write by the daughter of her white enslaver, was the first African American woman to author a book of poems. Her *Poems on Various Subjects, Religious and Moral* was published in London in 1773. Later she wrote odes to George Washington and Benjamin Franklin. In a letter to her on February 28, 1776, Washington called her "style and manner … striking proof of your great poetical Talents." During the war he asked Wheatley to visit with him at his military headquarters, and shortly after the visit he ordered that blacks be conscripted into the Continental Army. An estimated 5,000 black men – some slaves offered false promises of freedom by their owners for fighting – served under Washington in the Revolutionary War.

Still other African American women used abolitionist sentiment in the North to seek freedom. Trapped in slavery, they found their voices in defying the cruelty of human bondage. In 1716, Joan Jackson became the first enslaved woman to win her freedom through courts in New England, although she was unable to free her children. In 1780, slave Mum Bett was present in her town square for a reading of the newly ratified Massachusetts Constitution. On hearing the document's first article, "All men are born free and equal, and have certain natural, essential and unalienable rights," she determined to fight for her freedom. She and another slave hired abolitionist lawyer Theodore Sedgwick and won their case in court. The County Court of Common Pleas in Great Barrington found that the phrase "all men are born free and equal" meant that there could be "no such thing as perpetual servitude of a rational creature." A slave for thirty years, Mum Bett changed her name to Elizabeth Freeman (Fig. 1.2), serving as governess to the children of the lawyer who had represented her in court. And in 1796, while serving as president from the nation's capitol of Philadelphia, George Washington sat down to dinner as one of his wife's favorite slaves, 23-year-old Ona "Oney" Maria Judge, fled from the house. With help from the city's population of free blacks, she was walked or likely spirited through the streets of Philadelphia, boarding a ship to New Hampshire. Soon, she married a free black sailor named John Staines, bore three children, and spent the rest of her seventy-five years looking over her shoulder, living the life of the hunted. In 1796, George and Martha Washington, leaving for a summer trip to Mount Vernon between sessions of Congress, launched an intense campaign to recapture Ona Judge, offering a reward of $10 to any person, black or white, who would "bring her home."

Slavery and patriarchy, racism and sexism, all had survived the Revolution. Men had welcomed the patriotism, and sacrifices, offered by colonial women, shaming those who had failed to do their share. They had accepted, if grudgingly, the patriotism of black soldiers – a military necessity after the British offered to free any African Americans who fought on the loyalist side. But as Adams made clear, even amid the fervor of revolutionary rhetoric that championed egalitarian principles, men had no intention of repealing "our Masculine systems." Even in New Jersey, which in its constitution offered the vote to both women and free African Americans who were property owners – the same requirement for male voters – the privilege was designed to limit numbers of these newly enfranchised voters, and ensure that white male dominance, indeed that the political status quo, was preserved.

The New Jersey Exception

Like Massachusetts, New Jersey also wrote an early foundational document, ratifying its constitution on July 2, 1776. In the document, the new constitution offered the ballot to "all inhabitants of this colony of

Figure 1.2 Elizabeth Freeman, born in 1742, was one of the first African American slaves to sue in the courts – and win – her freedom, based on Article 1 of the Massachusetts Constitution stating, "All men are born free and equal, and have certain natural, essential and unalienable rights." Known during her slave years as Mum Bett, after winning her freedom she changed her name to Elizabeth Freeman. Miniature portrait, oil pastel on ivory, by Susan Anne Livingston Ridley Sedgwick, 1811, *Source:* Public Domain.

full age, who are worth £50." No records remain about legislative debate over this radical idea, and some have wondered if this provision was accidental, a deliberate attempt to empower women and blacks who owned property, or a mere oversight. The state constitution included other reforms popular among colonists, such as a bicameral legislature, that suggest the suffrage provision – which applied to free blacks as well as women – was intentional. Others have wondered if New Jersey's Quakers, who welcomed female speakers, may have been the impetus for this extension of the vote.

Either way, the new vote for women applied to only a small proportion of the population. Coverture laws meant women could not own property unless they were single (*feme sole*) or widowed, like Lydia Taft. Married women (*feme covert*) gave up rights to own property, which transferred to their husbands. No one knows how many single or widowed women of 21 years or older in New Jersey had amassed £50 worth in holdings by 1776. Pamphleteer William Griffith, who said he found it "perfectly disgusting" to watch women cast ballots, thought the number considerable, saying, "Of widows and spinsters above twenty one, there can not, I imagine, be fewer than 10,000." Others put the figure at 20,000.

Whenever new parties vied for power in the state – Patriots in 1776, Federalists in 1789, Republicans in 1797 – men reached out to female voters to expand their base. Women attended public rallies, lobbied for patronage jobs for their male relatives and family friends, raised money for political causes, actively campaigned for candidates and were invited to celebrations of George Washington's birthday. Politicians on all sides sought to endear themselves to these new voters, offering carriages to transport them to the polls.

But the guiding rule of suffrage history is that male politicians never cede power unless it advantages them. Griffith and other men in New Jersey always saw female voters as disorderly, accidental members of the polity. By the 1790s, after the French Revolution turned violent, its cries of "Liberté, Egalité, Fraternité" fading with the guillotining of the king and queen, politics in America grew more divisive. Washington and Alexander Hamilton saw the Revolution's Terror as a warning about the dangers of unbridled democracy. Jefferson and James Madison believed the excesses would right themselves, that France would become a republic. Gone were the warm feelings of camaraderie from the revolutionary era. Now the other side was the enemy, to be vanquished. During the war, some women had become avid patriots after watching British troops plunder their homes. Hanna Caldwell, of the renowned Ogden family in Newark and a mother of nine, resisted British attempts to burn her home and was shot. Now, amid what Rosemarie Zagarri has dubbed "a revolutionary backlash," they became easy scapegoats whenever outcomes differed from predictions.

In the early years, especially after the contentious 1800 election in which Thomas Jefferson finally bested Aaron Burr in the House of Representatives, men on both sides credited women. In Stony Hill they raised their glasses to "the fair daughters of Columbia, those who voted in behalf of Jefferson and Burr in particular." In Bloomfield they toasted "the Republican fair," adding, "May their patriotic conduct in the late elections add an irresistible zest to their charms." In Mendham too they prayed that the female "Republican conduct be pleasing and exemplary to their sisters of the Union." But in fact, both Federalists and Democratic-Republicans suspected women of aiding the opposing party, of voting wrong.

In 1802, Republicans complained when Federalists gained an equal number of representatives in the state legislature. They blamed illegal voting by a married woman and a black slave, tilting results toward Federalists in Hunterdon County. A legislative investigation found, indeed, that the married woman had been separated from her husband and paid taxes under her maiden name, a subversion of the laws. The inquiry also found that an African American woman suspected of being a slave had actually purchased her freedom from her owner. It remains unclear if either woman voted illegally, or if they had, whether it changed the election results. What is clear is that male partisans on all sides felt free to disparage them. Patriarchy held voting women as an abomination, a disorderly blight on public life. They were expendable, easy scapegoats in a political fight. Which is exactly how they lost the vote.

Thomas Jefferson had once said that American women, unlike their French counterparts, should be "too wise to wrinkle their foreheads with politics," and should instead be "contented to soothe and calm the minds of their husbands returning ruffled from political debate." Now his Republicans, also angry that Federalist women had cast a sizeable 150 votes for Jonathan Drayton in a Senate race, grew nostalgic for an earlier generation, when women were characterized by "chastity, prudence and industry." Critics disparaged the female voter and her insertion of "petticoat politics," hardly the Republican Motherhood founders envisioned. In a 1798 commentary, Griffith described female voting as a "mockery." One writer to the Republican newspaper *True American* expressed alarm at a "defect in our constitution" allowing "whole wagon loads of those 'privileged fair'" to show up at the polls. "In some townships I am told they made up *almost a fourth* of the total votes," he despaired, signing his letter "Friend to the Ladies." Calls grew to reclaim male privilege. In 1803, one observer claimed that women in Newark had "vied with men, and in some instances eclipsed them, in 'stuffing' the ballot box." Now, they were said to be corrupt, too easily swayed, not fit for the vote. By the turn of the century, there was a sharpening of the gender borders.

In 1804, with Jefferson seeking re-election, Republicans in the state offered "An Act for the Gradual Abolition of Slavery." In one of the party newspapers, the Newark *Centinel* [cq] *of Freedom*, editors referred to blacks as "gentlemen," published letters from "politicians of color," and authored poems with implicit messages of outreach. "Though black his skin as shades of night/His HEART is fair – His SOUL is White." Two years later, liberal Republicans in the state began agitating to extend the vote, saying "a widow's mite is property" but so is the life of any male "black, white, red or yellow" citizen. In a nation where, as John Adams said, "power always follows property," this return to gender preference must have been soothing to men outraged by the advent of female voting. Three years later, the state's thirty-year experiment of extending the vote to women came to an end.

The precipitating incident was a dispute in Essex County over where to put a new courthouse. Moderate Republicans favored Elizabeth Town. Liberal Republicans insisted on Newark. After Newark won, moderates protested that the election had been fraudulent, with allegations of ballot stuffing. For years there had been talk about illegal voting by wives and daughters who lived under the roof of their husbands and fathers, and by black men who were not worth £50. Now, critics saw an opening. Petitioning for annulment of the constitutional provision, they demanded that election laws be changed. Leading the fight was John Condict, a Republican congressman who believed he had nearly been defeated at the last election by the votes of seventy-five female Federalists.

"Whereas," began his bill, "doubts have been raised and great diversities in practice obtained throughout the state in regard to the admission of *aliens, females, and persons of color, or negroes* to vote in elections ... and whereas, it is highly necessary to the safety, quiet, good order and dignity of the state, to clear up the said doubts," New Jersey would reassert the interests of the state, and return to an electorate of free white men. Newark got its courthouse. Elizabeth Town got a new election law limiting the vote to white, male, tax-paying citizens over 21. And Condict won his revenge through this legislative compromise. No matter the rationale, the legislature saw, and welcomed, the opportunity to reclaim the "quiet, good order and dignity of our states." After thirty-one years of voting, after being courted by political parties and wooed by candidates, women were disenfranchised to give the Democratic-Republic Party advantage in the 1808 presidential election. Not surprisingly, the new party's candidate, James Madison, won decisively. That female protests were muted says much about the political climate. As quickly as it came, political equality for women in New Jersey disappeared as if it were a ghost standing on the shoulders of political whim, in the service of political interests.

As the New Jersey case demonstrated, the Federalists were losing power, and after the War of 1812, the party faded into oblivion. The birth of partisan parties led to toxic campaigns, mudslinging, and a new kind of ungentlemanly politics. Republicans in the thirteen original colonies, and in the eleven new ones who sought admission to the Union before 1830, now sought to change the shape and the color of the electorate. Because states controlled who voted, they drafted new constitutions redefining voting qualifications, in some cases granting the vote to white men without property – an idea that had been an anathema to Federalists. By the 1830s, seeking to eliminate a monopoly of government by elites, Andrew Jackson enfranchised white men without property, disenfranchised black men, and removed from the rolls Cherokee men who served those in power. Thus he expanded the electorate, seeking universal white male suffrage without tax requirements, making it whiter, poorer, less diverse.

For their part, Republicans deliberately excluded women and blacks. The case of Anna Gordon Martin further cemented this turn against women. In 1805, the Supreme Judicial Court of Massachusetts had considered the case of her son, who was trying to reclaim the land his mother had left behind when she and his father, loyalists to the crown, fled Massachusetts during the war. She had brought significant real estate holdings to the marriage. The court ruled that she had not been free to remain in Massachusetts, to proclaim herself a patriot. She was married, with no free will either as a property owner or as a political actor. The revolutionary rhetoric of the late eighteenth century now gave way to a new pragmatism in the early nineteenth century. As historian Linda Kerber noted, "Restricting women's politicization was one of a series of conservative choices that Americans made in the postwar years as they avoided the full implication of their own revolutionary radicalism."

As Virginia was redrafting its state constitution in 1829, one woman wrote to the *Richmond Enquirer* to protest. "Why is it that the pretentions of almost every other class of society have been duly weighed," wrote the woman, yet "*one half of the Society*" was still "cut off, at one throw from all share in the administration of government?" This missive by a reader, who signed herself as "A Virginia Freewoman," was an early indication that women began agitating for the vote long before the 1848 Women's Rights Convention in Seneca Falls, NY. Even at this early stage in the nation's evolution, they were asking to participate in the affairs of governance. Amid a trend in the states to ignore women's rights and instead grant manhood to white men no matter their wealth or holdings, many women, white and black, turned to knocking down barriers not to the ballot but to the schoolroom door.

Pursuing Education

For Jefferson, a new nation required a systematic procedure of educating the boys, "to instruct the mass of our citizens in these their rights, interests and duties, as men and citizens." Until then, women had been taught to read, but not to write. Now Benjamin Rush, a prominent Philadelphia physician and signer of the Declaration of Independence, spoke up for women. In his 1787 *Thoughts upon Female Education,* he argued, "A principal share of the instruction of children naturally devolves upon the women. It becomes us therefore to prepare them, by a suitable education, for the discharge of this important duty of mothers." It was up to "the ladies," he noted, "to concur in instructing their sons in the principles of liberty and government." But Rush also saw practical needs for educating women, suggesting they be schooled in "the more useful branches of literature," trained to be "stewards and guardians of their husbands' property," and to manage a household staff. He advocated teaching them to read English properly, write legibly, and keep figures and bookkeeping so that a wife could serve as executrix of an estate if her husband predeceased her. He also sought to counter what he saw as women's tendency toward superstition, suggesting rounding out female education with study of geography and history, even astronomy and natural philosophy, all to make her an "agreeable companion for the sensible man."

Many women rallied to the call for more equality in education, and some hailed their new role in educating the new generation. As Abigail Adams had written to her husband in 1776, "If we mean to have Heroes, Statesmen and Philosophers, we should have learned women." But if Republican Motherhood was the public rationale for educating women, it was not one they all shared. In 1793, Priscilla Mason graduated from Young Ladies Academy in Philadelphia, taking the podium as class valedictorian. Celebrating the victory of women "over ignorance," she castigated men for seizing power. "Our high and mighty Lords (thanks to their arbitrary constitutions) have denied us the means of knowledge and then reproached us for the want of it." Lamenting that "*Man,* despotic man" had closed to women the doors to "the Church, the Bar, and the Senate," she spoke of "the sources of knowledge ... gradually opening to our sex." She urged women to overcome male opposition "and take for themselves the schooling that was their due." That same year, Catherine Ferguson, a former slave who had purchased her freedom from her owner, began a school for the poor in New York, open to black and white children.

In 1802, Judith Sargent Murray (Fig. 1.3), a prominent political essayist who had overseen the education of twelve children including her daughter, helped open a school for girls in Dorchester, Massachusetts with her cousins Judith Foster Saunders and Clementina [cq] Beach. The oldest of eight children, Murray had taught herself history, philosophy, geography, and literature in the family's vast library. During the Revolution, she had written widely on the need for female education, and the right of women to control their earnings. One year before Wollstonecraft's *Vindication of the Rights of Woman,* Murray penned *On*

Figure 1.3 Judith Sargent Murray was an essayist, educator, and one of the first to argue, in *On the Equality of the Sexes*, that women, like men, should be empowered to achieve educational and economic independence. Portrait by John Singleton Copley, *Source:* Public Domain.

the Equality of the Sexes. Under a male pseudonym, she wrote columns in the local newspapers.

In the school's first advertisement, which Murray wrote, the two educators promised to teach "Reading, English, Grammar, Writing, Arithmetic, the French language, Geography, including the use of Globes, needle work in all its branches, painting, and hair work upon ivory." Over the next years, a number of female academies would spring up – including Mrs. Rowson's Academy, a boarding school, in downtown Boston – opened by Susan Rowson, a novelist and actress who shared Murray's views that "the human mind, whether possessed by man or woman, is capable of the highest refinement, and most brilliant acquirements." Hundreds and later thousands attended, entering the public domain as educators, writers, and reform-minded leaders of benevolent societies. Harriet Beecher Stowe, born in 1811, later author of *Uncle Tom's Cabin*, was schooled at Litchfield Academy, learning there the Western canon of literature that no doubt helped her write the best-selling novel of the nineteenth century.

By the 1800s, other institutions of greater academic ambition opened their doors to women. Emma Hart Willard established the Troy female Seminary in 1821, the first school to offer women a broad-based and rigorous education comparable to that taught at all-male academies. No longer limited to courses in French conversation and embroidery, ninety women attended the first lectures in mathematics, science, history, foreign language and literature. Chemist Mary Lyon founded Mount Holyoke Female Seminary in 1837 with the slogan, "Go where no one else goes, do what no one else will do." The first of the so-called Seven Sisters colleges of Ivy League reputation, the school prided itself on low tuition and rigorous entrance exams. On opening day in 1837, Lyon proclaimed a new "era in female education." It is hard to overestimate the revolutionary nature of this new era of female education. By one estimate, nearly two hundred female academies and seminaries opened in the North and South between 1790 and 1820, a number that nearly doubled by the Civil War.

Few of these institutions – no more than fifteen by one count – were open to African Americans, and a little over half of these to black women. Prudence Crandall, a white Quaker woman, defied racial boundaries in her small Connecticut town when, in 1833, she invited a young African American student, Sarah Harris, to enroll at her Canterbury Female Seminary. When white students fled, Crandall turned her seminary into an all black institution, the High School for Young Colored Ladies and Misses. The town's reaction – led by Andrew Judson, a state attorney, politician, and fervent believer that free blacks should be recolonized in Africa – laid bare its racist prejudices. White residents, fearful that New England might become "the Liberia of America," a site of black empowerment, poured manure into the school's water well, set its building on fire, and refused services – from groceries to medical care – to its staff and students. Rather than being hailed for extending educational opportunities to free black women, for teaching Christian principles and ethics to girls from 8 to 20, Crandall was prosecuted for violating a local law, the so-called Black Law, which banned teaching of out-of-state African American students. She spent a brief time in jail before her conviction was overturned. Later her students wrote about their "trial and struggles" in earning an education. One student delivered an address saying she and her sister students had "begun to enjoy what our minds have long desired; viz. the advantages of a good education." Another urged residents of Canterbury to "obey the voice of duty" and emulate Crandall, who "stepped from within the shadow of prejudice" to plead their cause, "in the midst of persecution, with great success." Another asked simply, "Where is justice?" Amid the violence, the school closed its doors in 1834.

All of the players in the Canterbury saga – the prosecutors, the defense attorneys, the trial judges, and the appellate court judges – were men. Crandall was barred from either attending or speaking at a town meeting called to discuss the case because of her gender. In his appeals to the court, Judson could not have made it clearer that the basis of his objection was white privilege, that he understood the existence of the school to be a threat to the hegemony of a white male nation. "I would appeal to this Court, to every American citizen," he argued, "and say that America is ours – it belongs to a race of white men."

Though only a minority of women, white or black, could avail themselves of these new opportunities, the impact of female learning on the male hierarchy was inevitably a threat. Often prevented from speaking as valedictorians, female graduates experienced a rebellion of will, bristling at limits on their voices. As abolitionist Sarah Grimke later observed, "Prepare women for duty and usefulness, and she will laugh at any boundaries man may set for her."

At its opening in 1833, Oberlin became the first college to offer women an education nearly equal to that offered men, two years later admitting African American students. Oberlin was the brainchild of two prominent men who had been much influenced by the Second Great Awakening – a religious revival movement in the nineteenth century that taught converts that to achieve salvation, they had to repent not only for their sins, but work toward the eradication of the nation's sins, chief among them the abolition of slavery and the achievement of women's rights. At first, women were restricted to courses of study in the female or teachers' departments. But by 1837, four women were admitted to the Collegiate Department, where they studied mathematics, natural science, philosophy, and general literature. Three women – Mary Caroline Rudd, Mary Hosford, and Elizabeth Prall – graduated in 1841. Nine years later, Lucy Sessions became the school's first black female graduate.

In 1843, at the age of 25, Lucy Stone went by train, steamship, and stagecoach to reach the college campus. She had saved her meager salary as a teacher to make the trip. It would steel her determination, and change the direction of the women's suffrage movement. As she once explained, "In education, in marriage, in religion, in everything, disappointment is the lot of women. It shall be the business of my life to deepen that disappointment in every woman's heart until she bows down to it no longer." The specter of women earning college degrees, schooled in the philosophical and literary canons that undergirded male education, was a direct threat to the patriarchy. On earning her bachelors degree from Oberlin in 1847, Lucy Stone became the first female college graduate from Massachusetts. Asked to write an honors paper to be read at graduation, as was customary, by a male faculty member, she declined, saying she would fight any policy that denied women "the privilege of being co-laborers with men in any sphere in which their ability makes them adequate." Later, after being hired by the Massachusetts Anti-Slavery Society to give lectures about abolition, she infuriated the society's male leaders by also speaking about the need for women's rights. The topic of empowering women was, if possible, the more controversial of the two. But Stone was so compelling as a speaker that the society agreed to a compromise – hiring her to lecture against slavery on weekends, when audiences were larger, leaving her to talk women's rights during the week. She had found her voice, and she would not now part with it.

While men may have viewed these efforts as part of the obligations of a Republican Motherhood, for many women education not only taught basic skills of literacy, but also connected them to a code of shared values, a community of interests. As Charlestown's Social Circle in Massachusetts announced, it was committed to the "pursuit of intellectual and moral excellence." In the decades to come, as persecution of Native Americans would propel women to again join the political debate and slavery of African Americans would wrench the nation toward Civil War, women got involved. As Lucy Stone later put it, "We discussed educational, political, moral and religious questions, and especially we learned to stand and speak, to put motions, how to treat amendments, etc."

Some of the earliest literary societies began among free African American women. In June 1832, abolitionist leader William Lloyd Garrison printed in his newspaper, the *Liberator*, an account of his visit to "a society of colored ladies, called the female literary society." He reported that "members assemble every Tuesday evening for the purpose of mutual improvement in moral and literary pursuits." He said that their weekly writings are put anonymously into a box, and later critiqued by a committee. "If the traducers of the colored race could be acquainted with the moral worth, just refinement and large intelligence of this association," he wrote, "their mouths would hereafter be dumb." For their part, members of the Female Literary Association of Philadelphia felt it their duty, "as daughters of a despised race – to use our utmost endeavors to enlighten the understanding," and "break down the strong barrier of prejudice, and raise ourselves to an equality with those of our fellow beings who differ from us in complexion." They hoped to cultivate intellect, because "the degraded station that we occupy in society is in great measure attributable to our want of education." Sarah Forten wrote for the *Liberator* under pennames. And Sarah Mapps Douglass, the daughter of black abolitionists and founder of an African American seminary, wrote of literary activity as a way of lifting a "wronged and neglected race." A Quaker, Douglass also confided to friends that African Americans were treated as second-class citizens in Quaker meetings, forced to sit apart from whites in a "Negro Pew." Her revelations would eventually be aired in public, piercing the veil of Quaker probity with the charge of hypocrisy.

The involvement of women in America's founding – the spinning bees, the enforcement of economic boycotts, the camp followers at the front, the early voting in New Jersey, the fight to gain freedom by enslaved women – was an early sign of political awakening. Their embrace of education, intended or not by the male establishment, further cemented their place in the nation's polity. And when they were summoned to support the great causes of the coming century – against the genocidal removal of Native Americans from their lands, the barbaric institution of enslaving human beings, and the denial to women of their rights as citizens – they turned to one of the oldest tools in American jurisprudence, the petition.

The First Amendment had affirmed an old principle of British Common Law, "the right of the people … to petition the Government for a redress of grievances." The practice dated back to the Magna Charta, signed by King John of England in 1215, which established what came to be called human rights – the right of the church to exist without government interference, the right of citizens not to be overtaxed, and the principle of due process before the law, which included the right to petition the king to hear and address injustices. Many colonial administrations, such as the Massachusetts Body of Liberties, adopted the practice and extended it to those without a voice in government. Women, prisoners, African Americans, both slave and free, Native Americans seeking their tribal land claims – all used the process. In one case, African American women petitioned the Colony of Virginia in 1769 to relieve them of a tax that had been applied to black men, white men, and black women – but exempted white women. Free blacks and mixed-race men and women supported the bill. The Virginia Assembly agreed, enacting a new bill exempting black women too. During its 1789 session, the South Carolina House of Representatives received seventeen petitions signed by more than 2,000 citizens asking for bills of various kinds.

There had been much debate by the founders about whether the First Amendment's petition clause – so widely practiced in the colonies – should be amended to become a right not to petition but to instruct legislators how to vote. Favored by North Carolina and Virginia, the idea was rejected 41–10 as too radical, as it would turn the new government from one where laws were enacted by legislators representing their constituents to one where citizens directed lawmakers how to behave. Petitioning the government seemed a far more popular idea. Soon petitions came in on all kinds of issues – requests for an end to enslavement, for recognition of intellectual property, and often for pensions and war debt reimbursements. Jehoaikim M*Toksin, a Native American with the Moheconnuck or Stockbridge Nation, petitioned Congress successfully for back pay for serving as an interpreter for the colonies during the Revolutionary War. So numerous were the petitions from military widows that from the 1790s until the beginning of the Civil War, Congress enacted seventy-six statutes granting cash pensions to tens of thousands of widows of soldiers, and to veterans, who had served the young nation in the Revolutionary War and the War of 1812.

In *Common Sense*, Tom Paine had likened petitioning to policy "formed not in the senate but in the field; and insisted on by the people, not granted by the crown." Amid this embrace of the practice by British and now American lawmakers, Abigail Adams had once jokingly written to Mercy Otis Warren, "I think I will get you to join me in a petition to Congress." Other women took the right of appeal to heart. Mary Katherine Goddard of Maryland asked the First Congress to be reinstated as postmistress of the city of Baltimore. She had been Baltimore's postmistress for over fourteen years when she was suddenly dismissed. She was also an early American publisher, the second printer to publish the Declaration of Independence – and the first one that listed the names of those who signed the document. Appealing to allies, some of them speculating she was being purged because of her political alliance with her brother William and other anti-Federalists, she drew signatures from two hundred businessmen in the city. This petition, along with George Washington's executive order naming her to the position, was submitted to Congress. She was not returned to office.

Often, these efforts to "stand and speak," to insert themselves into the fabric of the nation's governmental concerns, took the form of petitions. Relegated to the backrooms of the revolutionary experiment, American women soon began using the art of petitioning not for themselves but to press for reforms as disparate as abolition, anti-lynching, anti-polygamy, temperance, and women's suffrage. They found a space between the limitation of service on the home front and the promise of participation in the public square. In this civic society, women could not hold office or vote but they could conduct themselves as citizens. The ideology of Republican Motherhood that had isolated them within the domestic domain emboldened them as they found a way to maintain their cultural femininity while affecting the decisions of the political nation. With petitions, they could assert their claim not just as mothers of patriots, but as citizens of the republic. Female activism became an extension of their role as keepers of virtue, first in the home and now in the nation. Tentatively at first, later with moral and out-loud certainty, they joined the national conversation. In campaigns to come, Congress would be deluged with their appeals.

2

Female Activism in Antebellum America

From the early 1800s, the U.S. government pursued an official policy to expel American Native tribes from their lands. During the War of 1812, Andrew Jackson had become a hero for fighting both the British and the Indians. Defeating the Creeks in Alabama, Jackson captured 23 million acres of Indian land for the United States. By then, industrialization had increased global demand for cotton, and annual consumption worldwide was about 900 million pounds. U.S. exports accounted for half the production. With such riches at stake, and with African slaves for sale to do the work, squatters quickly filled the Creek land. White farmers pressured Washington to forcibly remove the Native Americans from other lands despite the fact that the United States had pledged to respect their borders in innumerable treaties. In his inaugural address in 1829, Jackson proposed an Indian Removal Act that would force the Cherokee, Muscogee, Seminole, Chickasaw, Choctaw, and Ponca nations from their homes to territory earmarked for them west of the Mississippi, in Oklahoma. Stripped of their heritage, fleeing their lands, Native Americans left on horseback, on foot, and by ship. Along the way, thousands – estimates range from 4,000 to 10,000 – died from starvation, murder or disease. Their journey would come to be known as the Trail of Tears.

Influenced by the religious revival known as the Second Great Awakening, which called on Christians to purify their own souls and rectify the nation's sins, women stirred to the horrors of this genocide.

And Yet They Persisted: How American Women Won the Right to Vote, First Edition. Johanna Neuman.
© 2020 John Wiley & Sons, Inc. Published 2020 by John Wiley & Sons, Inc.
Companion website: www.wiley.com/go/Neuman

For fear of rousing the patriarchy, they did not engage in overt, political behavior. What the women did – and even this they did secretly – was to collect signatures from women around the country, petitioning Congress "in the name of humanity and mercy" to stop the mistreatment of the Indians. Their assertion of policy interest pushed the boundaries of their role as guardians of civic virtue, and provoked a violent backlash.

Men had accommodated women's push into the public space as an extension of Republican Motherhood, approving their charitable efforts to raise money for orphans or minister to the poor. Even in the temperance movement, their involvement, as keepers of moral authority, was seen as key to the success of any campaign for abstinence. But now, as female activists joined the reform causes of their day, from abolition of slavery to labor reform for female workers to rights of Native Americans to their land, they risked being called "rampant women," code for fanatic or promiscuous. Some male progressives stood at their sides. But other men greeted their activism with violence, burning down meeting halls and assaulting female speakers. As Jacksonian democracy expanded the number of white men engaged in the partisan business of politics, they viewed with alarm any effort by women to join the exclusively male pursuit, mocking what one Massachusetts editor in 1830 called "this amazon march to manhood." Female empowerment was a threat because it would rob these men of their newfound status as members of the political inner circle.

The Indian Removal Policy

Native American women had been pleading with their elders for several decades "not to part with any more of our lands." As one petition to the Cherokee national council explained, "The land was given to us by the Great Spirit above as our common right, to raise our children upon, & to make support for our rising generations." Now, in the summer of 1831, the daughter of Chief Mat-ta-tas went to a meeting with American officials with "a stick in her hand," to demonstrate women's connection to the land. Indian culture was traditionally divided by gender – men hunted game, women farmed the land. The community so valued farming that most tribes practiced matrilineal heritage. Wealth and name descended from the mother, not the father. But when the chief's daughter from the Saukenak tribe in Illinois explained to Major General Edmund P. Gaines that women could not leave the earth they had cultivated, that corn was the foundation of their wealth, he had difficulty absorbing the news that Indian women controlled property and had a say in Native political life. Insulted that war leader Black Hawk had sent a woman to mediate, he called off negotiations.

If Edmund Gaines was deaf to the Indian appeals, Jeremiah Evarts was not. A lawyer, missionary, and evangelical Christian, Evarts was also a believer in the Second Great Awakening, which preached to converts in tent revivals that Christians could achieve salvation not only by atoning for their personal sins but also by repenting for the moral imperfections of society. Before President Jackson could act, Evarts meant to stop him. A Christian nation had promises to keep, treaties to honor, humanity to respect. He appealed to influential members of Congress to speak against Indian removal on the floor. In 1829 he wrote a widely circulated and passionate memo of resistance, called *The William Penn Essays*. If the United States sinned by removing the Cherokees from their land, he wrote, the country would forever after suffer God's wrath. He wanted to summon a groundswell of public protest. He asked Catharine Beecher to mount a petition drive among women.

Founder of the Hartford Female Seminary, Catharine Beecher (Fig. 2.1) was the daughter of Presbyterian minister Lyman Beecher and sister of Harriet Beecher Stowe, whose 1852 novel *Uncle Tom's Cabin* became a bestseller – and, as Abraham Lincoln told her, many believed had sparked the Civil War – by depicting the cruelties of slavery. Catharine Beecher was moved by Evarts' appeal. But mindful of the risks of being accused of female impropriety, she agreed to help only if her role could be kept a secret. And so it was agreed. She wrote a poignant letter on behalf of the Cherokee, conspiring with the printer to keep her involvement hidden. Then she convened a circle of friends – including Lydia Sigourney, her colleague at the Seminary, and Faith Wadsworth, whose husband Daniel was the school's architect and whose brother John Trumbull had painted the iconic *Declaration of Independence* in 1817 – to help her organize a petition drive among women. They too pledged secrecy.

Each contributed the names of female friends in the great cities of the country. "It was remarkable how large a number were thus collected," Catharine recalled in her memoirs. To mask their identities, they arranged to mail the petition not from Hartford but from four large cities, likely including Boston and New York. They asked each recipient to share the petition with "the most influential and benevolent ladies of her acquaintance." In her unsigned letter, "Circular to Benevolent Ladies of the United States," Catharine Beecher explained the mission. "It has become almost a certainty, that these people are to have their lands torn from them, and to be driven into western wilds and to final annihilation, unless the feelings of a humane and Christian nation shall be aroused to prevent the unhallowed sacrifice," she wrote. Anticipating that many women might hesitate to join a political cause, she added, "Have not then the females of this country some duties devolving upon

Thomas K.   William   Edward   Charles   Henry Ward
Isabella   Catharine   Lyman   Mary   Harriet
James   THE BEECHER FAMILY, 1855.

Figure 2.1   Catharine Beecher, founder of the Hartford Female Seminary, was a member of a prominent antebellum family that included Lyman Beecher, a renowned minister, and author Harriet Beecher Stowe. Harriet's 1852 novel, *Uncle Tom's Cabin*, so graphically depicted the cruelties of slavery that Abraham Lincoln quipped on meeting her that she was the little lady who started the Civil War. Deeply moved by the plight of Cherokee Indians being forced from their lands, in 1830 Catharine began a petition drive among women urging Congress to reject Andrew Jackson's proposal for the Indian Removal Act. Although unsuccessful, her petition marked the greatest participation by women in the nation's political debate since the founding. *Source:* Getty Images. Hulton Deutsch.

them in relation to this helpless race?" Though the author's identity was masked, there was no attempt to hide the fact that the circular had been written by a woman, and was addressed to women, in the name of compassion. "Let every woman who peruses it … endeavor by every suitable expedient to interest the feelings of her friends, relatives and acquaintances, in behalf of this people, that are ready to perish. A few weeks must decide this interesting and important question, and after that time, sympathy and regret will all be in vain."

The response "exceeded our most sanguine expectations," Catharine Beecher recalled. Women held prayer meetings. They invited male speakers to lecture. And they gathered petition signatures by the hundreds. From Pittsburgh came 670 signatures, delivered to the Senate. From Hartford came a Ladies Association for Supplicating Justice and Mercy Toward the Indians, which met periodically to send off still more petitions to Congress. And from Steubenville, Ohio came an addendum, seeking to justify, or perhaps soften, the blow of female activism. Acknowledging that some might find such "presumptuous interference ... wholly unbecoming the character of American females," the women of Steubenville insisted they had no intention of governing. But they also suggested that even their husbands and brothers would understand this departure from the norm. Because "*There are times* when duty and affection call on us to *advise and persuade*, as well as to cheer or to console." In humility in the "cause of mercy and humanity," they submitted their signatures.

Male political petitioning had been going on since at least 1799, when free black men in Philadelphia, led by the Reverend Absalom Jones and the wealthy sail-maker James Forten, wrote urging Congress to repeal the fugitive slave law that endangered free black men by making them vulnerable to kidnapping by Southerners intent on enslaving them. While stopping short of calling for an end to slavery, the petition also urged Congress to "prepare the way for the oppressed to go free." Since the Republic's founding, women too had used petitions to seek redress of individual grievances such as requests for divorce or for wartime pensions. But never before had American women used petitions to protest an act of politics. Not all women warmed to the idea – some recoiled at petitioning as a violation of feminine manners. Even among participants, motivations differed too, from those who welcomed political engagement – one activist said the nation "seemed to be on the watch towers of politics and philanthropy" – to those driven by religious teachings of morality, believing that "God holds us accountable for all the talents which he has committed to our keeping."

Gatekeepers of the nation's religious and political male establishments were not pleased at this political action by women. "God would preserve our Congress," said the *Christian Watchman.* No need for "all the females in the land ... to get a question righteously decided." Many in Congress also felt the female activism an intrusion on their male privilege, a threat to their power. Thomas Hart Benton, who chaired the Senate Committee on Indian Affairs, mocked women for their audacity and suggested they retreat to their domestic role. No reason, he said, for women to "douse their bonnets, and tuck up their coats for such a race" as the Cherokee. Instead, they should "sit down on the way side, and wait for the coming of the conquerors." Although petitions from women may not have commanded the same attention on Capitol Hill as those from men, the public outrage prompted heated debate in

Congress from February through May, when the Indian Removal Act narrowly passed and President Jackson quickly signed it. Evarts tried to get the bill repealed, to re-energize the petitions, to no avail. He died two years later, at the age of 50.

The female petition drive to save the Cherokee had failed, but its legacy was to awaken in a generation of women the possibilities of serving God, country, and home – and prepare them for the likely resistance from the male hierarchy. For Catharine Beecher, the constant threat of exposure shattered her nerves, and she confessed years later that anxiety over her stealth activism left her "utterly prostrated and unable to perform any school duty without extreme pain and such confusion of thought as seemed like approaching insanity." In coming decades, as women spoke up for other public causes, a chastened Beecher warned they would lose their moral compass, corrupted by power in the "arena of political collusion."

The Lowell Mill Girls

By the 1820s, the industrial revolution had moved many families from farm to city. With many men migrating West in search of riches and land, labor in the East was limited. Young women were recruited to work at the textile mills, including in Lowell, Massachusetts. Founded by Francis Cabot Lowell, the planned development became known as the City of Spindles, and by the end of the decade factories there employed 8,000 women and girls between the ages of 15 and 35, most from farming backgrounds, the nation's first nearly all female labor force. Well groomed and articulate, they were housed in chaperoned boarding houses with strict curfews meant to protect them from vice and quiet the fury of religious leaders who objected to the very idea of women working in the textile industry. Soon they attracted the moral approval of visitors such as Charles Dickens, who proclaimed Lowell's sanitary conditions far superior to filthy European industrial capitals such as Manchester, England. At first, earning a salary and living in shared housing gave them a rare degree of independence from families, and a measure of camaraderie. Despite thirteen-hour days, and six-day-a-week schedules, one textile worker, Lucy Larcom, wrote that it was "one of the privileges of my youth that I was permitted to grow up among these active, interesting girls."

But by 1837, amid declining prices for cotton and wool, factory owners cut wages, sped up the machines, and extended work hours. By then, conditions had deteriorated, or perhaps reports of them became more accurate. A mill worker named Amelia wrote that mill girls had it worse "than the poor peasant of Ireland or the Russian serf who labors from sun to sun." Larcom confided that at the age of 12 she "hated the confinement, noise, and lint-filled air, and regretted the time lost to education." The Lowell Mill Girls went on strike, marching to mills, attending outdoor rallies, and circulating a petition to owners saying, "We will not go back into the mills to work unless our wages are continued." In the face of their "turn-outs," or strikes, factory owners dismissed their protests as "an amizonian display" of aggression, one where the girls had been overtaken by "a spirit of evil omen." In 1842, after the Middlesex Manufacturing Company announced a speedup and resulting 20 percent pay cut, seventy female workers walked out. All were fired and blacklisted. Three years later, mill girls formed the Lowell Female Labor Reform Association. They sent petitions to the Massachusetts legislature demanding that the work day be reduced to ten hours to benefit women's health, as well as their "intellectual, moral and religious habits." Appealing to class over gender, they called on male unions to fight for improved conditions for female workers.

But perhaps the most controversial thing the Lowell Mill Girls did was to speak out in public. "One of the girls stood on a pump and gave vent to the feelings of her companions in a neat speech, declaring that it was their duty to resist all attempts at cutting down the wages," Harriet Hanson Robinson recalled fifty years later. "This was the first time a woman had spoken in public in Lowell, and the event caused surprise and consternation among her audience." Before 1829, women did not speak in public. They did not join political parties or give lectures from the town square. Such a breach of gender decorum would brand them as "unsexed," making them unmarriageable. One critic, reformer Orestes Brownson, claimed that three years in the factories ruined the reputation of the Lowell Mill Girls. "Few of them ever marry; fewer still ever return to their native places with reputations unimpaired," he wrote. The expression "she has worked in a factory," he added, "is almost enough to damn to infamy the most worthy and virtuous girl." The assertion of gender and class interest by the Lowell Mill Girls was a preview of coming waves of female activism, none more insistent than the call to abolish slavery. But it was the Lowell Mill Girls' example in walking to the podium "to stand and speak" that cast the longest shadow. In the next generation, as other women began to speak against slavery, their assertion that women should have a voice in the polity and a role in the policy decisions of their nation divided the abolitionist movement.

The Female Fight Against Slavery

Inspired by Quaker theologian Elias Hicks, Lucretia Coffin Mott became a minister in 1831 at the age of 28, giving sermons about the presence of the Divine in every individual, including slaves. She was so adamant about ending slavery that she, like other Quakers, refused to import cotton clothing, cane sugar, and slavery-produced goods from the South. Much as colonial women had stopped importing British imports during the Revolution, these boycott leaders hoped to choke off the taproot of slavery's economic power. Her husband James Mott, once a cotton trader, had likewise abandoned the business because of its links to slavery, instead becoming a wool merchant. Lucretia Mott often spoke at churches to challenge the clergy to support abolition as a matter of Christian faith. In one sermon in Philadelphia, she used the cruelties of slavery to prick the hypocrisy of religious leaders. Calling it "an unworthy application of the scriptures," she told of a Methodist leader who "tied up a slave woman and flogged her till the blood streamed down her back; and when he had finished his brutal task, he quoted to her the text, 'He that knoweth his master's will and doeth it not, shall be beaten with many stripes.'" In another speech, this one to a Unitarian Church in Washington, DC, she lamented, "The Bible has been quoted to authorize nearly every wrong." She called on all people of all denominations, and of none, to "contribute what we can to the advancement of practical righteousness in the earth."

By the time abolitionist William Lloyd Garrison formed the American Anti-Slavery Society (AASS) in Philadelphia in 1833, Mott was already such an accomplished speaker that she was the only woman invited to address the proceedings. By then, black women in Salem, Massachusetts had organized what is believed to be the first female anti-slavery society, in February 1832, followed by women in Rhode Island in July. The AASS, formed in the weeks before Christmas, had as its mission to "spare no exertions nor means to bring the whole nation to speedy repentance" over the sin of slavery. Although Mott and three other women – Lydia White, Esther Moore, and Sidney Ann Lewis – were observers at the conference, they were not invited to join as members or sign the society's founding document, only encouraged to begin their own, separate and unequal, female auxiliaries. Three days later Mott joined with black and white women to form the Philadelphia Female Anti-Slavery Society, which opposed both slavery and racism. Some 10 percent of its members were African American women, and among the group's officers the proportion was greater still.

For white members, the society's biracial identity lent credence to its goal of emancipating American slaves and securing their equality. For African American women, the opportunity to help the enslaved and impoverished of their race was key. But joining the Philadelphia Female Anti-Slavery Society also allowed them to demonstrate, half a century after the nation's founding, that free blacks had become upstanding members of Philadelphia's elite community. James Forten was born free in Philadelphia in 1766, and at the age of 15 joined the Continental navy. His great grandfather had been a slave, brought to Philadelphia by the Dutch. His grandfather purchased his own freedom. Captured by the British during the war, Forten was released after seven months on condition he not return to the fighting. He signed on instead as an apprentice to Philadelphia's premier sail-maker, eventually becoming one of the wealthiest men in Philadelphia, black or white, said to be worth $100,000, or about $2 billion in today's dollars. All of his nine children were raised in a home, at 92 Lombard Street, that welcomed visiting abolitionists. Margaretta Forten had helped write the anti-slavery society's constitution. Charlotte Forten was a member, along with sisters Harriet Forten Purvis and Sarah Forten Purvis, who had married into the prominent abolitionist Purvis family. Sarah Mapps Douglass was from another influential Philadelphia family. Her maternal great grandfather, Cyrus Bustill, had served as a baker for the Continental Army and was one of the founding members of the charitable Free African Society. Her mother Grace Bustill Douglass was a milliner who had started a school for blacks with James Forten.

These black women were educated and privileged, in stark contrast to one of the earliest female abolitionists. Born to free black parents in Hartford, Maria Stewart was one of the first African American women to speak publicly before a "promiscuous" audience, the term at the time for any mixed-gender group of men and women. Orphaned at five years old and "bound out" to a clergyman's family, she worked as a servant for ten years. Her only schooling was to attend the minister's Sabbath School, to imbibe the Bible. After the death of her mentor, Boston merchant David Walker, and her husband, shipping agent James W. Stewart, in 1830, she determined to become "a strong advocate for the cause of God and for the cause of freedom." In her speeches, she lashed out at white reformers for ignoring the sexual crimes committed against black women – "Thou hast caused the daughters of Africa to commit whoredoms and fornications" – and at free black men for failing to take advantage of the opportunities not available to slaves. "Had those men among us who had an opportunity, turned their attention as assiduously to mental and moral improvement as they had to gambling and dancing," she told an audience at the African Masonic Hall in 1833, "I might have remained quietly at home and they stood contending in my place." But she reserved her greatest thunder for black women, seeing them as the great moral influence on public opinion. "How long should the fair daughters of Africa be compelled to bury their minds and talents beneath a load of iron pots and kettles?" she asked. "Never will the chains of slavery and ignorance burst till we become united as one and cultivate among ourselves the pure principles of piety, morality and virtue." Urging black women to confront the power embodied by slavery and racism, she asked, "Who shall go forward, and take off the reproach that is cast upon the people of color? Shall it be a woman?"

Women still enslaved also played a role in the anti-slavery movement of the antebellum era. Arranging work slowdowns, feigning illness, and fleeing to freedom – all were signs of slave resistance. Once the Civil War began, these so-called bondswomen fled their plantations, often running off to freedom in Yankee camps with their mistresses' finest dresses, laces, ribbons, and trinkets, their first declarations of self-expression. When Stewart spoke of the need for free blacks to take advantage of their opportunities to lead, jeers often met her sermons, especially among female audiences. Perhaps she was thinking of the restraints on enslaved blacks, the limits on their agency. Stewart soon retired from the speaker's podium, spending the rest of her career as a teacher. Other female activists came in her place.

Scores of female anti-slavery societies soon proliferated – the largest formed in Boston and Philadelphia in 1833, followed by New York in 1835 – and the rifts within their ranks were a proxy for a wider debate about women's role in abolitionism. The Boston Female Anti-Slavery Society prided itself on a biracial membership, but religious, class, and racial conflicts often resulted. Women connected to the evangelical clergy, such as the group's president, Mary Parker, shunned formal political activities, while educators Maria Weston Chapman, Abby Kelley Foster, and Lydia Maria Child pushed for reform at state legislative sessions and court hearings, and lawsuits to challenge court rulings in favor of slaveholders. They were ridiculed by reporters as "petticoat politicians," causing discomfort to other members, more involved in their churches, hesitant to risk clerical rejection with such overt political behavior. The Ladies' New York City Anti-Slavery Society refused to admit African American members, and did not sanction female involvement in political activism. No matter their internal divisions, the prominence of these societies soon attracted the attention of vigilantes outraged at reports that white and black abolitionists were meeting together. The motives of these disrupters also varied. Some seethed at female activism as an affront to male political authority, as an effort to topple the founders' vision of a white America.

In 1833, Andrew Judson had led a fight to close down a school for black women in Canterbury, Connecticut, saying, "America is ours – it belongs to a race of white men." In 1834, fearful that elite reformers were trying to impose racial intermarriage or abolition of slavery on the city, rioters in New York targeted abolitionists' homes and churches, and the Farren Theater, where the English owner had been critical of Americans for not abolishing slavery. Now, one year later, crowds in Boston planned to attack a visiting speaker, British activist George Thompson, a leader in the London Anti-Slavery Society. Garrison had invited Thompson to lecture about abolitionism at a meeting of the Boston Female Anti-Slavery Society. Already, his appearances in nearby towns of Lowell, Lynn, and Abington had ended in riots. On learning of the impending violence, Garrison insisted that Thompson flee to safety. Rioters threatened the meeting anyway. Members of the Boston Female Anti-Slavery Society – who included wealthy women as well as blacks from Boston's Belknap Street neighborhood, members of the African Baptist and Zion churches, and workers newly arrived from rural New England – refused to leave. As Chapman put it, "If this is the last bulwark of freedom, we may as well die here as anywhere." Persuaded finally to exit, the black and white members walked arm-in-arm through the belligerent crowd. By his own account, Garrison, who filled in for Thompson as a speaker, was dragged through the street by the rioters until officials rescued him. Disguising him in new clothes, they went by a circuitous route to the city jail, where he was imprisoned overnight for his own protection.

Soon, Chapman reached out to the Philadelphia group, suggesting that the various societies form a "general executive committee" to coordinate strategy. As a result, on May 9, 1837, some seventy-one female abolitionists from twenty-five societies in seven states gathered in New York, in what is believed to be the first national convention of American women. One of them was Lydia Maria Child, a novelist who five years earlier had published *An Appeal in Favor of that Class of Americans Called Africans*, calling for the immediate emancipation of the slaves in the South and an end to racism in the North. At the convention, she was excited to meet the Grimke sisters. Born into a slave-owning family in Charleston, South Carolina, Angelina Grimke, 32, and her older sister Sarah, 45, were eager to give witness to the daily humiliations of slavery. As a young girl, Angelina (Fig. 2.2) had watched in class one day when a slave boy about her age was summoned to open a window. She saw he had been so "dreadfully whipped that he could barely walk." A friend told her that she lived near where the slaves were banished for punishment and "often heard screams of slaves under their torture." Sarah was severely punished once by their father for teaching a slave girl to read and write. Their brother Henry once gave the slave butler a blow to the head so severe he was subjected to epileptic seizures thereafter. They had fled the South to testify to these cruelties.

They had also left Charleston to find a new religion. Influenced by the Second Great Awakening, sure that their mother's Episcopalian faith was as culpable as the system of slavery it protected, they left for Pennsylvania, to convert to the Quaker religion that held slavery a sin.

Figure 2.2   Angelina Grimke and her sister Sarah were born to a slave-owning family in Charleston, South Carolina. As young girls, they had witnessed the daily humiliations of slavery. They came North to testify these cruelties. Both became passionate speakers against slavery and for women's rights, despite opposition of some men within the abolitionist movement to the idea of women speaking in public. Angelina in particular urged women to "do all that she can by her voice, and her pen, and her purse, and the influence of her example, to overthrow the horrible system of American slavery." *Source:* Library of Congress Prints and Photographs Division.

In 1835 Angelina had attended a lecture by British abolitionist George Thompson, joined the Philadelphia Female Anti-Slavery Society, and learned of abolitionist William Lloyd Garrison. In a letter Garrison published in his newspaper, *Liberator,* she declared, "It is my deep, solemn, deliberate conviction that this is a cause worth dying for." In her *Appeal to the Christian Women of the South* in 1836, Angelina urged women to persuade their legislators on the issue, "as a matter of morals and religion, not of expediency or politics." Citing the recent successful petitions against slavery in the British West Indies, she also made the issue one of special moment for women, not as keepers of a Republican Motherhood but as guardians of a religious one. "Have not *women* stood up in all the dignity, and strength of moral courage to be the leaders of the people, and to bear a faithful testimony for the truth whenever the providence of God has called them to do so?" she asked.

At the convention, both sisters offered resolutions targeting northern complicity in southern slavery – including cooperation in returning fugitive slaves. They gave witness to the sexual immorality of slavery – where white women were complicit in the sexual unions between their husbands and their slaves, in the name of producing more slaves. Angelina offered a resolution – ultimately passed but not unanimously – calling on women to leave the domestic sphere and "do all that she can by her voice, and her pen, and her purse, and the influence of her example, to overthrow the horrible system of American slavery."

Afterward the Grimke sisters left for a speaking trip that took them to sixty-seven cities in twenty-three weeks. In February 1838 Angelina became the first American woman to speak before a governing committee, addressing the Massachusetts legislature. "As soon as we entered we were received by clapping," she wrote a friend. But when she rose to speak she was "greeted by hisses," interrupted three times by loud disapproval. "No doubt great numbers who have attended them come out of mere curiosity; some to make fun of such a strange anomaly as a Woman addressing a Committee of the Legislature; they came despising me and my cause from the bottom of their hearts," she wrote. "But I trust the Lord will overrule all things to his own glory, the manumission of the slave and the elevation of woman." To another friend she wrote, "We Abolitionist Women are turning the world upside down."

The advent of the female abolitionist – one who organized, spoke, and wrote – did not escape the notice of men who resisted the idea of women entering the public square. The General Association of Mass Churches condemned female activism as "unchristian." Men, said the clergy, should not be encouraging women to abandon their families for politics. In a letter to their parishes, Congregational pastors condemned the Grimke sisters for defying New Testament commandments precluding female participation in public life. The idea of female advocacy also rankled some within abolitionism's ranks, who feared female speakers would muddy the anti-slavery campaign with an even less popular cause – that of women. In no small measure these critics of female abolitionist speakers helped push reformers toward a separate women's rights movement, a space where they could debate their own issues.

For now, Sarah Grimke addressed the church leaders, noting that the very Bible they were quoting was a product of the patriarchy that wrote it. "All I ask our brethren is that they will take their feet from off our necks, and permit us to stand upright on that ground which God designed us to occupy," she wrote. Angelina comprehended that the clergy were defending their turf. "If it can be fairly established that women *can lecture*, then why may they not preach, & if *they* can preach, then woe! Woe be unto that Clerical Denomination which now rules the world." In a letter to several abolitionists, including Theodore Weld, who would later become her husband, Angelina Grimke spelled out why it was important for women to speak, connecting the very voice of females to the cause of freedom for slaves. "If we surrender the right to *speak* to the public this year, we must surrender the right to petition next year & the right to write the year after &x," she wrote. "What *then* can *woman* do for the slave, when she herself is under the feet of man & shamed into *silence?*"

Perhaps the pinnacle of male resistance to female activism against slavery came in Philadelphia at the Anti-Slavery Convention of American Women in 1838. There, Angelina Grimke endured the stone-throwing rebellion of male anti-abolitionists who were enraged by the sight of black and white women meeting together. Explaining why women were particularly compelled to advocate for the anti-slavery cause, she said, "Men may settle this and other questions at the ballot box but you have no such right. It is only through petitions that you can reach the legislature. It is, therefore, peculiarly your duty to petition. Men who hold the rod over slaves rule in the councils of the nation; and they deny our right to petition and remonstrate against abuses of our sex and our kind. We have these rights, however, from our God. Only let us exercise them." A mob outside threatened to burn down Pennsylvania Hall, which had been dedicated as a meeting hall only months before by abolitionists, complete with its motto "Virtue, Liberty and Independence."

Abby Kelley, a friend of the Grimke sisters, was another Quaker educator who took up the cause of public speaking against slavery just as they were leaving it. The seventh daughter of Massachusetts farmers, she had borrowed money from her older sister to attend college. Later, teaching school in Lynn, she met other Quakers who had already adopted the dietary restrictions suggested by Sylvester Graham and already gravitated to the conviction of William Lloyd Garrison that slavery should be abolished. In 1837, she joined the local Female Anti-Slavery Society, which collected signatures of six thousand women, nearly half the women in Lynn, on an anti-slavery petition. Like Garrison, she condemned the U.S. Constitution as a pro-slavery document. And, after she married fellow abolitionist Stephen S. Foster, she and her husband offered their home, Liberty Farm in Worcester, Massachusetts, as a safe house on the Underground Railroad. The farm is now a national historic landmark.

Her first speech was to the same Anti-Slavery Convention of American Women where Angelina Grimke gave her last. With a mob threatening to burn down the building, Kelley talked of a "moral whirlwind" that also gripped the nation. Against these forces, she said, "it is the still small voice within, which may not be withstood, that bids me open my mouth for the dumb, – that bids me plead the cause of God's perishing poor – ay, God's poor." By the conference's third day, a menacing group of men prowled the perimeter, "examining the gas-pipes, and talking in an 'incendiary' manner to groups which they collected around them in the street." The mayor of Philadelphia, understanding that what enraged the mob was the meeting's biracial nature, ordered that the next day's proceedings be restricted to white women only. This the society refused to do. Instead, on the mayor's instructions, managers locked the doors, cancelling all meetings. Undeterred, the mob set the building on fire, which firefighters and police officials did little to impede. The riot continued for several days, as the mob burned down a black orphanage and damaged a black church. An official report by the city blamed the abolitionists, saying they had incited violence by their "race mixing."

Now Kelley joined Garrison's team of female orators, relentless, lecturing for two to three hours a day, for as many days as required, until her listeners enlisted. She dressed in Quaker gray – no bright colors or bowed embellishments allowed – and endured missiles of rotten eggs. "All the great family of mankind are bound up in one bundle," she once said. "When we aim a blow at our neighbor's rights our own are by the same blow destroyed. Can we look upon the wrongs of millions – can we see their flow of tears and grief and blood, and not feel our hearts drawn out in sympathy?" On another she reminded women of their debt to one another. "Sisters, bloody feet wore smooth the path by which you come up here."

Uncompromising in her views on abolition, she urged women to publicly confront ministers and leave their churches if the houses of God failed to renounce slavery, an appeal called "come-outerism." She was passionate not just about abolishing slavery but about ensuring that black Americans would be treated as equals in white society. She opposed military intervention to end slavery, saying this cruel institution should be defeated not with violence and bloodshed but with moral suasion. In many places, she was as likely to spark controversy as converts. When she spoke in Waterloo, New York in 1842, the local newspaper, the *Seneca Falls Democrat*, headlined her talk, "Treason! Treason!" Frederick Douglass, the former slave who would awe audiences with his eloquence, was just starting his speaking career when he encountered "the fascinating Abby Kelley" on tour. "Her youth and simple Quaker beauty, combined with her wonderful earnestness, her large knowledge and great logical power bore down all opposition wherever she spoke, though she was pelted with foul eggs and no less foul words from the noisy mobs which attended us," he recalled.

Mob violence complicated the ability of female abolitionists to continue their work. Business owners and church leaders who once rented them meeting space refused. For their meeting the following year, the Philadelphia Female Anti-Slavery Society met at the African American school headed by Sarah Mapps Douglass. With black membership falling, planners of the next Anti-Slavery Convention of American Women appealed to their "colored sisters" to participate, demonstrating their commitment to equality by visiting African American families throughout the city to help lift them out of "degradation, ignorance and poverty."

By this time, several prominent women in the abolitionist movement had concluded that they could be more effective rejoining the male abolitionist movement. Lydia Maria Child said female-only conventions were as effective as "half a pair of scissors." Abby Kelley too thought female conventions unnecessary. Given Kelley's record as a fundraiser for the cause and for newspapers such as the *Anti-Slavery Bugle*, in 1840 she ran for a position on the business committee of the American Anti-Slavery Society. The idea that a woman would participate in business meetings was so radical, so threatening to male hegemony, that a splinter group, headed by New Yorkers Lewis and Arthur Tappan, now formed a rival American and Foreign Anti-Slavery Society. Although the Tappan brothers were staunch abolitionists – they had underwritten the creation of the New York Female Anti-Slavery Society, and Arthur Tappan had married a black woman – they did not want women mixing in the serious business of male societies. Politics of any kind, abolitionism included, was for men.

Mob violence also doused willingness of female abolitionists to canvass neighborhoods in search of petition signatures to send to Congress. The effectiveness of petitioning had reached its peak in 1837, when the Anti-Slavery Convention of American Women undertook a massive national effort to influence congressional opinion. Assigning two or three members to every district in each city where it had an affiliated anti-slavery society, the group hoped that if "all the maids and matrons of the land knock at the door of Congress, our Statesmen must legislate." That year the Philadelphia Female Anti-Slavery Society alone collected 5,000 signatures, and by one estimate abolitionists had sent in 130,000 petition signatures nationally in 1837–1838. But by the end of the decade, amid a surge of mob violence against abolitionists, many women expressed fear about seeking signatures from private homes. As for Congress, southerners imposed a series of gag rules that tabled action on all resolutions relating to slavery, without a hearing. Having used petitions to try to persuade men against the evils of the Indian removal policy, of workplace exploitation of women and children, of alcoholism and of slavery, female activists now returned to the public podium.

Perhaps Abby Kelley Foster's greatest legacy is that she developed a fan base of "Abby Kelleyites," inspiring the activism of younger abolitionists and suffragists such as Lucy Stone and Susan B. Anthony. As Stone later recalled, "Abby Kelley earned for us all the right of free speech. The movement for equal rights began directly and emphatically with her."

Speaking for Women's Rights

Lucy Stone (Fig. 2.3) was 20 years old when she and her family went to a lecture by Abby Kelley. Ministers in their town of Brookfield, Massachusetts had recently issued a pastoral letter against offering church pulpits to anti-slavery speakers, especially women. Comparing women to a vine "whose strength and beauty it is to lean upon the trelliswork," the letter warned them against assuming "the independence and the overshadowing nature of the elm." Such gender confusion, the clergy said, could only hurt the vine, which would "not only cease to bear fruit but fall in shame and dishonor into the dust." On hearing the pastoral letter read aloud, Stone, then working as a teacher so she could save money to attend Oberlin College, "blazed with indignation." One clergyman in town, Deacon Henshaw, had defied the edict by inviting Kelley to use his pulpit for an anti-slavery speech. And so the Stone family, and most of Brookfield, had piled into wagons to make the three-mile trek. Later Deacon Henshaw faced charges of disobedience from the church hierarchy. As a member of his congregation, Stone attended his trial and raised her hand to vote in his favor. A minister insisted that women were not "voting members." Six times the question was put, and each time she raised her hand, only to be counted out. It made of her a feminist.

Angered by the Brookfield religious edict that discouraged women from engaging in public debate, Sarah Grimke authored *Letters on the Equality of the Sexes*, serialized in the *New England Spectator*. She likened the Brookfield clergy to Cotton Mather, minister of Boston's Old North Church, who had warned good Christians against the temptations of witchcraft. Grimke advocated universal, co-educational education, seeking for women "the same platform of human rights and moral dignity and intellectual improvement" as that of men. She warned women, "As long as we submit to be dressed like dolls, we never can rise to the stations of duty and usefulness from which they desire to exclude us." Stone read the *Letters*, predicting it would do the women's rights movement "lots of good."

Figure 2.3   The sixth child of a farming family where Francis Stone demanded much work and brooked no rebellion, Lucy Stone became one of the great lights of the fight for abolition and one of the first speakers for women's rights. She was the first woman in Massachusetts to earn a college degree, graduating from Oberlin College in Ohio, the first institution in the country to admit women and African Americans. Finishing at the top of her class, she was invited to write a commencement address for delivery by a male student. She declined. After the Civil War, she formed the American Woman Suffrage Association and the most important suffrage newspaper of the day, the Boston-based *Woman's Journal*. *Source:* Getty Images. Bettmann.

The sixth child of a farming family where Francis Stone demanded much work and brooked no rebellion, Lucy Stone became one of the great lights of the fight for abolition and "the morning star" of women's rights. For four years she had attended Oberlin College in Ohio, the first such institution in the country to admit women and African Americans. Finishing at the top of her class, she was invited to write a commencement address for delivery by a male student. She declined. On graduation she became the first woman in Massachusetts to earn a college degree. In her senior year, a visiting Abby Kelley Foster had suggested to Stone that she lecture for the Massachusetts Anti-Slavery Society, then recruiting new speakers.

By the summer of 1847, Stone began lecturing for the Anti-Slavery Society, provoking much anger by men in the audience, who pelted the stage with prayer books, rotten fruit, and sometimes on a winter's day, cold water. Amid the din, one reporter found poetry. "I have never, anywhere, heard a speaker whose style of eloquence I more admired," he wrote. "The pride of her acquaintances, the ideal of the crowd, wherever she goes, the people *en masse* turn out to hear Lucy Stone." One male critic was captivated by her voice. He had arrived to scoff and left full of conviction. "The moment that that woman spoke to me she had me at complete command," he said. "I would have done anything for her ... she has the voice of an angel, and with that voice, she can't be anything but a good woman."

Traveling to five or six different locations a week, she was usually subjected to ridicule. Once, on publicizing her speech in Malden, a suburb of Boston, a local clergyman announced from his pulpit, "This evening, at the Town Hall, a hen will attempt to crow!" Often she shared the program with far more prominent speakers, such as Wendell Phillips, Stephen Foster, and Parker Pillsbury. Once in Cape Cod, an angry crowd stormed the stage. Much as she had as a teacher addressing a school bully in one of her classes, Stone asked one of the attackers to escort her outside. The man not only ushered her to safety outside, he also stood guard as she climbed a tree stump and continued to lecture. In its annual report of 1848, the Anti-Slavery Society said she had been "of very high value" to the cause, attributing her popularity to the "thoroughness of preparation ... and the gentleness of demeanor."

She was not a thunder and brimstone speaker, in the fashion of the popular evangelicals, but a teacher, using the detail to make the grander point. She told stories that sprang from her devotion to the abolitionist cause. In one she related a father's ordeal as he tried to lead his family in escape from slavery, only to watch in despair as their hiding place was discovered and they were all recaptured. On another occasion, at Boston's Faneuil Hall, she invited to the stage an escaped slave, telling her, "Bless you my sister." For her, slavery was a disease on the nation's soul, one that "cursed us spiritually, morally and materially." Women were oppressed not by physical chains and whippings but by male arrogance and power, she argued, and both were subjected to indignities that lashed the spirit. Her stories about fugitive mothers often moved her audience to tears. In 1853, one audience member, Henry Browne Blackwell, was smitten, and asked Garrison for a letter of introduction. As Blackwell courted her, Lucy Stone resisted marriage, fearful she would lose her voice, her individuality. In 1855, she acquiesced, and they were married in a special ceremony in which he renounced the legal rights of property conferred on a husband and she elected to keep her maiden name. In fact, the Stone–Blackwell union may be one of the few marriages to take place under duress, with bride and groom issuing a personal protest against laws which give the husband "custody of the wife's person, the control and guardianship of their children" and any wages she might earn, as well as laws that precluded her from signing a will or inheriting property.

Soon, officials at the Anti-Slavery Society protested her mingling of the two causes. Samuel May, a wealthy activist who backed abolition as well as labor reforms, was the society's recording secretary. Now he confronted her about complaints they had received. "The people came to hear anti-slavery, and not woman's rights; and it isn't right." To this Stone replied, "I was a woman before I was an abolitionist." She offered to resign, to devote herself solely to defending women's rights. Neither was happy with this outcome – Stone did not mean to abandon abolitionism, and May could not afford to lose such a popular speaker. So they agreed that she would receive a reduced fee – from $6 to $4 a week – for lectures on Saturdays and Sundays to advance the cause of the slave. And then on weekdays, when fewer came to hear lectures, she could speak about equality for women. In this way she became the first woman in the country to make a living as a lecturer for women's rights.

She spoke at a time when the question of whether women were entitled to equal treatment in the law was gaining traction as a matter of public debate. Ideas that once sounded novel or even radical – that mothers, for instance, should have as much authority in the raising of children as fathers – were beginning to percolate up from the grassroots. Ever since the 1830s, when Andrew Jackson expanded the white electorate to include working-class men, the idea of women voting had gained a grasp within progressive circles. In 1846, as New York convened a state constitutional convention, petitioners from at least three counties called for delegates to enact a provision granting women the right to vote. Among them were six women from Jefferson County. And in Michigan that year, Ernestine Rose addressed her legislature, arguing that female reformers needed the right to vote.

In 1848, Lucretia Mott and Elizabeth Cady Stanton would call a convention on women's rights at a Methodist chapel in Seneca Falls, New York. Nearly 300 male and female delegates attended. Susan B. Anthony, member of a progressive Rochester Quaker family, was not one of the delegates, though several of her relatives were, and they told her enthusiastically about its particulars. Anthony was holding back, shy about her ability to persuade audiences, resisting Abby Kelley's entreaties to join her cadre of anti-slavery speakers. She was a teacher, not a preacher. Her chance meeting with Stanton in 1851 came in Seneca Falls, where she had traveled not to hear calls for women's suffrage but to hear Garrison and Thompson speak about slavery. More than Stanton, she was a proté-gée of the abolitionist movement, a Quaker who believed in reforming society through moral example.

Joining the anti-slavery cause had taught women the art of organization and argument, the advantages of moral suasion and the risks of male violence. For black women and white, the female anti-slavery societies that formed autonomous female-run organizations within the abolitionist movement offered a way to learn the needed if dull minutiae of politics, from note taking to parliamentary procedure. This was their foothold into the public sphere, their introduction to the ways of male power. Along the way, they had been assaulted, their assembly halls burned to the ground, their speakers hunted through the streets. They were mocked as "rampant women," ridiculed for seeking reforms because they were too unattractive to find a husband and raise a family, or too wild to deserve one. Progressive men who stood with them, often called "Miss Nancys," or "man milliners," were likewise denigrated for opening the gates of male power, for lacking virility. Abby Kelley and other white women had made some progress in penetrating the male power structures of the abolition movement, but African American men and women rarely did. The abolitionist movement would be the last major biracial coalition for change for more than a century.

Now, the reform efforts of benevolence and religion gave way to demands for equal rights. They had learned much from the fight against slavery, from the painstaking work of building coalitions to the prosaic stuff of running meetings. But they had also observed that a male establishment would not cede power unless it was met by power on the other side. From the abolitionist movement Elizabeth Cady Stanton took rhetorical inspiration and tactical instructions. But from her own biography she took passion for overturning the patriarchy that had restricted her life. What animated her activism was a sense that women were enslaved by laws that preserved their husbands' control over money, property, and children. With no right to divorce a drunken or abusive husband, no right to pursue an education or career of her own choosing, no right to vote out of office political men who perpetuated this entrapment, women in Stanton's view were as aggrieved as slaves. She was no religionist, but Stanton hoped her words would launch a rebellion, in churches and in homes. "By the foolishness of preaching," she said, "must all moral revolutions be achieved."

3

From Female Influence
to Women's Rights

As the American delegation sailed for London in 1840 to attend the first World Anti-Slavery Convention, there were signs of progress. Only a few years before, Britain had officially abolished slavery, although the cruel institution would persist for decades in parts of the vast British Empire. In America, most northern states were working toward gradual emancipation of slaves, though the slave population, with its economic benefits to growers, was increasing in the South. More, the cause of the slaves, known as abolitionism, was attracting new converts, as female anti-slavery societies proliferated in America and abolitionist sentiment spread in Europe. Called for the purpose of "stamping out the vestiges of the international slave trade and to undermining American slavery," the World Anti-Slavery Convention, however, would be remembered less for the vigor of its abolitionist agenda than for its view of women's rights as a threat to male power.

The first question to be addressed, though it was not on the agenda, was whether to seat the seven female abolitionists who had arrived unexpectedly as part of the official delegation of William Lloyd Garrison's American Anti-Slavery Society. Their inclusion had already divided the American abolitionist movement, so angering New Yorker Lewis Tappan that a few months earlier he had bolted from the AASS to form a rival group that banned women as members. There were other issues that divided the two organizations – including whether the moral question of slavery could be resolved politically – but it was the issue of female

And Yet They Persisted: How American Women Won the Right to Vote, First Edition. Johanna Neuman.
© 2020 John Wiley & Sons, Inc. Published 2020 by John Wiley & Sons, Inc.
Companion website: www.wiley.com/go/Neuman

activists that ignited the most animosity between the two sides. Debate in London was equally heated.

British delegates suggested the Americans should heed local custom and abide by a men-only policy. Americans countered that Britain had a Queen on the throne, and anyway that it was not a matter of custom but of morality. British delegates took great offense that the Americans seemed to be lecturing *them* on a matter of conscience, they who had already ended the slave trade. Dismissing women's rights as an unworthy topic for an anti-slavery convention, they urged male delegates to reject such an infringement on their authority. As British Reverend C. Stout put it, "Are we not met here pledged to sacrifice all but everything, in order that we may do something against slavery, and shall we be divided on this *paltry question* and suffer the whole tide of benevolence to be stopped by *a straw*? No! You talk of being men, then be men!" British hosts succeeded in banishing the women to a separate section to watch the proceedings from the gallery, with no rights to speak. In solidarity, Garrison and American abolitionist Nathaniel P. Rogers, editor of the Concord, New Hampshire *Herald of Freedom*, sat with them. Voting against the American women, sitting on the convention floor with the men, was Henry Brewster Stanton, an American abolitionist whose wife later looked back at this convention as one of the turning points in her life.

Elizabeth Cady Stanton was a 24-year-old bride, spending her honeymoon with a man whose passionate speeches against slavery had swept her off her feet. Over her father's misgivings about the ability of the near penniless Stanton to provide for his daughter, the two had married, in a ceremony in which the word "obey" was dropped from the oath. They had sailed almost at once for London. Elizabeth was not a delegate to the convention, only an observer, but she was outraged that the American women had been silenced. "It struck me as very remarkable that abolitionists who felt so keenly the wrongs of the slave should be so oblivious to the equal wrongs of their own mothers, wives and sisters," she wrote. Unlike many delegates, she had not participated in the abolitionist movement, was neither a Quaker nor an evangelical. But she thrilled at the chance to meet 47-year-old Lucretia Mott, the first woman she had ever heard make a public speech. "It was the realization of an oft repeated, happy dream," she recalled. "I felt at once a newborn sense of dignity and freedom." According to Stanton – there is no record to this in Mott's diary – the two went for a walk along Great Queen Street in London one evening, the Quaker preacher and her admirer, musing that perhaps one day they would host a convention for women's rights in America.

In 1848, they did. Later, in their three-volume *History of Woman Suffrage*, Stanton and Susan B. Anthony (Fig. 3.1) would tout the Seneca Falls meeting as the first marker in the American feminist movement. Ignoring or slighting the pioneering work done by Maria Stewart, Abby Kelley Foster, and others, they sought to cement their own place as the movement's matriarchs, to craft what historians call an origins myth about its founding. They could have opened their account of the birth of women's rights with the black women who resisted slavery and rape, the Lowell Mill textile workers who demanded fair wages, the six women in upstate New York who appealed to the state constitutional

Figure 3.1 Elizabeth Cady Stanton (left), seen here with her great partner for women's rights, Susan B. Anthony, was the first to call publicly for women to have the right to vote. For a convention at Seneca Falls, NY in 1848, she wrote a Declaration of Rights and Sentiments that included a suffrage plank. On hearing of the idea, Lucretia Mott, a Quaker activist and co-founder of the convention, told her, "Why Lizzie, thee will make us ridiculous!" Henry Stanton, fearing his wife's call for the vote was so toxic it would rebound negatively on his aspirations for a political career, boycotted the meeting. A debate over animal rights, observed abolitionist orator Frederick Douglass, would have been far less controversial. *Source:* Library of Congress Prints and Photographs.

convention for a right to vote. They could have begun the story with the Grimke sisters' testimony as eyewitnesses to the evils of slavery in the 1830s or with Lucy Stone's pioneering lectures for women's rights in 1847. Instead they chose to fix the movement's birth at the convention in Seneca Falls.

But if others were as deserving of designation as the first mothers of suffrage, Seneca Falls and its many aftershocks did leave important legacies that would follow the cause throughout its history. Chief among them was that the battle to win political rights for women, as demonstrated so pointedly at the 1840 World Anti-Slavery Convention in London, would anger the male polity, making the struggle for suffrage long and trying. Second, that the cause required women to wrest the podium from their male allies, to assert their own rights. Whether it was Stanton lobbying the New York state legislature to enact property rights for married women, or Mexican women demanding recognition for their rights to ancestral lands, or African American women seeking to participate in church-led abolitionist groups, the first stage of activism, the one that would lead them to the vote, was that they stood up and spoke.

The Legacy of Seneca Falls

Throughout the 1830s and 1840s, women had been broadening the boundaries of their moral influence. Female literary societies had awakened women to the injustices of their homes, and their nation. Early organizations of benevolence, with names such as the Female Association for the Relief of Women and Children in Reduced Circumstances and the New York Female Moral Reform Society, had educated them to festering degradations, from poverty to prostitution. They had used the First Amendment right to petition to join the national conversation against slavery, the Indian Removal Policy, and exploitation of female workers. Now, female activists hosted a series of conventions that allowed women – and male supporters – to consider an agenda of educational, property, and marital reforms for women. The most controversial of these, the one that provoked the most pushback from the political establishment, was the idea that women, like men, should have the right to vote.

When Stanton first suggested to organizers of the Seneca Falls convention that they include the right to vote in their Declaration of Rights and Sentiments, Mott told her, "Why Lizzie, thee will make us ridiculous!" Henry Stanton, fearing his wife's call for the vote would rebound negatively on his aspirations for a political career, boycotted the meeting. Legend has it that her father Judge Daniel Cady, on hearing of this radical proposal, took a train up to Seneca Falls to ask her if she had lost her mind. A debate over animal rights, observed abolitionist orator Frederick Douglass, would have been far less controversial.

Their fears were well grounded. In later press reports, the misogyny of the political class was on full display. Praising women who tended to home and family, the Philadelphia *Public Ledger* disparaged the woman who called for equal rights as "a nobody." The *Oneida Whig* mused that if women continued to indulge in such "unnatural" demands, men might have to go without dinner. Perhaps to strike fear into the hearts of its male readers, the *New York Herald* warned that if Lucretia Mott got the vote, she might get it into her head that she was qualified to seek the presidency. Delegates were castigated as "sour old maids," childless women" or "divorced wives." To the *Syracuse Recorder*, the convention was "excessively silly."

The call for the vote was not the only thing on the program at Seneca Falls that July. In writing its demands, Stanton – the only non-Quaker among the convention's organizers – had consciously played on the nation's foundational principles, enunciated seventy-two years earlier. Parroting the language of the Declaration of Independence, she wrote in the preamble, "We hold these truths to be self-evident: that all men and women are created equal; that they are endowed by their Creator with certain inalienable rights." Like Thomas Jefferson, she laid out the case against the ruling power – not the British king but the American man. Man "has compelled her to submit to laws, in the formation of which she has no voice," Stanton read in her litany of charges against mankind. "He has made her, if married, in the eye of the law, civilly dead." She then enunciated ten planks to rectify the wrongs committed. Seeking equality with men, the declaration asked that women be given equality in the law with men, that they be allowed to own property and keep their own wages, that they be allowed to pursue an education and a career, and to seek a divorce. For Stanton and Mott and their allies, "no taxation without representation" was an affront, and "consent of the governed" a principle. Most controversially, they demanded the right to vote – afforded to "the most ignorant and degraded men," those convicted of crimes or known to be mentally ill. They sought to reassure the male polity that their enfranchisement would elevate the electorate. They were not trying to expand the rolls with "ignorant and degraded" women, but with those who, like their male counterparts, were respectable. It was an unfortunate oversight that the founders had excluded them seventy-two years earlier. Now they would be restored.

Stanton came to these understandings as a child, reading in her father's ample library of law books. A lawyer and judge with a touch for politics,

Daniel Cady had grieved the death of his only son, telling the young Elizabeth that he wished she had been a boy. In reading, she grew angry at the legal constraints placed on women. One case involved a woman who had purchased a farm and later married. On her husband's death, he willed the land to their son. Seeking redress, the woman came to Judge Cady, who told her the law was clear, there were no options. On reading of the case, Stanton took a knife and excised the pertinent section from her father's law books. The judge explained to his daughter that laws could only be erased by legislation. She dedicated the rest of her life to enacting those new laws. By the time organizers planned the Seneca Falls convention, Stanton's knowledge of the law fueled the passion of her words. As she wrote in the Declaration of Rights and Sentiments, men had declared married women "civilly dead," they had "taken from her all right in property, even to the wages she earns," and they had "deprived her of this first right of a citizen," the right to vote, "leaving her without representation in the halls of legislation," "oppressed ... on all sides."

Fearful of the controversy that might ensue if they had asked a woman to chair the meeting, at Seneca Falls, female activists called on Lucretia's husband James Mott, "tall and dignified, in Quaker costume," to chair the proceedings. And only after Frederick Douglass spoke with great passion about the justice in enfranchising women did the measure pass. Suffrage was the only plank at Seneca Falls not to win unanimous approval, passing with votes of sixty-eight women and thirty-two men. So explosive was the issue – and the backlash they received from family and community – that several delegates later withdrew their signatures. Perhaps sensing the public fury, many delegates gathered for the convention – the audience was estimated at between 240 and 300 – chose not to cast a vote. That the measure passed at all owed much to Douglass, a staunch abolitionist and suffragist who once explained, "When I ran away from slavery, it was for myself; when I advocated emancipation, it was for my people; but when I stood up for the rights of woman, self was out of the question, and I found a little nobility in the act." In years to come, when the relationship between white and black suffragists would be frayed to the breaking point, the memory of Seneca Falls reminded all of them of the interracial history of the movement's first call to action.

Women of Color and Their Rights

The meeting at the Wesleyan Chapel in Seneca Falls, NY was not the only convention taking place that year, not the only one to acknowledge the birth of a women's rights agenda from the movement to abolish slavery. At the National Convention of Colored Freedmen in Cleveland, delegates debated such issues as whether to take up arms against slavery, how to help fugitives flee to safety, and the need to finance the advocacy of black newspapers. But the issue that roiled the membership unexpectedly was a call by delegates Frederick Douglass and Martin Delany for women to be invited to speak and vote at the group's meetings. For Delany, it was evident that both African Americans and women were subjected to "despotic actions of legislation," and to ridicule. Many delegates pushed back, some arguing for the primacy of the race agenda, others citing the Biblical injunction for women to serve her husband and her home. But Delany was persistent, and members finally approved the idea, in the end shouting, "Three cheers for woman's rights." It would prove a Pyrrhic victory.

Many African American leaders despaired over this pivot away from female benevolence, toward a clash between female activists and the country's political ruling class. Addressing a Sunday School Benevolent Society in Buffalo, New York, James Whitfield suggested that women would be better off barred from "the turmoil of politics." William Nell, an abolitionist and founder of the Adelphic Union Literary Society in Boston, approved of female activism against slavery, calling it their "appropriate sphere," but nothing more. At the Connecticut State Convention of Colored Men, also in 1848, women were not invited to participate, instead reminded to complete their "duties" to "influence" the young at home.

By 1849, at the State Convention of the Colored Citizens of Ohio, African American activists threatened to walk out if they were not given the privileges of membership. Marginalized by black churchmen and white activists, African American women carved out their own role in politics. A delegate named Jane P. Merritt called it "wrong and shameful" to rob women of a voice. "We will attend no more after tonight, unless the privilege is extended," said her resolution. After a debate, the men extended voting privileges to women, who added a discussion of black female academies and seminaries to the agenda. As a result, the convention condemned the Seward Seminary in Rochester for expelling Frederick Douglass's daughter Rosetta, who had passed the school's entrance exam, because of the objections of one white parent, Horatio Warner, publisher of the *Rochester Courier*.

The year 1848 also marked the entry into the political conversation of Mexican women who were swept into the American umbrella by the Treaty of Guadalupe Hidalgo. The treaty, which officially ended the Mexican–American War, was a boon to the land-grabbing Americans, who picked up an additional 525,000 acres in land that made up part or all of what is now Arizona, California, Colorado, Nevada, New Mexico, Utah, and Wyoming. In addition, Mexico abandoned all claims to

Texas, recognizing the Rio Grande River as the boundary between the United States and its southern neighbor. For this windfall, the United States paid $15 million, about half a billion dollars in today's terms, and promised to prevent and punish raids into Mexico by Comanche and Apache Indians, which proved problematic.

Many American reformers inveighed against the war, arguing the United States had no right to take over foreign lands by force. Women were active in several such groups – the American Peace Society and the League of Universal Brotherhood. Jane Swisshelm, who had established her own anti-slavery newspaper in Pittsburgh, the *Saturday Visiter*, took up the Mexican cause in its pages. Publishing a series of "war letters," she accused southern slaveholders and northern businessmen of backing the war to acquire new territory for slavery. For Mexican women, the treaty marked a loss of economic power and rights. Before 1848, under the inherited Spanish colonial and later Mexican law, Mexican women could own and inherit property, without consent from men. Although they experienced a different kind of patriarchy, they were recognized as property owners. After the treaty, they came under U.S. rule, citizens in name only, and the patriarchal wards of their husbands or fathers.

When Mexico gained independence from Spain in 1821, the new country's civil law gave legal identity to women outside of patriarchal relationships. They could petition for land grants, work as artisans, inherit property, and be recognized as head of households. The Treaty of Guadalupe Hidalgo, signed on July 4, 1848, gave U.S. citizenship rights to residents of the newly annexed lands, meaning their property rights would now be protected by the U.S. government. At the last minute Congress deleted Article X from the treaty, stripping away protections for landowners. If Mexican women could not prove their claims, their land would become public domain. Among the first to rise to defend their rights was Maria de Valencia. She and her sisters sought recognition of the land grant awarded to their mother, Senora Teodora Peralta. Under the treaty, her claim to ownership, already recognized by the Mexican government, should have been "inviolably protected." Instead, U.S. officials demanded more documentation and courts repeatedly ruled against them. Other women – such as Maria Gallegos y Garcia – appealed to the U.S. Surveyor General to recover their lands. Heir to the El Tajo Grant in Bernalillo County, New Mexico, Garcia claimed that she was the property owner, entitled to payment. Maria Cleofas Bone de Lopez likewise testified that she had inherited land, and that she had the papers from her mother. U.S. courts compromised their property rights. Much like Native American women whose ties to the land were questioned by U.S. officials, these Mexican American women lost their property rights, and with them their power to carve out independent livelihoods.

The Conventions

In May of 1850, at the conclusion of the New England Anti-Slavery Convention, a group of activists met to organize the first national women's rights convention. Seneca Falls had been a regional affair, catching public attention locally. But this was to be the first national convention to promote women's rights. Within the abolitionist movement, both male and female reformers had come to believe that women could more effectively promote change in the nation's politics if they came not as petitioners appealing for reform but as constituents demanding it. Even abolitionists who believed the U.S. government so evil in its complicity with slavery that it was immoral for reformers to seek political solutions saw the benefits. "The first thing to be done by the women of this country is to demand their political enfranchisement," William Lloyd Garrison said at the organizing session. "It is not for me or for any man dogmatically to judge as to what is or what is not a sinful act, or to say to others you shall not exercise the right to think for yourselves," he told female delegates. "I want the women to have the right to vote, and I call upon them to demand it perseveringly until they possess it.... [Then] it will be for them to say whether they exercise it or not."

Over the next ten years, silenced later only by the guns of war, the conventions would prompt national debate about the enfranchisement of women, and its implications for men. For Stanton these conventions provided intellectual stimulation and "a community of discourse" that defined the rights and privileges of citizenship. Friends criticized her for taking her seven children to an Episcopal church on Sundays, even as she questioned its teachings. Other allies who were Quakers berated her choice of clothing – theatrical, even feminine. Often she was too busy with raising children to attend, but sent missives and proposals read prominently into the record. Although these early women's rights meetings provoked angry male critics to heckle and attack them, other men viewed the conventions as "efficient manufactories of public opinion," not a threat to the state governments or political parties that they controlled. They reasoned that these gatherings would defuse female activism while proving little challenge to the patriarchy. As it was not until 1920, some seventy years later, when most American women succeeded in getting the vote, perhaps they were right. Or perhaps the more accurate way to describe the impact of conventions is to say that they were like chisels on marble, chipping away at male resistance one piece at a time.

Held in Worcester, Massachusetts, the first national Woman's Rights Convention took place in October 1850. Organizers posted the announcement widely, and response was overwhelming. Some 1,000 people attended the two-day conference, from eleven states, including California, which had been admitted to the Union only weeks before. Lucy Stone invested much energy in lining up speakers. "We need all the women who are accustomed to speak in public – every stick of timber that is sound," Stone wrote Antoinette Brown, a friend from Oberlin College. They did not disappoint. Paulina Wright Davis, who with her husband Francis Wright had resigned from their church to protest its pro-slavery stance, chaired the meeting and delivered its opening address. She appealed for "the emancipation of a class, the redemption of half the world, and a conforming re-organization of all social, political and industrial interests and institutions." And she called women's rights "perhaps the very last grand movement of humanity towards its highest destiny." Abby Kelley Foster was equally thunderous, shocking many when she called for women "to revolt against tyranny," much as the nation's founding generation had rebelled against King George III, defending their right "to cut the tyrants' throats." Urging co-education, she predicted that one day a woman would be president of the United States. Press coverage was mocking – many found her ideas subversive, "an insurrection in petticoats."

This new militant rhetoric about women's rights could not disguise the festering tension within the crusade to end slavery. One resolution, authored by abolitionist Wendell Phillips, called for emancipation of "the million and a half of slave women" in the South, "grossly wronged and foully outraged." The proposal met with hostility from abolitionist Jane Swisshelm, editor of the Pittsburgh *Saturday Visiter*, whose objections exposed the fissures between abolitionism and women's rights. "The question of color has no right to a hearing" in a women's rights convention, she wrote. It was hard enough to convince men to empower women, she argued. Mingling the two causes would only hurt both of them. While women might lend the black man "an oar or show him how to make one," she wrote, "we do not want him in our boat. Let him row his own craft!"

Swisshelm was no friend of slavery. As a young wife in Kentucky, a slave state, she had concluded that the real victim of the cruel institution was the female slave, often sexually abused, then separated from children she had given birth to. Later, in the 1840s, she became one of the first women to run a newspaper, campaigning against the Fugitive Slave Law and exposing Daniel Webster for his hypocrisy in fathering a family of mixed-race children while urging northerners to compromise on slavery. But she was also an aggrieved wife who had weathered her husband's pressure – and that of her mother-in-law – to end her career so she could better tend to her husband. Though many delegates at the first national Woman's Rights Convention, like Swisshelm, had learned their activism from the abolitionist cause or the temperance movement, they now wanted a platform to air their own, distinct, grievances.

For African American women, the move toward feminism came at a moment of extreme danger for the black community. The Fugitive Slave Act, passed by Congress in 1850, legalized the odious practice of slave catching, making all African Americans, slave or free, vulnerable to being captured and enslaved. The need to flee to safety was the priority, and many now did, nearly 20,000 American blacks escaping to Canada, joining the thousands who had already arrived via the Underground Railroad. Seven years later, in an opinion many scholars consider the most misguided in its history, the Supreme Court ruled in the Dred Scott case that African Americans were not citizens, ensuring that slave owners could take their slaves into free states without fear of emancipating them. For some states, such as California, having just joined the Union as a free state, this insistence on importing slavery was the tinder that lighted the match toward the Civil War four years later. In the eyes of many abolitionists, these assaults on black identity further cemented the primacy of anti-slavery over the cause of women's rights and, for African American women, the painful intersectionality of race and gender. During the 1854 convention, many black delegates likely stayed in the streets to witness and protest the capture of runaway Anthony Burns, a Baptist minister living as a free man in Boston. Activist Charlotte Forten (Fig. 3.2), part of the prominent Forten-Purvis family and a founder member of the Salem Anti-Slavery Society, may have been one of them. She recorded in her diary her sadness that abolitionists had failed to rescue him. "A cloud seems hanging over me, all our persecuted race, which nothing can dispel," she wrote.

These conventions generated much public interest, their agendas reflecting the range of grievances women now brought to the fore. The advent of the conventions also coincided with a proliferation of women's rights newspapers throughout the country, often one-woman shops aimed at filling the void from a mainstream media diet of hostility. From 1851 to 1853, Elizabeth Aldrich published *Genius of Liberty* in Cincinnati. In 1852, a newspaper called the *Pioneer and Woman's Advocate* appeared in Providence, Rhode Island. Technology had made it cheaper and faster to print newspapers, and there was interest from an increasingly literate public. Connecting readers to a wider world, these early newspapers represented a new form of political communication, a bridge to readers in isolated cities.

Figure 3.2   Charlotte Forten was a member of a prominent, wealthy African American family of abolitionists and women's rights activists. Her grandfather, James Forten, was a wealthy sail-maker in Philadelphia who petitioned Congress in 1799 to repeal the fugitive slave law that endangered free black men. Her grandmother Charlotte and three of her aunts were founding members of the Philadelphia Female Anti-Slavery Society. A poet, educator, and influential activist, she was a founding member of the Salem Anti-Slavery Society. In 1878, she married Francis James Grimke, a Presbyterian minister, and helped him in charitable causes and education at the Fifteenth Street Presbyterian Church in Washington, DC. Her husband was born to South Carolina plantation owner Henry Grimke and his slave, Nancy Weston. After Henry's death, activists Angelina and Sarah Grimke helped support Francis and his brothers, their mixed-race nephews. Schomburg Center for Research in Black Culture, Photographs and Prints Division, *Source:* New York Public Library. Digital Collections.

Like Stone, many delegates were teachers who had experienced the insult of being paid half the salary of male counterparts, many of them not as well trained. Now they called for equality in salary and property, for greater job and educational opportunities, temperance reform and marital rights, and the vote. By the second national convention, in Worcester, Massachusetts in October 1851, the resolution adopted by delegates made clear how central the campaign for the vote had become to movement leaders. "While we would not undervalue other methods, the Right of Suffrage for Women is, in our opinion, the corner-stone of this enterprise, since we do not seek to protect woman, but rather to place her in a position to protect herself," read its opening lines. "It will be woman's fault if, the ballot once in her hand, all the barbarous, demoralizing and unequal laws relating to marriage and property do not speedily vanish from the statute-book."

For the next ten years, national conventions were held annually, and regional ones at the call of local activists, organized by white and black activists. And for ten years, female reformers were greeted, heckled, and assaulted by men angered by the audacity of women in rising to speak. The editor of *Harper's* regularly castigated these "hybrid conventions" and bemoaned the fact that women had been given the podium. "I suffer a woman not to teach," he often wrote, suggesting that women be banned from "engaging in the life of the forum."

In 1853, male hecklers at the Broadway Tabernacle in New York directed all manner of shouts, hisses, feet stamping, and guttural noises toward the stage, whether speakers were men or women. "You prove one thing to-night," said an outraged Wendell Phillips, "that the men of New York do not understand the meaning of civil liberty and free discussion." What the men of New York had also demonstrated, however, was that they could obstruct and shut down a meeting – and expect cheering from an equally misogynist press corps. Editors at New York's *Herald* mocked the gathering as the "Women's Wrong Convention," calling its delegates "a gathering of unsexed women … entirely devoid of personal attraction." In 1854, Harriet Forten Purvis and her sister Margaret Forten, both from a wealthy African American family in Philadelphia, were instrumental in organizing the fifth national convention, held in their hometown. Delegates debated – but rejected – a proposal to launch a national women's rights newspaper, deciding instead to urge movement leaders to publish rebuttals and opinion pieces in the national newspapers. The *New York Times* called it "Amazonian wisdom" for the women to reject a national newspaper. Using familiar racial and sexual slurs, the *Times* ridiculed other groups that had started their own media outlets. The convention also elicited debate about the Bible – and whether it prohibited or encouraged female participation in public life. The Reverend Henry Grew cited passages he said had been misconstrued to enable female rights. Lucretia Mott argued the clergy had long raised this objection to female activism in temperance, anti-slavery, and now women's rights. "The pulpit has been prostituted, the Bible has been ill-used," she said. Deconstructing the very passages Grew had cited, she accused critics of hurling "passage after passage of the Bible, never intended to be so used."

In a preview of postwar politics, the last Woman's Rights Convention before the Civil War also featured a heated debate over an issue never before debated at one of these meetings. Comparing marriage to a

business partnership, a civic contract to be dissolved whenever its signers wanted, Stanton argued that one of the essential rights of woman
was to obtain a divorce. This call for marriage reform, for liberalized
divorce law and marital choice for women, was hardly a new argument
for Stanton. A mother of seven, in 1852 she had become president of
the Woman's State Temperance Society, learning firsthand of abusive
husbands who ravaged their families by chronic drinking and abusive
behavior. Then, she had scandalized some within the temperance
movement by suggesting that drunkenness should be grounds for
divorce. Now, she horrified friends within the women's movement by
equating marriage with business, provoking attacks on her as an advocate
of free love. Likening it to a contract between "parties of mature age,"
Stanton said marriage as currently constructed is "a mere outward
tie," its insides riddled "with every possible inequality of condition and
development." Unequal marriage, she argued, undercut female ability
to serve as guardians of civic valor. "The family, that great conservator
of national virtue and strength, how can you hope to build it up in
the midst of violence, debauchery and excess?" Ernestine Rose stood to
agree, calling for a divorce law that would allow a woman to leave a cruel
marriage and to pursue more educational opportunities that would promote her independence, so "she will not be obliged to marry for a home
and a subsistence."

In churches where morality was the central teaching, the term
"free love" was, as one advocate put it, "a synonym for promiscuity."
Olympia Brown was one of the nation's first female ordained ministers,
a graduate of Antioch College and one of the first women to attend
theological school at St. Lawrence University. At every step, she had
faced discrimination, fighting to win admission, to earn a degree, to
compete with men, to achieve by their standards. Born in 1835, she was
also one of the few suffragists from the Reconstruction era who would
live long enough to cast a vote. Now she lamented that the issue of
free love was being held against women, many temperance advocates,
who simply wanted to reform the divorce laws. "One could hardly speak
in the most academic or speculative way of the marriage or divorce
question without being accused of free love bias," she observed.

To movement staples such as Wendell Phillips, divorce was hardly an
appropriate topic at a woman's rights convention, an assault on patriarchy and a political hot button issue that could only inflame the anger
of male lawmakers. Calling it politically "premature and unwise" even
to discuss the matter of divorce, he moved that the conversation be
stricken from the convention's records. "Those who use this platform
to make speeches on this question ... do far worse than take more than
their fair share of the time; they open a gulf into which our distinctive

movement will be plunged, and its success postponed." Anthony, who had elected not to marry for fear of surrendering her independence, argued not to delete the conversation from the record. "The discussion is perfectly in order," she said, "since nearly all the wrongs of which we complain grow out of the inequality, the injustice of the marriage laws, that rob the wife of the right to herself and her children – that make her the slave of the man she marries." Phillips' call to expunge the record was defeated. A number of women agreed with Phillips. To Antoinette Brown Blackwell, an ordained minister who had befriended Lucy Stone at Oberlin and was now her sister-in-law, liberalizing divorce laws was an anathema. Marriage was a holy contract, not a civil one, divine in the eyes of God.

New York's newspapers were far less polite. The *Evening Post* thought it unseemly to liken marriage to a business contract. The *New York Observer* declared that Stanton's words "would turn the world into one vast brothel." And at the *Tribune*, editor Horace Greeley, once a supporter, now a bitter foe enraged by Stanton's use of his wife as a political prop, said the Woman's Rights Convention title should be changed, the word "Woman" replaced by "Wives Discontented." The wound that most stung came from Phillips. "With all his excellence and nobility, Wendell Phillips is a man," she wrote Anthony. "His words, tones and manner came down on me like a clap of thunder." She insisted they had been right to raise the issue at the convention, writing another friend, "Those sad-faced women who struggled up to press my hand, who were speechless with emotion, know better than the greatest of our masculine speakers and editors who has struck the blow for them in the right place." And she reassured Anthony, who may not have welcomed the news, "I shall not grow conservative with age. I feel a growing indifference to the praise and blame of my race."

Amid the flurry of conventions, reformers also pursued progress in state legislatures. After Stanton appealed to lawmakers in Albany, they passed a bill in 1860 giving married women the right to inherit, to leave wills bequeathing their wealth to beneficiaries of their own choosing, and to do business in their own names. Activists also tried to integrate movements whose doors had until then been closed to women. One was temperance. During the antebellum years, inebriation was seen as a sin of character. In the early 1800s, with water supplies often polluted and milk not always available, alcohol was an embedded part of the American diet. By the 1820s, male evangelical reformers, casting over-indulgence as an impediment to good citizenship, called for abstinence from hard liquor. By the 1840s, a group calling itself the Washingtonians pledged complete abstinence, using tools of personal appeal to persuade other men to eliminate all kinds of alcohol from their diets. In

May 1853, a group calling itself Friends of Temperance issued a call for the first world's convention on the topic in New York. To the annoyance of the movement's male leaders, female delegates showed up too. One of them was Lucy Stone. She wrote a friend that the Rev. Hewitt called it "a burning shame for women to be there, ... taking the ground that women should be nowhere but at home." She also reported the Rev. E. M. Jackson went further, charging that the women who came to the meeting "came there expressly to disturb." When one female delegate, perhaps Stone, suggested that Susan B. Anthony, a longtime temperance advocate, be named to a committee, Mayor Amos Barstow of Providence, Rhode Island announced he "would resign rather than do it." In September, when Antoinette Brown, the first woman ordained as a mainstream Protestant minister, attended another "World Temperance Convention," resentment over the idea that women would try to invade this male space had abated not at all. In a piece dripping with sarcasm, Horace Greeley, editor of the New York *Tribune*, noted, "This convention has completed three of its four business sessions, and the results may be summed up as follows: First Day – Crowding a woman off the platform. Second Day – Gagging her. Third Day – Voting that she shall stay gagged. Having thus dismissed of the main question, we presume the incidentals will be finished this morning."

In response to anger from male activists keen to protect their turf, women began their own temperance newspapers – notably *The Lily*, which first appeared in January 1849, published and edited by Amelia Jenks Bloomer – and formed their own organizations. "We have been obliged to preach woman's rights, because many, instead of listening to what we had to say on temperance, have questioned the right of a woman to speak on any subject," Stanton said on forming the Woman's State Temperance Society in New York.

Since Seneca Falls in 1848, women had been organizing around the country, a network of grassroots activists agitating at the local and state level, often provoking a male backlash. Perhaps the most famous of these state conventions took place in Akron, Ohio in 1851. The political climate was not hospitable. Male critics had descended on the meeting, intent on disruption. They hooted, heckled, and sometimes shouted out speeches about the teachings of Jesus and the weakness of women. Their heckling so enraged Sojourner Truth that she advanced to the stage to preach to them. Born into slavery in New York as Isabella Baumfree in 1797 and escaped with her infant daughter in 1826, Baumfree two years later won a court case to reclaim a son who had been sold away from her. In 1843 on hearing God's summons, she changed her name to Sojourner Truth (Fig. 3.3) and began to speak against slavery and for women's equality, "testifying of the hope that was in her." Now, having

I SELL THE SHADOW TO SUPPORT THE SUBSTANCE.
SOJOURNER TRUTH.

Randall

East Grand Circus Park,
DETROIT.

Figure 3.3 Isabella Baumfree was born a slave in upstate New York, but escaped with her infant daughter in 1826. Two years later she went to court to recover her son, becoming the first black woman to win such a case against a white man. In 1843 she took the name Sojourner Truth because she believed God had called her to talk about what she had seen, "testifying of the hope that was in her." She gave one of the seminal speeches of the 1850s era of women's rights conventions, upbraiding men in the audience for belittling the cause. "Why children, if you have woman's rights, give it to her and you will feel better," she said. Though contemporary versions mischaracterized this talk as the "Ain't I A Woman" speech, recent histories suggest that Sojourner did not speak in dialect. *Source:* Public Domain.

listened to the conference speeches, and the heckling, for two days, she rose to speak.

There is some dispute about what Sojourner Truth said that day, and how. Organizer Frances Gage left an account that reported Truth's words in Negro dialect, an account since discredited. Truth's very biography belied the claim that she was helpless, or unschooled. As a slave, she had negotiated with her enslaver to win her freedom, under the Gradual

Emancipation Law in New York. Passed in 1817, the law promised freedom to slaves born before 1799, but delayed their emancipation for ten years. And as a free black woman she had again used the courts to win custody of her son, asserting the free will of both of them. "You need not be afraid to give us our rights for fear we will take too much, for we can't take more than our [share]," she said that day, according to the most trusted account. "The poor men seem to be all in confusion, and don't know what to do. Why children, if you have woman's rights, give it to her and you will feel better. You will have your own rights, and they won't be so much trouble. I can't read, but I can hear. I have heard the bible and have learned that Eve caused man to sin. Well if woman upset the world, do give her a chance to set it right side up again." By all accounts, Truth's words did quiet critics in the auditorium. But the warring accounts of her words, the deliberate skewering of her biography, also exposed the rifts within the movement, between the abolitionist cause and the women's rights movement it had birthed. After the Civil War, these fissures would divide reformers, white from black, men from women, abolitionists from feminists. For now, they simmered.

Civil War

In the runup to war, women continued organizing petitions against slavery. In 1837, a 17-year-old Susan Brownell Anthony had collected signatures against the gag rule Congress enacted to thwart a hearing on the petitions. She was a temperance activist first, and a committed abolitionist – confiding to her diary that she had "fitted out a fugitive slave for Canada with the help of Harriet Tubman," the escaped black slave who had started the Underground Railroad to help others flee. But Anthony was also a teacher concerned that her female students' opportunities were being stunted by an educational system that valued them little. After she attended a regional abolitionist meeting in Seneca Falls in 1851, a chance encounter with Elizabeth Cady Stanton – they were introduced on the street by Amelia Bloomer – led to a lifelong partnership for women's rights and women's suffrage.

Their fabled friendship featured a division of labor perfectly suited to their distinct talents – Stanton as the movement's intellectual, Anthony as its chief organizer. Anthony, who had eschewed marriage, often served as surrogate mother to Stanton's seven children so that Elizabeth could carve out time to write the majestic speeches that would keep them both inspiring audiences. Even after the Civil War began, Anthony was eager to continue the work against slavery and for women's rights. But by early 1861, mobs in Syracuse attacked her with rotten eggs as benches were broken in loud protest. In a letter to Lucy Stone, Anthony wrote, "The Men, even the *best* of them, seem to think the Women's Rights question should be waived for the present. So let us do our own work, and in our own way."

As the cannons from Fort Sumter summoned the nation to a war that had been so long postponed, Stanton convinced Anthony that they should suspend work for women's rights during the conflict. Within two years, however, Anthony, tending to her family farm in Rochester, became bored with inaction. Stanton, who had only recently moved her family to New York City, was worried about signs from Albany that legislators were walking back earlier gains for women in property and parental rights. So in May 1863 the two put out a call for a new organization, the Woman's National Loyalty League, dedicated to ensuring that a postwar nation would reward "true loyalty" with true equality. With many Union women doing volunteer work during the war, Stanton and Anthony sought to reframe the purpose of their service, to engage them in "labor for a principle." At the Loyalty League's inaugural convention, Anthony read a series of resolutions, likely written by Stanton, which outlined their hope for the postwar liberation of both African Americans and women. "There can never be true peace in this republic until the civil and political rights of all citizens of African descent and all Women are practically established," the declaration read. Applauding President Lincoln for signing the Emancipation Proclamation that would free four million African American slaves if the Union won the war, the two suffragists said, "Shame on us if we do not make it a war to establish the negro in freedom."

In the coming years, Stanton and Anthony would part from this pact of solidarity with black Americans, splintering the movement for women's rights into a schism over race. But for now, their embrace of the emancipation of the slaves came as joyous news to some suffragists who had arrived at their passion for women's rights through the prism of abolitionism. "I rejoice exceedingly that that resolution should combine us with the negro, [for] … we have been with him, … the iron [of his chains] has entered into our souls," said Angelina Grimke Weld. "True, we have not felt the slave-holder's lash; true, we have not had our hands manacled, but our *hearts* have been crushed." To applause she added, "I want to be identified with the negro; until he gets his rights, we never shall have ours."

Some delegates objected, on pragmatic grounds, that organizers risked alienating patriotic supporters by muddying their message about loyalty with other causes. Still clinging to the perception that the Civil War was being fought over the constitutional principle of secession of the states, one delegate from Wisconsin said Ladies Loyal Leagues in her area had succeeded because "we have kept them sacred from Anti-Slavery, Women's Rights, Temperance and everything else, good though they may be." But for Stanton, Anthony, Lucy Stone, and other early suffragists, the links between the two causes were visceral, and historic. Noting "the sad mistake" that the founders made in leaving slavery, "this one great wrong in the land," Stone urged officials not to repeat the same mistake now by ignoring the rights of women. "Leave them out, and we take the same backward step that our fathers took when they left out slavery. If justice to the negro and to woman is right, it can not hurt our loyalty to the country and the Union." They were interested in showcasing their loyalty not to reknit the boundaries of the union in some sort of geographical compact. They were hoping, as Anthony put it, to "enunciate the principles of democracy and republicanism."

After the convention, the Women's Loyal League began what turned out to be the largest petition drive by women in the nation's history, collecting almost 400,000 signatures to abolish slavery. Each state sent in a petition on yellow paper, closed with a red ribbon. In its entirety, the petition read, "The undersigned, women of the United States above the age of eighteen years, earnestly pray that your honorable body will pass at the earliest practicable day an act emancipating all persons of African descent held to involuntary service or labor in the United States." A separate petition was sent from each state signed by "men above the age of eighteen years." Perhaps because the petition was organized and circulated by women, they outnumbered men in most states. New York, for instance, sent in 17,706 signatures, 11,187 from women and 6,519 from men, 63 percent to 37 percent. Massachusetts Senator Charles Sumner presented the first installment of 100,000 signatures to the Senate. "Here they are, a might army, one hundred thousand strong, without arms or banners, the advance guard of a yet larger army," he said. "They ask nothing less than universal emancipation." Sumner, who had been caned nearly to death on the Senate floor by a House member from South Carolina, concluded by saying the petitions indicted slavery as "a *national enemy*."

After the war was won, Stanton assured Anthony, they would be rewarded for their patriotic loyalty. The cause of the slave and the cause of the woman would be connected by the common bounds of history and injustice. Then, Stanton felt sure, women and African Americans would be welcomed into the U.S. Constitution as the equals of white men. Enslaved blacks who had donned the blue uniform of the Union Army would join the millions of women who had been working toward their own empowerment to experience the franchise together. As she put it, "Would it not be wiser to keep our lamps trimmed and burning, and when the constitutional door is open, avail ourselves of the strong arm and blue uniform of the black soldier to walk in by his side, and thus make the gap so wide that no privileged class could ever again close it against the humblest citizen of the republic?"

4

The Fifteenth Amendment

After the Civil War, the South lay in ruins, physically and financially. Newly freed slaves were completely without resources, appealing to the new federal Freedmen's Bureau for literacy, land, and help in locating relatives sold from their embrace on the auction block. Northern carpetbaggers descended too, seeking to exploit a chaotic economy for riches and reward.

Amid the turmoil, little more than a year after the shocking assassination of Abraham Lincoln, reformers met at the Church of the Puritans in New York's Union Square. They had convened on May 10, 1866 for the first National Woman's Rights Convention since the war had ended. It soon became apparent that loyalties among them would divide over the question of race. "You white women speak here of rights, I speak of wrongs," began Frances Ellen Watkins Harper (Fig. 4.1), an African American poet, novelist, civil rights activist, and suffragist, born free in Baltimore. "I, as a colored woman, have had in this country an education which has made me feel as if I were in the situation of Ishmael, my hand against every man, and every man's hand against me." After Harper's piercing remarks, delegates voted to create a new organization, the American Equal Rights Association, dedicated to winning "Equal Rights to all American citizens, especially the right of suffrage, irrespective of race, color or sex." Three weeks later, the group held its first meeting, in Boston. But the association's early commitment to interracial cooperation for the vote soon disintegrated. Within three

And Yet They Persisted: How American Women Won the Right to Vote, First Edition. Johanna Neuman.
© 2020 John Wiley & Sons, Inc. Published 2020 by John Wiley & Sons, Inc.
Companion website: www.wiley.com/go/Neuman

MRS. FRANCIS E. W. HARPER.
See p. 755.

Figure 4.1 Frances Ellen Watkins Harper, an African American poet, novelist, civil rights activist, and suffragist, set the tone for the first woman's rights convention after the Civil War, saying, "You white women speak here of rights, I speak of wrongs." The Fifteenth Amendment eliminated barriers to the vote for black males, sparking a schism within the suffrage movement that was foreshadowed at this convention. Harper, Lucy Stone, Harriet Beecher Stowe, and other abolitionists supported the Fifteenth Amendment, arguing that women would get the vote next. Elizabeth Cady Stanton and Susan B. Anthony disagreed, forming their own suffrage association and campaigning against the Fifteenth Amendment. *Source:* Library of Congress Prints and Photographs Division.

years, the organization would cease to exist, torn apart by conflict between black rights and female rights, between abolition and suffrage.

In the Civil War's aftermath, reformers in Congress enacted three constitutional amendments meant to end the nation's entanglement with slavery. The Thirteenth outlawed slavery. The Fourteenth, an attempt to overrule the Supreme Court's Dred Scott decision, proclaimed all those born or naturalized in the United States to be citizens, adding that all male citizens of 21 years or older were entitled to vote. With the exception of Tennessee, every Confederate state refused to ratify this amendment, prompting Congress to make its ratification a condition of their acceptance back into the Union. The Fifteenth said simply, "The right of citizens of the United States to vote shall not be denied or abridged by the United States or by any state on account of race, color, or previous condition of servitude."

Stanton and Anthony were infuriated that in crafting the Fourteenth Amendment, reformers in Congress had introduced the word "male" for the first time into the constitutional requirements for voting. They were even more furious when Congress enacted the Fifteenth Amendment – which they expected to enfranchise both blacks and women at the same time – without any mention of the rights of their sex. As Wendell Phillips, abolitionism's "Golden Trumpet," explained, "This is 'the Negro's hour,'" a time when the sacrifices of blacks in both slavery and war had earned them the right to march first into the polls. For women there would be a Sixteenth Amendment. "Causes have their crises," said Phillips. "That of the Negro has come; that of the woman's rights movement has not yet come." To Frederick Douglass, the only man to defend Stanton's call for women's suffrage at Seneca Falls twenty years earlier, black voting rights were a matter of life and death, while those for women were not. There are no Ku Klux Klans "seeking the lives of women," he said at one of the last meetings of the American Equal Rights Association. Fearing newly freed African American men were facing mob violence, he added that the ballot "is with us a matter of life and death and therefore can not be postponed." He had long "championed woman's right to vote," he noted, but "the present claim for the negro is one of the most *urgent* necessity." For all the talk of whether blacks or women most needed the vote, raw politics drove this compromise of principle. In the 1868 elections, Democrats had picked up twenty seats in Congress, cutting in to Republican margins that had elected Abraham Lincoln and leaving reformers with a reduced majority. Odds were always long for women to win the vote after the Civil War – their liberation was not a priority to male lawmakers. Any chance they had, what one scholar called a "fighting chance," all but evaporated in this loss of Republican political muscle.

Ironically, it was both the Fourteenth and the Fifteenth Amendments that sparked a spontaneous attempt by women, black and white, all over the country, to show up at the polls to vote. The ploy was shut down by a Supreme Court decision that not only barred women from voting but opened the door to disenfranchisement of many categories of voter, at the discretion of the states. It was also these amendments that prompted the first female candidate to run for the U.S. presidency, and splintered the women's suffrage movement into two rival organizations in a feud over race that would cloud the campaign's progress for at least twenty years. But first, suffragists faced a key electorate test in "Bleeding Kansas," where abolitionist and pro-slavery forces had battled violently before the Civil War. Now, in its aftermath, voters would decide whether women and African Americans should be granted the vote in the state.

Battle Lines

The state legislature in Kansas had placed two unprecedented measures on the November 1867 ballot, with national implications. The first stripped the word "white" from voting requirements, enfranchising the state's African American men, who at the 1860 Census numbered fewer than three hundred. The second eliminated the word "male" from the state constitution. If passed by the state's fifty thousand white male voters, this second measure would make Kansas the first state to enact women's suffrage since New Jersey's revolutionary-era experiment with female voting. A laboratory for the sectional politics that had sparked the Civil War, Kansas now stoked its still-hot embers.

Weathering "all manner of discomforts in traveling, eating and sleeping," Stanton led a team of East Coast luminaries, including Lucy Stone, to the campaign trail. "As we went to the very verge of civilization, wherever two dozen voters could be assembled, we had a taste of pioneer life," Stanton recalled in a memoir published thirty years later. "We spoke in log cabins, in depots, unfinished schoolhouses, churches, hotels, barns, and in the open air." Often, she and the other activists for women encountered rivals, sparking a kind of impromptu debate across the four positions, pro and con, female and black.

Lucy Stone and her husband Henry Blackwell arrived from Boston in April, the first wave of crusaders who would stump the state during the next eight months. They came with great excitement and reams of paper – "brimming with optimism and armed with two hundred fifty pounds of suffrage tracts." Their early enthusiasm must have cheered Stanton and Anthony. "We have on our side all the shrewdest politicians and all the best class of men and women in this state," Blackwell wrote Stanton. "I think we shall probably succeed in Kansas next fall if the State is thoroughly canvassed, not else." Stone was even more effusive, writing Anthony after an inspiring reception in Atchison that "impartial Suffrage, without regard to color or sex, will succeed by overwhelming majorities. Kansas rules the world!"

Stanton and Anthony arrived in September, dividing their itineraries to maximize their impact. As Stanton noted, Kansas had already liberalized some laws for women – allowing them to vote in school board elections and reclaim children from abusive fathers. She liked to chide male voters, teasing that they did not oppose women's vote because they "fear it will drag women down" but because "women will lift suffrage so far into the realm of purity and morality that they will never be able to offer themselves as candidates for office."

By October it was clear that the spirited effort – Stanton had managed to put a speaker or at least a trove of women's rights literature in every county in the state – was unlikely to succeed. In the campaign's last few weeks, as they felt the effort sinking, Stanton and Anthony made a strategic decision to partner with Democratic maverick George Francis Train, a "flamboyant racist" given to wearing gold-buttoned coats and lavender kid gloves. Train was more of an entertainer than a politician, one who promised an infusion of both campaign money and white immigrant supporters. But it was a tactical miscalculation. As Stanton, a brilliant intellectual who pioneered and promoted the idea of women's suffrage, descended to this racist plank, friends deserted. The assertion that women's rights had to be won at any cost, even at the risk of denying black men their rights, alienated many of her abolitionist allies, including Stone, who called Train "a lunatic, wild and ranting," whose association with the cause of women's suffrage "was enough to condemn it in the minds of all persons not already convinced." Garrison accused them of having "taken leave of good sense and departed so far from true self-respect, as to be traveling companions and associate lecturers with that crack-brained harlequin and semi-lunatic." Lucretia Mott, who had been Stanton's co-sponsor at Seneca Falls in 1848, was so upset she resigned as president of the American Equal Rights Association. It had been a mistake, she now suggested, to try to link the two causes, to think that the slave's plight and that of the woman were equal. As Anthony wrote after the election, "All the old friends, with scarce an exception, are sure we are wrong. Only time can tell, but I believe we are right and hence bound to succeed."

Tensions between the two causes – of black suffrage and women's suffrage – had been simmering throughout the campaign. In April, Lucy Stone campaigned in Lawrence, with a sizeable black population, reporting that she found much support for the women's cause, except for "an ignorant Black preacher" who campaigned for black rights and against those of women. By October, George Train's presence inflamed the debate further. Often, before Irish audiences, he pronounced it absurd to grant the vote to blacks, especially if white women were not enfranchised. No longer pretending to campaign for both, an angry Stanton lashed out at the abolitionists, such as Frederick Douglass, who had failed to come to Kansas to campaign for women's vote. In Kansas, she said, "it was the utter desertion of our cause by those to whom we had a right to look for aid that forced us to our present affiliations." Republicans in Topeka were sending out speakers who talked up black suffrage while belittling voting rights for women. Republicans in Washington were nowhere to be found, their influential newspapers silent – especially the New York *Tribune*, where editor Horace Greeley was still smarting over a stunt Stanton and Anthony had embarrassed him with earlier in the year. At a state constitutional convention he chaired, female New Yorkers flooded the mails with 20,000 signatures on a petition for the vote. Stanton and Anthony arranged for one delegate to announce that the first signature on the petition from his Westchester County belonged to the editor's wife, Mary Cheney Greeley. Once an advocate, Greeley never again backed women's suffrage, and until his death in 1872, made sure neither Stanton's name nor her cause was much covered. Despite the effort in Kansas, both measures went down to defeat. The woman's cause fared worse, losing 19,857 to 9,070, garnering one thousand fewer votes than suffrage for African American men.

The turmoil within the abolitionist movement in Kansas was also reflected in the halls of Congress. In the 1860s, it was the Republican Party, with its support mostly from the North and the West, which opposed slavery. Democrats were divided between those in the South, who supported the Confederacy, and those in the North, who opposed slavery's expansion. But in 1868, Republicans lost twenty seats in Congress in the elections, cutting in to Republican margins in favor of enfranchising blacks. Mindful of their dwindling clout and eager to boost the party's future health by enfranchising millions of freed black men, in 1869 Republicans used a lame duck session to enact the Fifteenth Amendment, prohibiting governments from denying a citizen the right to vote on grounds of "race, color, or previous condition of servitude." Proposals to ban literary tests and property requirements on one side and to keep foreign-born immigrants from the polls on the other were all rejected. Now the measure would go to the states for ratification, with three-fourths required for approval.

Because the Fifteenth Amendment did not contain protections against poll taxes and literacy tests, its stated intention to enfranchise African American men eventually faltered. Still, to many abolitionists, its enactment was the culmination of a lifelong ambition, the final victory over a cruel institution that had blotted the nation's ideals from its founding. The nation had invested much blood in liberating the slaves. The Republican Party had invested much capital in validating Lincoln's war. But for Stanton and other advocates, the women's cause had always been the priority. Embedding black suffrage in the Constitution without female suffrage was in their view a travesty, and they prepared to fight its ratification.

Stanton and Anthony felt that white women, after their Civil War loyalty, had been betrayed. Worse, they felt they had been stabbed in the back not by their enemies but by their friends. Appealing to bigotry, they now campaigned against the Fifteenth Amendment, favoring suffrage for the educated, brazen in their call for a white vote. Stanton criticized Republicans for ignoring the rights of fifteen million women while empowering two million black men who "do not know the difference between a Monarchy or a Republic, who never read the Declaration of Independence or Webster's spelling book." As Anthony explained in a letter to the *New York Times*, "By the Fifteenth Amendment, the Republican Party has elevated the very last of the most ignorant and degraded classes of men to the position of master over the very first and most educated and elevated classes of women." After the debacle in Kansas, Train funded a newspaper for Stanton and Anthony, *Revolution*. Now Stanton used its pages to continue the assault. "American women of wealth, education, virtue and refinement, if you do not wish the lower orders of Chinese, Africans, Germans and Irish, with their low ideas of womanhood to make laws for you and your daughters ... demand that women too shall be represented in government," she wrote. The ideals of Jeffersonian liberalism that she had brought to Seneca Falls and celebrated to cheering crowds in Kansas were giving way, in the anger of defeat, to the racial overtones of social Darwinism. Often she railed about laws affecting women being legislated by blacks and immigrants, by "Patrick and Sambo and Hans and Yung Tung who do not know the difference between a Monarchy and a Republic." Hers was a call not for universal suffrage but for educated suffrage, for white privilege.

Their advocacy against the Fifteenth Amendment infuriated former allies, anger erupting at the last meeting ever held by the American Equal Rights Association, in 1869. Stephen S. Foster denounced the association with Train by Stanton and Anthony, refusing to back their re-nomination as officers. Douglass objected to Stanton's use of the word "Sambo" to describe black men. Debate degenerated from there. "I do not see how anyone can pretend that there is the same urgency in giving the ballot to the woman as to the negro," Douglass argued. "When women, because they are women, are hunted down ... when they are dragged from their houses and hung upon lampposts; when their children are torn from their arms and their brains dashed out upon the pavement; when they are objects of insult and outrage at every turn; when they are in danger of having their homes burnt down over their heads; when their children are not allowed to enter schools; then they will have an urgency to obtain the ballot equal to our own." Robert Purvis was the only black man who stood with Stanton and Anthony, saying, in their account, that "he would rather that his son never be enfranchised, unless his daughter could be also, that, as she bore the double curse of sex and color, on every principle of justice she should first be protected."

Lucy Stone begged for cooperation. "We are lost if we turn away from the middle principle and argue for one class," she said. But Stanton was in no mood to compromise, or to pretend any longer that she believed white women should wait as those without their skills or education cast ballots. She chastised her critics, insisting that she did not want "ignorant negroes and foreigners" to enact laws that would affect her life. In marginalizing black women such as Frances Watkins Harper who had been leaders in the great coalition around abolition of slavery, Stanton chose class over race, privileging whiteness. This was not the first sign of racism from white suffrage leaders, nor would it be the last.

Two days later, Stanton and Anthony bolted from the anti-slavery movement that had nurtured their activism. Tarred by the voter rejection in Kansas, stunned by hostility from those who were once their friends, they formed a new women's rights organization, the National Woman Suffrage Association. They were also angry that Phillips had taken the $50,000 bequest left by Boston dry goods merchant Charles Hovey for both causes and allocated it almost exclusively to the cause of abolitionism. They continued to campaign against ratification of the amendment. As Stanton said, "The struggle of the last thirty years has not been merely on the black man as such, but on the broader ground of his humanity." In some sense they were attempting to redefine abolitionism, recasting it from a platform against the enslavement of African Americans to a cause of liberation for all. "Some think this is harvest time for the black man and seed-sowing time for woman," Anthony said at the inaugural American Equal Rights Association meeting. "Others, with whom I agree, think we have been sowing the seed of individual rights, the foundation idea of a republic for the last century, and that this is the harvest time for all citizens who pay taxes, obey the laws and are loyal to the government."

Six months later, Lucy Stone created a rival group in Boston, the American Woman Suffrage Association, winning support from Mott and Julia Ward Howe, who in 1861, after observing Union troops, had authored "The Battle Hymn of the Republic." Unlike Stanton and Anthony, Stone supported the Fifteenth Amendment. "I thank God for that XV," she said. She also founded the *Woman's Journal,* soon the largest women's newspaper in the United States. And unlike the National Woman Suffrage Association, the American Woman Suffrage Association welcomed men as members and officers and as editors of the *Journal.*

Stanton's political calculation that the post-Civil War environment offered a rare opportunity for women's suffrage may not have been wrong. After all, although Wendell Phillips had promised to support a new amendment for women, it took another fifty years before the Nineteenth Amendment was enacted. Still, the wrenching schism within the movement – between New York and Boston, between militant tactics in one camp and coalition building in the other – led to a war of words and a diffusion of energy that would delay progress at the state and federal level and blunt the effectiveness of both for decades.

After the split with abolitionist friends who now denounced them, Stanton and Anthony resumed their advocacy for women's rights. Stanton, whose marriage was strained, moved to broaden the agenda to include divorce reform, birth control, and the misogyny of the church. Critics called it "social utopianism." Anthony, who had never married, wanted to focus exclusively on women's right to vote, convinced that being identified as a party of free love would only hurt the cause. The episode that tested these discordant strategies and frayed their friendship involved the first woman ever to run for president of the United States.

Victoria Woodhull

Victoria California Claflin Woodhull (Fig. 4.2) was the seventh of ten children of a charming con man, Reuben "Old Buck" Claflin, whose various nefarious schemes forced him and his family to leave many a town in debt, one step ahead of authorities and the aggrieved. After a failed marriage at the age of 15 to an alcoholic husband, whose chronic drinking she blamed for leaving one of their children mentally impaired, Victoria joined her sister, Tennessee "Tennie" Claflin, in a new business venture. They would combine their father's gift for beguiling the public with their unschooled mother's avowed belief in spiritualism. They would set up shop in Cincinnati, offering herbal cures for illness and clairvoyant predictions for the future. As male customers were seen entering dark rooms with the attractive sisters for séances, keepers of the local honor objected. Soon the two decamped for New York, seeking their father's help to secure customers. Old Buck came through, delivering the richest man in America.

The year was 1868 and the 73-year-old Cornelius Vanderbilt, called the Commodore, had enjoyed a colorful life as one of the nation's largest railroad and shipping magnates. His pluck in climbing his way to the top from an impoverished upbringing had earned him grudging admirers, even among those who scoffed at his meager education, shrewd tactics, and uncouth manners. Recently his luck had gone sour – his wife Sophia had died, and he had lost a humiliating and costly battle for control of the Erie Railroad to Jay Gould, the most savage of the Gilded Age's robber barons. Tennessee, 22, practiced her "laying on of hands" on his temples. Victoria, 30, using her spiritual talents, advised him on stock picks. Vanderbilt was so impressed with the results he set them up as the first female stockbrokers on Wall Street. Polite society disparaged them for conducting business unchaperoned, code for moral impropriety. But to press and public, Woodhull, Claflin & Company was an

Figure 4.2 Victoria Claflin Woodhull was one of the most charismatic figures in the women's suffrage movement. A spiritualist, a vegetarian, and a newspaper publisher, she was the first woman to testify before Congress, telling the House Judiciary Committee in 1871 that the Fourteenth and Fifteenth Amendments, meant to protect black male voting rights, in effect enfranchised women. This concept, called the New Departure, prompted women all over the country, black and white, to attempt to register. Among them were Susan B. Anthony and African American activist Mary Ann Shadd Cary. In 1872, Woodhull became the first woman to run for president, felled by her belief in free love, the freedom to marry, divorce, and bear children without government intervention, and by her decision to publish scandalous news that the Reverend Henry Ward Beecher, who often preached against adultery, was conducting an adulterous affair with one of his parishioners, Elizabeth Tilton. *Source:* Getty Images. Hulton Archive.

immediate sensation. The *New York Herald* called the two sisters "the Queens of Finance," or "the Bewitching Brokers." Ignoring the critics, a delighted Victoria Woodhull, at last financially secure, made good on her hopes of joining the women's rights crusade.

She would start by creating a newspaper. First published in 1870, the same year as Lucy Stone's *Woman's Journal*, the *Woodhull & Claflin Weekly* served as a megaphone for Woodhull's eclectic philosophical affections and political ambitions. Spiritualism, vegetarianism, and women's suffrage were all on full display, and the newspaper was the first to publish, in English, Karl Marx's *Communist Manifesto*. A member of the International Workingman's Association of trade unions and socialist groups, Woodhull was a capitalist who was fascinated by Marx. She argued for a "complete revolution" in corporations and banks, urging access for all to the opportunity within their walls. She believed women were the equal of men, and should be granted the same rights as men under the law, including the right to vote. Eager to expound on her theories, she left for Washington, DC. Making the rounds on Capitol Hill, she convinced Senator Benjamin Butler of Massachusetts to invite her to address the Judiciary Committee, which he would later chair. On January 11, 1871, she became the first woman in U.S. history to address a congressional committee.

Speaking before the House Judiciary Committee, she suggested that since women, "white and black," were citizens of the United States, they were subject to the laws of its Constitution, including the Fourteenth Amendment. And they were further included because the Fifteenth Amendment had commanded that no American could be robbed of the vote because of "race, color or previous condition of servitude." Well, women of all colors were citizens, she said. Women of all colors should not be robbed. All that remained, she argued, was for Congress to recognize its own handiwork, to declare women's suffrage settled law.

With that, according to the *Cincinnati Enquirer*, Victoria Woodhull "gave the committee one of her blandest smiles and bowed graciously." Electrified by her celebrity, reporters flocked to her side. Publicity was enormous. Suffragists set up headquarters on Capitol Hill to lobby for the proposal. In the end, only two members of the committee – Benjamin Butler of Massachusetts and William Loughridge of Iowa – voted for the idea. For the moment, Woodhull's testimony had made of her a suffrage star. As the *Galveston Daily News* put it, "Mrs. Woodhull has at last risen to rightful place as the legitimate leader of the Woman Suffrage movement." That prediction proved overwrought. But her suggestion that the Fifteenth Amendment might empower women to vote had enormous consequences. In its wake came a nationwide campaign to test the theory that suffrage leaders called "the new departure," and a showdown at the U.S. Supreme Court.

The New Departure

For several years, women all over the country had been testing the proposition that the Fourteenth Amendment – passed by Congress on June 8, 1866 and ratified by a sufficient number of states two years later – entitled them to vote. Its very first sentence states, "All persons born or naturalized in the United States, and subject to the laws thereof, are citizens of the United States and of the State wherein they reside." In a subsequent section, called the Equal Protection Clause, the amendment states that no state can deny to any person within its jurisdiction "the equal protection of the laws." To 55-year-old Portia Kellogg Gage, living in Vineland, New Jersey, this seemed a propitious time to test the nation's ideals. She had already organized the biracial New Jersey Woman Suffrage Association. Now, with her husband John, she went to the polls in 1867 to test the limits of her own rights.

"I was induced to offer a vote first, because I felt it a duty, and second, out of curiosity," she said. "We have always been told that it was a dangerous place, … that the very atmosphere at the polls was freighted with pollution for women." In the end, she reported, "my fears were groundless, as the men whom I there met were quiet and well behaved, and treated me as respectfully as though I were in a Church or lecture room."

She presented her ballot to the chairman of the board of registry, John Kandle. Though "blushing" at this incursion of femininity into a male purview, according to one account, he informed her that no one could vote unless they were registered. According to one witness, "she acquiesced in the decision very readily, saying she only wished to test a principle, and retired very quietly from the hall." In fact, she vowed to return the following year with other women, to again test their rights. And so she did, arriving on November 3, 1868 with 171 other women, four of them African American, and their own ballot box. Sitting at a table opposite the male registrars, the women voted, deposited their ballots at the woman's table, and often went to the homes of female friends, to mind their children so they too could cast a protest vote. Asked by a male friend why she was bothering, as the votes would not count, Gage replied, "You say there will not be five women there. We will show you that you are mistaken, that women do want to vote, and it will strengthen them for action in the future."

That same year, Lucy Stone arrived at the polls in Roseville Park, NJ with her mother-in-law, Hannah Blackwell. Both were taxpayers, and both intended to vote. Lucy Stone, one of the great orators of the antebellum era, who had withstood rotten vegetables and loud protests in speaking against slavery and for women's rights, now addressed a three-judge panel of election registrars. With a crowd of male onlookers listening attentively, she argued that since New Jersey's original constitution, adopted in 1776, had enfranchised women, the legislation in 1807 stripping their rights had been invalid. A new constitution in 1844 was also invalid, she argued, because women, enfranchised by the original constitution, had not been consulted. One judge agreed to accept the ballots, but the other two objected.

This testing of the limits of the Constitution also reached the Far West and the Midwest. In fact in the five years between 1868 and 1873, at least 700 women – white and black – marched to polling places in California, Connecticut, Illinois, Kansas, Maine, Michigan, New Hampshire, New Jersey, New York, Pennsylvania, and South Carolina, where it is believed that several recently freed African American slaves tried to vote. The idea had first occurred to Mary Olney Brown in 1867, when she wrote to "some prominent women of the towns" in Washington territory. "I was looked upon as a fanatic and the idea of a woman voting an absurdity," she recalled. Two years later she went to the polls with her husband, daughter, and son-in-law to read the Fourteenth Amendment to registrars. They were unimpressed, one of them noting that the laws of the United States did not then apply to a territory like Washington, which would not gain statehood until 1889. In a nearby town, its name and hers unknown, Mary's sister found more success, apparently registering to vote.

In Washington, DC one of the suffragists on hand to hear Woodhull's testimony in January 1871 had been Mary Ann Shadd Cary. Born in Delaware as the first of thirteen children, Mary Ann Shadd was a descendant of a white Hessian soldier who had fought for the British during the French and Indian Wars and had married an African American woman who cared for him after he was wounded. As racial tensions increased in the runup to the Civil War, state officials made it illegal to educate black children in Delaware, so the Shadd family moved to Pennsylvania, where Mary Ann attended a Quaker school. And when in 1850 the federal government enacted the Fugitive Slave Act, which rewarded bounty hunters for forcing free blacks and escaped slaves into bondage, Mary Ann and her brother Isaac moved to Ontario, Canada. There, she ran a newspaper, *The Provincial Freeman*, making her the first black female newspaper publisher in North America. Her father Abraham Shadd, a shoemaker and veteran of the Revolutionary War, had served as "a conductor" on the Underground Railroad, escorting slaves from the South to freedom in the North.

After the Civil War, Shadd Cary returned to the United States to teach school children in Wilmington, Delaware and finally, Washington, DC. She was the first female student at Howard University's law school but was not allowed to graduate with her class in 1872 because the District of Columbia Bar only admitted men. Later, the DC bar admitted women, and Shadd Cary returned to Howard, to receive her law degree, at the age of 60.

On the eve of the District's first territorial elections in April 1871, Shadd Cary and famed orator Frederick Douglass led a delegation of sixty women, black and white, to the courthouse seeking to register. By some accounts, she managed to register, though was never allowed to vote. In an affidavit, Shadd Cary wrote that her request had been "wrongfully refused." Three years later she petitioned the House Judiciary Committee on behalf of 600 women in the District of Columbia who sought the vote. Embracing Victoria Woodhull's testimony that the two amendments had already enfranchised them, she urged Congress not to forget black women during their debate. Although black women might have been "silent" until now, they were not "indifferent to their own just claims under the amendments." All over the country, black women joined white women in the New Departure strategy, including Mary Beatty, a black activist who joined three white suffragists in a trip to the polls in Portland, Oregon in November 1872. The election judge in Oregon accepted their four ballots, though he neatly tucked them "under the [ballot box] and not inside."

In Rochester, New York, Susan B. Anthony, perhaps the city's most famous resident, went to the registrar's office with her three sisters and ten other women. Arriving at the makeshift office set up in a general store on November 1, 1872, they were at first refused. So Anthony made a speech, quoting the Fourteenth Amendment, and the New York Constitution section on voting, which made no mention of sex. One account suggested that she also threatened to sue. To her surprise, her application was accepted as a voter in Rochester's eighth ward. The *Rochester Union and Advertiser* suggested that election officials be arrested and prosecuted to the full extent of the law. "Citizenship no more carries the right to vote than it carries the power to fly to the moon," the paper said. Four days later, on November 5, 1872, she and eight other women arrived at the West End News Depot polling place to cast votes for Congress. At first, Republican registrars accepted their ballots, in Anthony's telling because they calculated the women were Republicans whose votes would help the party's candidates. But Sylvester Lewis, a poll watcher, challenged their right to vote, and the ballots were discarded. The three election inspectors were later arrested, tried, and convicted of violating the Enforcement Act of 1870, requiring fidelity to election laws. Ultimately President Grant, who first won office that year, pardoned them. As for Anthony, she was arrested and tried for voter fraud in a courtroom setting that became a stage for her advocacy in a much-anticipated, much-covered trial of a woman's right to vote. Prosecutors had moved the trial to the County Courthouse in Canandaigua, New York, in part to avoid pre-trial publicity stirred up by Anthony's speeches. Ward Hunt, an associate justice of the U.S. Supreme Court, presided over the case while riding circuit in New York, a common practice that required Supreme Court justices to take over some of local caseload.

Having instructed the jury to find the defendant guilty, Hunt asked her if she had anything to say in her defense. She did. "Yes, your honor, I have many things to say," Anthony replied, "For in your ordered verdict of guilty, you have trampled under foot every vital principle of our government. My natural rights, my civil rights, my political rights, my judicial rights, are all alike ignored. Robbed of the fundamental privilege of citizenship, I am degraded from the status of a citizen to that of a subject; and not only myself individually, but all of my sex are, by your honor's verdict, doomed to political subjection under this so-called, form of government." The judge ordered her to stop arguing the case, noting she had already been found guilty. She replied: "Your denial of a citizen's right to vote, is the denial of my right of consent as one of the governed, the denial of my right of representation as one of the taxed, the denial of my right to a trial by a jury of my peers ... the denial of my sacred rights to life, liberty, property..." Before she could add "and the pursuit of happiness," the judge silenced her. He found her guilty, ordered her to pay a fine of $100 and the costs of prosecution. This she refused to do, declaring that she would "never pay a dollar of your unjust penalty."

The Anthony legal team had hoped her refusal to pay the fine would land her in jail, allowing her lawyer, Henry Selden, to file a writ of *habeas corpus*, a protest of unlawful imprisonment. This course would have gained her a hearing before the Supreme Court. Hunt, a former chief judge of the New York Court of Appeals well familiar with the legal process, closed off that option by refusing to imprison her. The other fourteen women arrested with her were never prosecuted, leaving the appeal to the Supreme Court for another day, in another state.

Two weeks before Anthony had arrived at the general store in Rochester to register to vote, Virginia Louisa Minor (Fig. 4.3) had gone to the registrar's office at 2004 Market Street in St. Louis to become a voter. In fact it was her husband Francis, a lawyer wholly sympathetic to the cause of women's suffrage, who first suggested to Anthony that she try to test the application of the Fourteenth Amendment. Described as "beautiful, intelligent and charming," Virginia Minor was a southerner who had supported the Union cause. On news that Union solders had come down with scurvy, she hunted for cherries on their farm and made them into preserves for the troops at Benton Barracks, three miles away. After the accidental gun death of the couple's only child, 14-year-old Francis, she poured her grief into the cause of suffrage. Two years before Anthony, Stanton, and Stone had created their rival national suffrage organizations, Minor co-founded and became president of the Woman Suffrage Association of Missouri in 1867. Now, on October 15, 1872, she attempted to register.

Figure 4.3 Virginia Minor, one of the founders of the Missouri Woman Suffrage Association, was described as "beautiful, intelligent and charming," a southerner who supported the Union cause. She was one of the women, arguably the most important, who attempted to vote in 1872 in what movement leaders called the New Departure. Represented by her husband Francis Minor, her case went all the way to the Supreme Court. In *Minor v. Happersett*, the court ruled that the Constitution largely left electoral decisions to the states. *Source:* Getty Images. Kean Collection.

The St. Louis registrar, Reese Happersett, informed Virginia Minor that only male citizens could vote. The couple filed suit in Missouri that December, alleging that provisions in the Missouri state constitution reserving voting privileges only to men were in violation of the U.S. Constitution's Fourteenth Amendment. They lost and appealed to the U.S. Supreme Court, where they added an additional argument: that the intent of the original U.S. Constitution was to enfranchise women as well as men. Personally arguing the case on February 9, 1875, Francis Minor noted that women had voted in New Jersey from the state's founding until 1807, though the state constitution did not mention men or women by name, saying only that those citizens qualified by property holdings and residency could vote. As Virginia Minor was a citizen, he said, the rights of citizenship, including the right to vote, were implicitly hers. Denying suffrage to women, he suggested, was not embedded in law but in custom. More, he said, the Fifteenth Amendment shifted responsibility for suffrage from the states to the federal government, making it a national, not state, privilege.

In an opinion written by Chief Justice Morrison Waite and released on March 29, 1875, the U.S. Supreme Court conceded that Virginia Minor was a citizen. But the court ruled that the United States government had "no voters in the States of its own creation." More, the justices held unanimously, the intent of the authors of the Fourteenth Amendment was to give voting rights to former male slaves, not women. As for the intent of the founders, wrote Waite, "It cannot for a moment be doubted that if it had been intended to make all citizens of the United States voters, the framers of the Constitution would not have left it to implication. So important a change in the condition of citizenship as it actually existed, if intended, would have been expressly declared." The quixotic attempt by female activists to turn to their advantage a postwar strategic opening had ended. More, it had set a legal precedent, codifying the Founding Fathers' intent to delegate these thorny issues and paving the way for states to litigate the business of who was entitled to vote.

A Run for the Presidency, and a Sex Scandal

Within a few months of her testimony before Congress, Woodhull announced her intention to run for the presidency. She cast herself as a doer. "While others of my sex devoted themselves to a crusade against the laws that shackle the women of the country, I asserted my individual independence," she wrote to the *New York Herald.* Others might argue that women were the equal of men, but she had lived the veracity of the claim. "I boldly entered the arena of politics and business and exercised [my] rights," she wrote. Pledging to "speak for the unenfranchised women of the country," she announced her campaign.

The Equal Rights Party, a vehicle she had formed, nominated her for president on May 10. Delegates designated Frederick Douglass as her vice presidential running mate. Although Douglass never acknowledged the nomination, the very idea of a mixed-race, mixed-gender ticket sparked controversy, stirring fears of normalizing interracial marriage. One newspaper described the ticket as "a shameless prostitute and a Negro." Even more radical was the party platform. Advocating universal suffrage, a strong welfare state, and social equality, the party nominated Woodhull by acclamation, though she would not reach her 35th birthday, the constitutionally mandated age for the presidency, until several months after the new president's inauguration. Women were not then entitled to vote – except in the territories of Wyoming and Utah – but nothing in the law prevented them from holding office. "Whoever is set up to be President of the United States is just set up to have his character torn off from his back in shreds, and to be mauled, pummeled, and covered with dirt by every filthy paper all over the country," warned Harriet Beecher Stowe, author of *Uncle Tom's Cabin*. "And no woman that was not willing to be dragged through every kennel, and slopped into every dirty pail of water like an old mop, would ever consent to run as a candidate."

Despite Woodhull's unprecedented run for the presidency and her appearance before Congress, the issue for which she became infamous – one that led to her personal undoing and that of her candidacy – was her advocacy of sexual freedom between consenting adults. Defending a woman's right to live with a man without commitment to marriage or children, the twice-married Woodhull now declared, "Yes, I am a Free Lover. I have an inalienable, constitutional and natural right to love whom I may, to love as long or as short a period as I can; to change that love every day if I please, and with that right neither you nor any law you can frame have any right to interfere." She called free love the "highest, purest sense as the only cure for immorality, the deep damnation by which men corrupt and disfigure God's most holy institution of sexual relations." In a letter to the *New York Times* in 1871 she added, "It is not marriage, but sexual intercourse, then, that is God's most holy institution."

Seizing on these heretical views, newspapers exploited the toxic mix of sex and suffrage. "Mrs. Woodhull Claims the Right to Change Her Husband Every Day," the *New York Herald* headlined after one of her speeches at Steinway Hall in New York drew a crowd of three thousand. Thomas Nast, the cartoonist whose iconic rendering of Santa Claus has lasted the ages, portrayed Woodhull as "Mrs. Satan." Other newspapers called her "Queen of the Prostitutes." Horace Greeley wrote that his view of the sanctity of marriage now made the likelihood of him becoming a suffragist "a moral impossibility."

After meeting her in 1871, Stanton was sympathetic toward Woodhull, seeing in the press slurs all the usual weapons men used to assail assertive women. "We have had women enough sacrificed to this sentimental, hypocritical prating about purity," Stanton wrote to a friend. Woodhull "has done a work for women that none of us could have done. She has faced and dared men to call her names that make women shudder." By then Stanton and her husband Henry were maintaining separate households, their relationship frayed by her opposition to the Fifteenth Amendment. When women finally win the right to vote, said Stanton, Woodhull's name "will have its own high place as a deliverer."

But suffragists for the most tried to distance themselves from her. At one National Woman Suffrage Association convention, Anthony sat Woodhull between herself and Stanton, so no one else would risk association with her. Her speech did nothing to calm tempers. If Congress did not enfranchise women at the next legislative session, Woodhull warned, "We mean treason ... We will overthrow this bogus government."

Ridiculed by the press that sold newspapers over her controversial utterances, disdained by the political establishment that had once welcomed her into the inner halls of congressional power, estranged from most in the suffrage cause, and struggling financially to keep *Woodhull & Claflin* solvent, Woodhull now took aim at a popular man of the cloth. She would skewer him not because of his extramarital affair with a congregant, but for his moral hypocrisy. A man who preached fidelity and disparaged women who wandered would be held to account.

The Reverend Henry Ward Beecher, whose eminent sisters included Harriet Beecher Stowe, Catharine Beecher, and suffragist Isabella Beecher Hooker, was an unconventional preacher. Pastor of the Plymouth Congregational Church in Brooklyn, he had opened its doors to the Underground Railroad, part of his conviction that slavery was immoral. Before the Civil War he had raised money to free slaves by paying their owners, and sent rifles to abolitionists in Kansas, saying they could do more good than Bibles. The press nicknamed them "Beecher's Bibles." His writings in *The New York Independent,* a newspaper he had helped found, were as influential as his sermons, and reached a readership of 75,000 in 1870, when he retired as editor. He then began editing *The Christian Union*, a journal with the goal of uniting all Christian denominations around "Christian charity, love and sympathy." He was often on the road delivering sermons, and during the Civil War, President Lincoln sent him to Europe to build popular support for the Union, to keep Britain from recognizing the Confederacy as a separate nation. In 1865, as the cannons were silenced, Lincoln again sent Beecher on a mission, this time to Fort Sumter, where the war began, to mark the return of the American flag. "If it had not been for Beecher," Lincoln said, "there would have been no flag to raise."

Beecher had long inveighed against free love, preaching instead the "gospel of love," holding women closer to God than men, more vulnerable to the whims of godly nature. Now, he and Woodhull engaged in moral mudslinging, perhaps to boost the circulation of both his *Christian Union* and her *Woodhull & Claflin Weekly*. After the *Weekly* published a "Lord's Prayer for Adults," Beecher blasted "the incredible depths of folly and blasphemy into which Modern Spiritualism is plunging its followers." On learning from Stanton that one of his congregants had written a private letter accusing Beecher of seducing her, Woodhull plotted her revenge. In a speech to the American Association of Spiritualists in Boston in 1872, she disclosed the liaison between Beecher and Elizabeth Tilton, wife of Theodore Tilton, one of Beecher's protégés. Then Woodhull published a detailed account of the affair in the October 28, 1872 issue of *Woodhull & Claflin's Weekly*, generating enormous public interest – copies, normally 10 cents an issue, were said to be selling on the street for $40 each. The disclosure greatly damaged Beecher's reputation and sent her own status as a presidential candidate and advocate for women's suffrage into free fall. On November 2, three days before the election, she and Tennie were arrested for sending obscenity, in the pages of the *Weekly*, through the mails. Though a jury found them not guilty, the ignominy lasted. At the polls November 5, Republican Ulysses S. Grant was elected president, Democrat Horace Greeley was defeated (and died weeks later), and Equal Rights Party candidate Victoria Woodhull received not a single Electoral College vote. Still, she had achieved a marker in feminist history, becoming the first woman to run for the presidency, establishing a beachhead, and perhaps a warning, for women in future generations seeking a role in national American political life.

The Beecher–Tilton scandal, as it came to be known, doused the reputations of almost everyone who had touched its controversies. Tilton sued Beecher, who had to withstand a trial for adultery. The six-month trial, the longest in the nation's history to that point and one that captivated press attention, ended in a hung jury. Beecher asked for a verdict from his Congregationalist peers, who cleared him of wrongdoing and welcomed him back to Plymouth Church, though they excommunicated Theodore Tilton. Stanton called the church's edict "a holocaust of womanhood." The Tiltons divorced and Elizabeth Tilton withdrew from society, while Theodore Tilton moved to France, his career as a writer far less prestigious than its initial promise had suggested. After a few years Woodhull moved to England, denounced her free love advocacy, and married a British aristocrat. The scandal divided Beecher's family – his sisters Harriet and Catharine supported him, while his sister Isabella backed Woodhull. But of all the repercussions, none was worse than that visited on the women's suffrage movement, now affiliated in the public mind with sexual radicalism.

It was not hard to see why. Beecher was serving as president of the American Woman Suffrage Association. Tilton had at one point headed the National Woman Suffrage Association. Woodhull was running for president as the candidate for women's suffrage. Given the cast of characters, it was perhaps inevitable that the idea of free love would tarnish suffrage as the cause of upstanding reformers. After one Woodhull speech, a newspaper headline may have summed up the dilemma when it declared, "Died of Free Love, November 25th In Steinway Hall, the Woman Suffrage Movement."

To Lucy Stone, the public's view of suffragists as free love advocates was a curse, "the heaviest millstone we carry." Olympia Brown agreed the Beecher scandal had caused "great injury" to the cause. So eager was Susan B. Anthony to keep Woodhull from the podium at an 1872 meeting that she ordered a janitor to douse the gaslights, ending the session. Alice Stone Blackwell, in an assessment she no doubt inherited from her mother, observed, "The effect upon the movement was devastating. The cause was overwhelmed with a weight of odium which took years to wear away." Memberships in the national suffrage organizations plummeted. Women began forming their own local and state groups, eager to distance themselves from the national brush with scandal. The first anti-suffrage protests, organized by women, popped up. By 1875, the schism, the Supreme Court defeat of the New Departure, the Beecher–Tilton scandal – all these tempests of the post-Civil War era left the women's suffrage movement looking over its shoulder, back toward the states, now numbering thirty-seven, where the Founding Fathers had vested the power to enfranchise.

5

The States as Incubators for Social Change

On July 4, 1876, the United States celebrated its first centennial, seen as an opportunity to heal a nation wrenched apart by the Civil War. Outside Independence Hall in Philadelphia, where the U.S. Constitution had been debated, soldiers from each of the Thirteen Colonies marched in a procession commanded by two generals who had fought in the Civil War, Ambrose Burnside from the North and Henry Heth from the South. Inside the hall, Richard Henry Lee of Virginia read an original copy of the Declaration of Independence that two of his ancestors had signed. The crowd drowned out his words with wild cheers at the sight of the "faded and crumbling" document. When he finished, Susan B. Anthony, Matilda Joslyn Gage, and other suffragists rose from their seats and made their way to the podium. They had requested time on the program, and been denied. Now they carried out a rogue action, handing the surprised presiding officer their Declaration of the Rights of Women, written on parchment and "nicely rolled up & tied with red, white and blue ribbons."

Many suffrage activists had urged a boycott of the festivities. As one woman wrote the *Woman's Journal,* "As long as men do not allow her equal rights, why should she help celebrate masculine independence? No proud, independent woman can be sincere in helping such a jubilee." Anthony was convinced they would win much favorable publicity. Instead, the gambit backfired. An editorial in Greeley's New York *Tribune* called the Fourth of July theatrics by Team Anthony an example

And Yet They Persisted: How American Women Won the Right to Vote, First Edition. Johanna Neuman.
© 2020 John Wiley & Sons, Inc. Published 2020 by John Wiley & Sons, Inc.
Companion website: www.wiley.com/go/Neuman

of the kind of violence that would erupt if women won the vote. "Through a very discourteous interruption, it prefigures new forms of violence and disregard of order which may accompany the participation of women in active partisan politics," said the paper. Calling the suffragists "agitators," the *St. Louis Times* agreed, writing, "The women have had their Centennial say – that is, several of them have."

Even supporters of the cause faulted the suffragists for using an occasion of national celebration to launch a case against the government. "Woman suffrage is a sure thing of the near future," wrote the *New York Independent*. "But because we have not attained to it in the last century is no reason we should neglect to celebrate the grand things that have been accomplished." Worse, as one newspaper noted, suffragists seemed out of step with the times. After the Civil War, Americans were on the move. The nation was transitioning from the farm to the city, and expanding its borders west with the promise of gold and land. Industrialization was changing the smoke-filled skyline of urban America, and immigrants from Ireland and Germany were changing the nation's demographic profile. Men were marching in the streets to support political parties – or participating in labor strikes by steel workers and farmers. And women were joining reform efforts to work for temperance, clean streets, and better schools. Unlike the campaign for the vote, these issues were not overtly political, not likely to upset gender equilibrium or provoke opposition to their involvement. In the wake of the Beecher–Tilton affair, the cause of women's suffrage had the taint of scandal. "There is a prevailing indifference to their cause," said a *New York Evening Post* columnist. "And unluckily for them, the indifference is very largely feminine."

Against this backdrop of indifference, in January 1878, Senator Aaron Sargent of California introduced what he called the Sixteenth Amendment to the U.S. Constitution. Its twenty-nine words, borrowing from the words of the Fifteenth Amendment that ten years earlier had divided suffragists into rival groups, were succinct: "The right of citizens of the United States to vote shall not be denied or abridged by the United States or by any State on account of sex. Congress shall have power to enforce this article by appropriate legislation." Here, finally, was the bill that Republicans had been promising since the end of the Civil War, when they assured suffragists that this was "the Negro's Hour," that women's rights would come after the enfranchisement of African American men. Ten years later, "the Woman's Hour" had arrived, at least on paper. In fact, this measure, eventually to become the Nineteenth Amendment, would be introduced in identical language in each of the next forty-one years until it was finally enacted in 1919, and ratified by a sufficient number of states in 1920. Each year, suffrage advocates would descend on Washington, DC to lobby for its passage. And each year, pleas went unheeded, sometimes ignored altogether. In 1884, one member of Congress – his name is not recorded – suggested to Anthony that she stop bothering Congress and take the campaign to the states. If suffrage won in the states, female voters would help elect the next Congress. They would come to be seen not as ideologues with a small following but as constituents with the power to vote lawmakers out of office.

The idea of working toward the vote state by state had long been the policy of the Boston-based American Woman Suffrage Association, where Lucy Stone felt that a Congress composed of men without female constituents was unlikely to honor their appeal. More, she calculated that limited resources would be better deployed toward campaigns at the grassroots level. Anthony, exhausted by grueling and losing campaigns in Kansas, Nebraska, and Michigan, longed for a federal solution that in one broad brush would enfranchise all the nation's women. In dismissing the congressman's suggestion, she inadvertently confirmed claims of critics that the movement represented a small cohort. "We have neither the women, nor the Money to make the canvasses of the 38 states, school district by school district to educate each individual man out of the old belief that woman was created to be his subject," she scoffed. Anthony also betrayed her resentment about waiting for the vote after former slaves and immigrants, about having to plead with male voters for a human right. "When you insist that we shall beg at the feet of each of the states, native and foreign, Black and white, learned and ignorant, you doom us to incalculable hardships and sacrifices and to most exasperating insults and humiliations," she said. Better for Congress to enact a constitutional amendment requiring ratification by three-fourths of the states, which would "lift the decision of our question from the vote of the populace to that of the legislatures."

Rebuffed by Congress, ignored by the press and public, Anthony and her supporters had no choice but to turn to the states. They would have to renew their efforts at the local level, seeking approval of male legislators to put referenda on the ballot and of male voters to accept them. It would not be easy. Efforts to win the vote by appealing to state constitutional conventions in the 19th Century would all fail. Campaigns to win at the polls – convincing legislatures to place the issue before the voters in statewide initiatives – fared little better, winning in three states, losing in twenty. But in the attempt, activists stirred a debate about women's rights that gradually shifted the issue of suffrage from a concern of a radical few to the interest of the many. More, their agitation for the vote at the state level, while often defeated, won modest gains in local voting rights, a concession that female taxpayers and mothers of schoolchildren merited representation in the halls of local governments. This too would soften male opposition, assuring men that women could be both voters and wives.

School, Tax, and Municipal Suffrage

In towns and municipalities all over the country the argument gained ground that women merited a say in the doings of their local governments and school boards. School suffrage was especially popular, reinforcing a cultural view of Republican Motherhood. First promoted after the Revolution, the concept held that women were to organize the home and educate the next generation of patriots, while men served as the family's public and political face. To many male voters, advocates of women's suffrage represented a radical extreme of "old maids" or "spinsters," intent on bucking a gendered society that had cast them aside. But the school was an extension of the home, a secondary source of inculcating a new generation into essential American values. While the idea of women becoming political actors might threaten male pride or violate a gendered code of conduct, school suffrage for women did not. First enacted in Kentucky for widows in 1838, by century's end the local franchise had been extended to women, single, married, and widowed, in twenty other states.

Often, participation in school board issues propelled new female voters toward their own electoral victories. New York joined the list of states adopting school suffrage for women in 1880. Twenty-five years later, in 1905, Katherine Duer Mackay became the first woman to win election to the Rosslyn, Long Island school board. The wealthy and fashionably dressed Mackay later became the first member of High Society to embrace the women's suffrage cause, helping to mainstream the issue and defuse critics who feared the vote would emasculate men. During the campaign, her male opponent, Dr. J. H. Bogart, had belittled her for representing "petticoat rule." After she defeated him, Mackay pushed a reform agenda that included an end to corporal punishment, making her an immediate favorite with students, who scrawled on fences, sidewalks, and barn doors the schoolboy graffiti, "Mrs. Mackay is All Right." Demonstrating considerable political acumen, Mackay persuaded Bogart to run for an open seat at the next election. This he did, winning the race, giving Mackay a reliable ally for her reforms and proving her a savvy politico. As the *New York Herald* put it, "His attitude toward the proposals that come from the woman who read him out of the school board and then read him back in again is now said to be as distinctly respectful and considerate as that clever woman could wish."

Municipal suffrage – the right to vote in all local elections – was usually the fallback goal of suffragists defeated in efforts to win equal suffrage in all elections. After the failed campaign in Kansas in 1867, suffragists regrouped to work for the right to vote locally. Twenty years later, 1887, women went to the polls for the first time to vote in city and town elections there. Hoping to humiliate the female temperance activists who were being encouraged to turn out and vote, men opposed to both female voting and prohibition opted for hardball tactics. They arranged for the name of temperance activist Susanna Madora "Dora" Salter to be put on the ballot of a small Quaker town called Argonia, figuring male voters would reject any female or temperance candidates. They hoped this embarrassment would douse any further appetite by temperance advocates for the male sport of politics. Salter, whose husband was the city clerk, had no idea she was on the ballot until a delegation arrived at her home on Election Day to ask her if, indeed, she was willing to serve. She said yes, and won the election by a two-thirds majority, becoming the first woman in the nation elected mayor. She served one uneventful term, declining to run for re-election. A New York *Sun* correspondent who was sent to cover her first city council meeting reported that she presided with decorum, showing an aptitude for parliamentary procedure and for curbing irrelevant chatter.

Most municipalities still required voters to meet property qualifications. So the issue of taxation became a rallying cry for women, either single or widowed, who were required to pay taxes on land they inherited. Tax suffrage gained some converts – in 1887 Montana granted taxpaying women the right to vote on all questions submitted to taxpayers. Iowa followed suit in 1893, Louisiana in 1898. Lucy Stone had long preached against paying taxes without having a vote. Susan B. Anthony had recently joined the effort. But perhaps the most famous of the tax holdouts were the Smith sisters of Glastonbury, Connecticut.

Abby Hadassah Smith, 76, and Julia Evelina Smith, 81 (Fig. 5.1), were the last of five daughters of Zephaniah Hollister Smith, a graduate of Yale, ordained minister and lawyer, and Hannah Hadassah Hickcock Smith, a linguist and abolitionist. Born in Glastonbury, Connecticut, a town of 3,000 south of Hartford, they had been raised by their unusual parents to defy convention. Educated by tutors, Julia was fluent in Greek, Hebrew, and Latin, translating the King James Bible into each language, teaching French, Latin, and arithmetic at the Emma Willard School in Troy, New York. Like Elizabeth Cady Stanton, she had read widely in her father's law books, viewed by town folk as an expert on William Blackstone's legal treatises.

Now, these two seniors, the town's largest taxpayers, decided they would no longer pay taxes until the town let them vote in town meeting.

Figure 5.1 Abby Hadassah Smith, 76, and Julia Evelina Smith, 81, were the last of five daughters of Zephaniah Hollister Smith, a graduate of Yale, ordained minister and lawyer, and Hannah Hadassah Hickcock Smith, a linguist and abolitionist. Born in Glastonbury, Connecticut, a town of 3,000 south of Hartford, they had been raised by their unusual parents to defy convention. Educated by tutors, Julia was fluent in Greek, Hebrew, and Latin, translating the King James Bible into each language, teaching French, Latin, and arithmetic at the Emma Willard School in Troy, New York. When these two seniors, the town's largest taxpayers, decided they would no longer pay taxes until the town let them vote, they set off one of the greatest protests of "no taxation without representation" in the country's history. By the time the confrontation ended, the town had confiscated their cows, and made them famous. *Source:* Public Domain.

They were particularly aggrieved when authorities taxed them double in 1869 – explaining that otherwise highway officials could not pay the laborers building a road. In October 1873 they traveled to New York, among 1,200 people who attended the convention of Lucy Stone's American Woman Suffrage Association. They were especially moved by the comments of Frances Ellen Watkins Harper, an African American suffragist who appealed to white activists to fight for the rights of black women. Often when they canvassed Glastonbury for female signatures on anti-slavery petitions, they were surprised the women felt compelled to ask their husbands' permission. Now they came home to discover that men whose election they had no voice in had raised their property taxes – although no property owned by a man had been similarly reassessed.

The next month, they appeared at Glastonbury's town meeting. Like Lydia Taft, who had arrived at the Uxbridge town meeting in Massachusetts more than a century earlier, the Smith sisters were the town's largest taxpayers. Abby won permission to speak. "All we ask of the town is not to rule over them as they rule over us, but to be on an equality with them," she said. Her speech was met by utter silence. On their return home, the Smith sisters decided they would no longer pay taxes until they were allowed to vote in town meeting. As their protest wound its way through the courts, Glastonbury confiscated and auctioned off their dairy cows, farm land, suffrage memorabilia, and even Julia's "The Holy Bible: Containing the Old and New Testaments; Translated Literally from Original Tongues," the first translation of the scripture into English by a woman. The Smith sisters and their cows – including two they dubbed Taxey and Votey – became famous. The *Hartford Courant* reprinted Abby Smith's remarks, and the *Springfield Republican* set up a defense fund. In 1876, their plea of "No Taxation Without Representation" was noted at centennial celebrations across the country. But their lawsuit took eight years to wind through the courts, by which time Abby had died and Julia had married. Lawyers won the lawsuit on technical grounds, never testing the principle that no one could be taxed unless they had a vote on the matter.

The final chapter of municipal suffrage in the nineteenth century came in Michigan. Women in Detroit, where they paid taxes on an estimated $20 million in property, or about one-seventh of the city's landed wealth, were especially aggrieved about the injustice of taxation without representation. They wrote a petition, asking for a voice in making the laws they were compelled to follow in filling the city's coffers each year. In 1893 the legislature agreed, and women won the right to vote in local elections. Activist Octavia Williams Bates called it "the new jewel" in women's empowerment. But the Michigan Supreme Court overturned the decision, holding that the "Legislature has no authority to create a new class of voters." That is precisely the authority given to the states by the U.S. Constitution, but the case was never appealed. The idea of municipal suffrage withered until World War I, when the role of women in protecting the home front and volunteering for war service raised it anew.

Awakening Suffrage Foes

Even before that unnamed congressman suggested to Anthony in 1884 that she renew the campaign in the states, the suffrage movement had already suffered quite a few setbacks. Over the previous two decades, male voters in Kansas, Nebraska, Vermont, Michigan, the Dakotas, Oregon, and Colorado had rejected the idea of women voting, often with margins of 2 to 1. In Michigan in 1874, the anti-suffrage vote was overwhelming – 135,957 to 40,077, for a 77 percent to 22 percent margin. Anthony, who had spent forty days campaigning there, tried her best to distance herself from the tarnish of free love association. But when she arrived for a speech in Hillsdale, Michigan, she found local suffragists had refused to help with arrangements, arguing her presence would "do more harm than good." Likewise in Iowa, local activists asked both Anthony and Stanton to stay away from the state, for fear their very presence would remind voters of Woodhull and the movement's association with sexual adventurism. With the American Woman Suffrage Association (AWSA) and the National Woman Suffrage Association (NWSA) often running rival campaigns in the states, local advocates worried that the chief impact of this input from Boston and New York had been to awaken the opposition.

Chief among the opponents was the liquor lobby. As the nation grew more urban, liquor consumption spiked. In 1864, some 80,000 retailers sold liquor. Within ten years, the number had grown to 200,000, and 4,131 breweries were producing nine million barrels a year. Men often drank their salaries, and then abused wives and children in alcoholic rages. In 1873, women in Hillsboro, Ohio, inspired by a sermon given by visiting Boston minister Diocletian Lewis, gathered in churches to sing hymns and pray for the souls of the inebriated. Then they marched to saloons where they asked owners to destroy their booze and shutter their businesses. Soon this moral campaign against liquor spread to other cities.

The next year, in 1874, the Woman's [cq] Christian Temperance Union was founded to target moral decay, urging abstinence from the destructive power of alcohol. Five years later, Frances Willard (Fig. 5.2), a former teacher with frameless eyeglasses and a feminine demeanor, changed the organization from one dedicated to a moral crusade to a more muscular lobbying force. Heading the organization from 1879 until her death in 1898 at the age of 58, Willard understood that women feared for their safety at home, and she gave them permission, under the umbrella of female morality, to seek temperance legislation and other legal rights to protect themselves, their children, and their community. She urged members to "Do Everything" in the

Figure 5.2 Frances Willard was an educator and reformer who, as president of the Woman's Christian Temperance Union (WCTU), promoted a philosophy to "Do Everything" for the cause, from petitioning to educating. In 1880, she endorsed women's suffrage under the WCTU cause of "Home Protection," seeking to protect families from the "devastation of legalized traffic in strong drink." With what Susan B. Anthony called "an army of 250,000," the WCTU was a powerful infusion of troops whose endorsement was a game changer for women's suffrage. But the WCTU embrace also awakened opponents, especially the liquor lobby, which now mounted a fierce battle against suffrage in almost every state where it was on the ballot. *Source:* Public Domain. Library of Congress's Prints and Photographs division.

name of "Home Protection." She did not confine the agenda to alcoholism – pushing to limit workdays to eight hours and to raise the age of consent for young women in marriage or sex. Although there was a political element to her activism, all was couched in the terminology of domestic service, "For God and Home and Native Land."

No matter how Willard framed it, male protesters perceived female activism against inebriation as a threat to their sovereignty. Hecklers threw beer and sausages at temperance activists in Ohio, and set dogs on anti-liquor women in Cleveland. Municipal lawmakers sided with the men, passing ordinances against temperance marchers in Portland, Cleveland, and Cincinnati, and blocking women from praying for abstinence at the beer garden in Ohio.

In 1880, the Woman's Christian Temperance Union (WCTU) endorsed women's suffrage, deciding after years of avoiding the political fray that the ballot was the most effective way to target the ruinous effects of alcoholism and the abuse that often resulted. The WCTU endorsement was a game changer for the women's suffrage movement. Anthony admired Willard's success, calling her, a bit ruefully, "a General with an army of 250,000." NWSA by contrast was losing members. Where Anthony schooled supporters to seek the vote as citizens, Willard urged her members to embrace the franchise as an opportunity to lead a moral transformation of politics, to encourage "good behavior" in all citizens.

Where Victoria Woodhull and her free love associations had tainted the suffrage movement, Frances Willard and her moral crusade against alcoholism made the fight for women's rights respectable. The move swelled the ranks of suffragists by hundreds of thousands, but also awakened two groups whose opposition would further bedevil the cause. Female anti-suffragists now organized to demand that lawmakers protect their purview as guardians of the domestic good, insisting they did not want the vote. And the liquor lobby, fearing female voters would legislate to prohibit manufacture and consumption of alcohol, now alerted saloon owners, brewers, manufacturers, politicians, corporate interests, and male voters to the consequences of enfranchising women. Awakened to the threat this social change could pose to their business, the liquor industry muscled up into a fighting force that appealed to men's thirst and committed huge budgets to defeat women's suffrage in state after state.

Fresh attention to the issue of female voting rights had already roused the opposition. In Lancaster, Massachusetts, a group of more than 200 women had petitioned the state legislature not to extend the franchise to women, on grounds it would rob them of their moral high ground. "It would diminish the purity, the dignity and the moral influence of woman [cq] and bring into the family circle a dangerous element of discord," argued their petition. In 1882, female activists were again agitating in Massachusetts, this time for municipal suffrage. As momentum built for this bill that would have allowed women to vote in local elections, Senator George Crocker approached Nancy Manning Houghton to seek her help in defeating the measure, urging her to remonstrate against it. A leading social figure in Boston whose husband Henry Oscar Houghton had founded the publishing house Houghton Mifflin, Nancy Houghton was of "old colonial stock," tracing her name to early records in Watertown and Cambridge. She began collecting signatures of her friends on a petition to forestall "the imposition of any further political duties upon women." So successful was this drive that two years later, in 1884, she formed the Massachusetts Association Opposed to the Further

Extension of Suffrage to Women (MAOFESW). No fewer than 1,500 women became members the first year, and twice that by the second. The organization influenced elections around the country, circulating literature to like-minded women – called antis – in Iowa, Kansas, New York, Ohio, Vermont, and of course Massachusetts. Eventually a national organization was formed, which battled suffrage until 1920, when it lost a final battle to test the constitutionality of the Nineteenth Amendment in the courts.

The Nineteenth-Century Battle in the States

The first test came in Oregon, which placed women's suffrage on the ballot in November 1884. Led by Abigail Scott Duniway, the state had first wrestled with the issue in late 1871, after Susan B. Anthony's speaking tour throughout the Pacific Northwest. A journalist and orator, Duniway, whose brother Harvey W. Scott was editor of the *Oregonian*, used her own newspaper, the *New Northwest*, to stoke activism among readers. But she was often in conflict with suffrage supporters from the WCTU, fearing their involvement would trigger opposition from the liquor lobby and hurt the initiative's chances. By campaign's end, money had poured in from both suffragists and anti-suffragists. Saloon owners also raised money against the measure, which was defeated 28,176 to 11,223, or 71.5 percent to 28.4 percent.

One year later, in 1885, the Dakota territorial legislature enfranchised the state's 50,000 female residents. But the newly appointed territorial governor, Gilbert Pierce, vetoed the bill "with one stroke of his pen," arguing that such a provision would weaken Dakota's application for statehood a few years later. Likewise in Rhode Island in 1887, activists convinced legislators to pass the provision, only to have it defeated by the voters. Paulina Wright Davis, whose husband Thomas was a wealthy manufacturer, had co-founded the Rhode Island Woman's Suffrage Association and created the first women's newspaper in the nation, the *Una*, out of Providence. She had convinced the General Assembly to support the issue – meeting the required two-third majority in two successive sessions to win its placement on the ballot. On April 6, 1887, voters went to the polls and voted against it – 21,957 to 6,889, or 76 percent to 24 percent. As the *Newport Daily News* put it, "The woman suffrage amendment was simply buried, completely overwhelmed by an April snow storm of ballots."

In Washington, the first territorial legislature, meeting on February 27, 1854, had defeated by one vote a proposal to grant suffrage to all white women in the territory. Several legislators were married to Native

American women, and it is believed they may have voted against the measure. Advocacy did not stir again until Susan B. Anthony's trip through the region in 1871 – which included a speech before the Washington legislature, the first such speech by a woman to the Olympia statehouse. In her wake, local suffrage organizations formed, clubwomen debated the issue, and the liquor industry warned of dire consequences. One newspaper, hardly friendly, called the idea of women's suffrage "worse than the smallpox and chills and fever combined." While some lauded her advocacy as "graceful and elegant," other lawmakers were alarmed. In November they passed a bill, signed by the governor, stating that "hereafter no female shall have the right of ballot or vote at any poll … until the Congress of the United States of America shall … declare the same to be the supreme law of the land." Some women did vote in 1883 to 1886 after the legislature passed a bill saying that "wherever the word 'his' occurs … it shall be construed to mean 'his or her,' as the case may be." In 1884, some 8,000 women went to the polls to vote, 16 percent of an electorate of 50,000. Women also used this short opening to serve on juries, before the courts overturned the "his or her" bill. In its decision, the Washington Supreme Court held that family organization "is found in the divine ordinance, as well as in the nature of things." Women, said Judge George Turner, were to stay at home, in civil law, in nature, and in the teachings of the Bible.

By the time Washingtonians were again asked to vote on the matter, this history was still fresh in social memory. Adella Parker, writing a suffragist leaflet, blamed gambling and liquor interests for plotting to end the brief experiment with the vote. Women "voted in '85 and '86," she wrote, "and they voted so well they drove most of the thugs and gamblers over into British Columbia." Now, in 1889, Washington's territorial powers organized a convention to enact a constitution as a first step toward statehood. A newly formed Advocates of Equal Suffrage met at Olympia, the territorial capitol, to marshal for the fight. Seeking votes for the territory's 20,000 women, the new organization complained about the current lineup of voters that included "patrons of the prize-ring, wife beaters, tramps, bummers and drunkards." In the end, delegates did not include women in the document's definition of citizenship, but did attach an amendment that did so, if voters approved.

Borrowing from the New Departure campaign in 1872, in which women across the country tried to use the Fourteenth and Fifteenth Amendments to vote, the Equal Suffrage League of Walla Walla and other organizations urged women to show up at the polls and cast their votes for the amendment. League members were confident that while local election officials might mark the ballots "rejected," they would be counted later. Instead, male voters dashed their chances, voting 34,513 to 16,527, or 68 percent to 32 percent against the amendment.

The first bright star in the suffrage firmament came in Wyoming, which extended the franchise to women when it first became a territory in 1869. Now, twenty years later, the territory applied for statehood with a constitution that continued to empower women. Eager to welcome women to the sparsely populated area, Wyoming's political establishment recognized that the inclusion of women at the ballot box would bolster its power in Congress. Democrats in Congress, eyeing the territory's Republican leanings, decided to reject the application unless Wyoming dropped women from the voting rolls. This, officials refused to do, with one saying Wyoming would stay out of the Union rather than abandon its female voters, a move that would have diminished its political muscle. As happened in 1807 when New Jersey reneged on its constitutional pledge of women's suffrage, female suffrage became part of a political calculus about advantage. Holding its ground, Wyoming was the first to enter the Union, in 1890, as an equal suffrage state.

One victory against so many defeats was a depressing legacy, born of male hostility and strategic experimentation. Elizabeth Cady Stanton became so exasperated that at the 1889 meeting of the National Woman Suffrage Association, she criticized the frequent proclamations of gratitude issued to politicians for modest concessions to women's rights, such as property rights and educational opportunities. "I do not see any occasion for gratitude to these honorable gentlemen, who, after robbing us of our fundamental rights as citizens, propose to restore a few minor privileges," she said. At 73, Stanton had not lost the passion for reform, eager for an agenda that included the vote, divorce reform, and guardianship over children. But she had lost her appetite for the organized suffrage movement, with its tiresome parliamentary procedure and little progress. "There is not one impulse of gratitude in my soul for any of the fragmentary privileges which by slow degrees we have wrung out of our oppressors during the last half century," she added.

In 1890, amid dwindling memberships, younger activists suggested reuniting the two rival suffrage organizations. Anthony and Stone were not at first interested, as much animus had built between them. Stone resented the three-volume *History of Woman Suffrage* that Stanton and Anthony had written, which made scant mention of her efforts or those of her organization. Anthony resented the modest success of the *Woman's Journal* that Stone was still publishing, perhaps because it took her ten years to pay off the debt of the *Revolution* that she and Stanton had briefly published. Then too, Anthony, who never married, resented Stone's decision to keep her own name on marriage to Henry Blackwell. At one meeting Anthony criticized Stone for focusing solely on the vote to the exclusion of marriage reform. She speculated that perhaps Stone was unsuited to fight on the marriage issue because in rewriting her own vows, she had dropped the "honor and obey" language. Stone had, Anthony charged, thus "refused to submit to the legal form of marriage." The mutual ill will was evident within suffrage circles – one activist called it "a duel in the dark" – and hardly flattering to either of them. Now, they swallowed their pride and reunited for a new effort, merging their two organizations into the National American Woman Suffrage Association (NAWSA). Stanton, in absentia (she was in England), was named president. Stone was named chair of its executive committee. But Anthony was the power. Ignoring dissidents who left in protest, she steered NAWSA from its formation in 1890 to her retirement in 1900 and beyond.

South Dakota held an election on women's suffrage in 1890. Anthony came early and stayed through the election. "All the best speakers, all the best workers in the woman's suffrage ranks in the United States are to be turned into the field of South Dakota," she told one reporter, predicting, "We have every assurance that we are going to carry the day." The new state, welcomed to the Union only the year before, had adopted as its slogan, "Under God the People Rule." Suffragists adroitly piggybacked on the idea, taking as their motto, "Under God the People Rule. Women Are People." During the driest and hottest summer on record, there were many hardships. Distances between towns meant speakers – and the audience – often had to travel thirty miles or more. None of the state political parties endorsed women's suffrage, even those, such as the Farmers' Alliance and the Knights of Labor, who had pledged their support earlier. At some speeches Anthony faced groups of Russian immigrants sporting big yellow badges that said, "Against Woman Suffrage and Susan B. Anthony." The measure was defeated in a rout – 45,682 to 22,792, or 66 percent to 34 percent. Other ballot issues may have encouraged parties to barter away their support for women's suffrage in exchange for votes. One was the hard-fought battle over where to locate the state capital, with Pierre winning over Huron, 41,969 to 34,610, or 55 percent to 45 percent. A measure to restrict voting by Native Americans was close, 43 percent in favor, 47 percent against, with indications that some voters who thought they were restricting Indian rights were approving them.

Finally in 1893, suffragists won their first big victory after a string of defeats. As usual, political calculation played a role. In fact the state had been born of political ambition. Republican leaders had calculated that Rutherford B. Hayes might not win the presidency in 1876 without Colorado's three electoral votes. So Congress pushed through the territory's application for statehood in 1875. During the state's constitutional convention, delegates had defeated efforts to grant women the right to vote, but agreed to place an amendment on the ballot in 1877. There, the measure was defeated, 14,053 to 6,612.

Reeling from defeat, Albina Washburn and Mary Shields, veterans of these early Colorado losses, concluded that the idea of women voting was still too controversial. They had pitched the vote on the basis of equal rights, arguing that women should be granted their natural rights as citizens. Most male voters viewed women as guardians of the home, and they didn't want them mucking around in politics. So the two disbanded their suffrage society and established a new organization – the Colorado Woman Christian Temperance Union.

Their opportunity came in 1893, when Ellis Meredith, a reporter for the *Rocky Mountain News*, organized a group of twenty-eight women (one was her mother) to quietly shepherd a suffrage initiative through the Colorado legislature. They had taken turns quietly nursing it through committees and both houses, and watched as newly elected governor Davis Hanson Waite – a rare Populist to win office – signed it. Now voters in November would face a decision, so Meredith reached out to Anthony for campaign advice. Anthony was convinced that Kansas offered a far more promising venue, and a far better use of campaign resources. Still bruised by their reception in Colorado in 1877, when the electorate rejected the idea of women voting by a 68 percent to 32 percent margin, suffrage leaders were in no mood to return. Anthony blamed Mexican Americans in southern Colorado for the earlier defeat. So dubious was she about winning in Colorado she now asked Meredith, "Are all those Mexicans dead?"

Meredith instead turned to one of Anthony's young lieutenants, Carrie Chapman Catt, who at first declined to help, sharing the conventional wisdom that Kansas would be the next suffrage state. But Catt kept musing about Meredith's plea for advice, and started to commit her ideas to paper. Keep a low profile, so as not to stir up the opposition. Emphasize a quiet band of men and women working together. Reach out not to diehard supporters who tend to shout but quiet leaders in each precinct, preferably male. In plotting out the campaign, Catt grew excited. She agreed to travel to the state. Given the vast distances between Colorado towns, she asked for help in scheduling speeches. She would open in Denver but then spread around the state, eventually logging one thousand miles. Wary of being tagged as an outside agitator, Catt insisted local activists run the campaign.

This they did. Iona Hanna, wife of a prominent banker and the first elected official of the Denver School District, recruited elite social figures, "the best people," to the cause. She discouraged women who were "not intelligent and respectable." As the quiet campaign of the wealthy made inroads in Denver, so did Washburn, Shields, and other temperance supporters in the vast stretches of land that defined Colorado. They all made allies of Populists, pressured Republicans and

Democrats, reached out to men in the Grange, the Farmers' Alliance, and Knights of Labor. All over the state, women formed study groups to awaken interest in suffrage. In Longmont, Mary Carr, Orpha Bacon, Rosetta Webb, and Jane Lincoln explored the issue of property rights of women, demonstrating the necessity of the vote. Elizabeth Piper Ensley, an African American educator who had moved to Denver from Washington, DC, served as treasurer of the Colorado Non-Partisan Equal Suffrage Association, raising funds for the cause. All of these efforts, a stealth campaign of disparate communities fueled by a coalition of interests, snuck up on critics, and caught the liquor interests during a rare nap until just before the election. On November 7, male voters in Colorado, including those in Longmont, became the first in the nation to approve women's suffrage at the ballot box – passing the measure 35,798 to 29,451 or 55 percent to 45 percent.

In Kansas, where Anthony had placed her money and hopes for 1890, Annie Diggs convinced the state House to pass an amendment but the effort had faltered in the Senate. She and other activists marshaled the troops for a new election that in 1894 would bring every major national suffrage figure into the state. Amid the worst economic depression in the nation's history, prompted by an overextended railroads and a run on the banks, they capitalized on the surge of interest in populism and temperance. Carry Nation, the whiskey-smashing agitator who had threatened to vote illegally in her home state of Oklahoma, joined the battle, as did Laura Johnson, Lucy B. Johnston, and Catherine Hoffman of the Kansas Equal Suffrage Association and Fanny Rastall and Lillian Mitchner of the Kansas WCTU, who pledged the support of 9,000 "faithful allies" for the cause. National suffrage leaders arrived to work, including Catt, who steered a horse-drawn wagon by herself for four hours across an empty plain. Applauded for her remarkable feat, Catt called it "a heartbreaking defeat" when voters rejected the measure 130,139 to 95,302. National suffragists blamed "a mesh of political rivalries" in Kansas. Locals blamed the infighting between Anthony and others on NAWSA's executive committee for dashing their hopes. Susan B. Anthony's brother agreed with the critics. Daniel Anthony, a Kansas publisher, had urged her to leave the scene, saying, "Susan, you're a damn fool – go home!" In 1912 Kansas again voted on the issue. Heeding advice from suffragists in California and Washington, local activists did not invite national leaders to join the campaign. This time, they won.

Women in New York were also organizing in 1894, this time for a massive petition drive to a constitutional convention that was considering revisions. Anthony had called for one million signatures to sway delegates. Though she and supporters fell short of the goal, they mustered 600,000 signatures to send to Albany. More important, the effort generated enormous and unexpected pockets of activism, on both sides. Elite women joined the campaign, giving speeches in their own homes. So intoxicating was the sight of wealthy women discussing politics that "parlor meetings" often overflowed, and reporters flocked to the scene. They also gathered signatures for the cause at what the *New York Times* called "the dainty white and gold atmosphere" of Sherry's at Fifth Avenue and 37th Street, not known for its political radicalism. The campaign also energized anti-suffragists, who began an active campaign of their own to persuade the convention not to extend voting rights to women. As usual, politics doomed the effort. Suffragists had cheered when Joseph H. Choate, a New York lawyer and legislator, was named president of the convention. His wife Caroline had been active in collecting signatures for the petition. But Choate had his eye on the governor's race, and packed the Suffrage Committee with known anti-suffragists, sure he would be rewarded with their support. He lost his gamble, never invited by his party to run for governor. Suffrage lost too, as delegates voted 98–58 against an amendment enfranchising women.

In 1896, Utah became the third state – after Wyoming and Colorado – to enact equal suffrage. It had been a bumpy road. When Utah became a territory in 1870, it offered women the right to vote, though not to hold office. Brigham Young, the church leader, believed that enfranchising women would complicate the image of Mormon women as manipulated by their polygamous husband. For seventeen years, women in Utah voted. They did not, as critics of the Mormon Church had hoped, vote to outlaw polygamy. In 1887, Congress did, as well as dissolving the Mormon Church and confiscating the property of any churches worth more than $50,000. The bill, directed at Utah, also annulled territorial laws allowing illegitimate children to inherit and repealed women's right to vote. Here was a prime example of legislators in Utah enfranchising women to increase their own hold on power, and of lawmakers in Washington using polygamy as a rationale to disenfranchise women in a way that also robbed the Mormon Church of its wealth and ability to produce armies of future voters. Self-interest was at the heart of male political action by both sides.

By 1890, the church itself had passed a manifesto officially ending its policy of plural marriage. This in turn allowed Congress, in 1894, to pass the enabling legislation that led Utah to apply for statehood. Activists opened organizations in most of the territory's twenty-seven counties, making sure that no one involved in polygamous marriages was named as a leader. An unofficial publication for Mormons, the *Woman's Exponent*, championed the cause. At a constitutional convention in 1895, some delegates argued that if Utah enfranchised women, Congress would reject its application for statehood. Others countered that women were a moral force in politics, and had voted for seventeen years without ill effect. A provision for equality in "all civil, political and religious rights and privileges" was embedded into the constitution. The following year, in 1896, male voters overwhelmingly approved, 28,618 to 2,687, making Utah the third equal suffrage state. Idaho, a neighboring state with a sizeable Mormon population, followed close behind. On November 3, 1896, women stood outside polling places all day, braving ankle-deep snow. Senate Joint Resolution 2, a constitutional amendment extending the vote to women, passed 12,126 to 6,282, or 66 percent to 34 percent. The fourth state, all in the West, one by constitutional edict and three by popular vote, was won (Fig. 5.3).

The last great effort for suffrage in the nineteenth century came in California in 1896. It was the largest campaign in suffrage history, supported by such well-connected women as Jane Stanford, who with her husband Leland, an industrialist, had founded Stanford University, and Phoebe Apperson Hearst, mother of William Randolph Hearst, publisher of the *New York Journal* and the *San Francisco Examiner*. At one point during the campaign, Anthony wrote to William Randolph Hearst, seeking the newspaper's endorsement. "I pray you for the love of justice, for the love of your mother, and for the sake of California – lead the way

Figure 5.3   In this 1915 cartoon, "The Awakening," *Puck Magazine* portrayed early suffrage victories, with women in the rest of the nation looking toward their liberators in the West, carrying the torch of women's suffrage to the eastern states. *Source:* Getty Images. Library of Congress.

for the Democratic Party of your state to advocate the suffrage amendment." He declined, understanding that his readers were not inclined to support the idea, even if his mother was.

It was the temperance clubwomen who led the fight in California, women such as Sarah Severance and Beaumelle Sturtevant-Peet, who first petitioned the legislature in 1890 for school, municipal, and full suffrage. On July Fourth they celebrated Wyoming's admission to the Union as an equal suffrage state. One year later, Sturtevant-Peet, state president of the Woman's Christian Temperance Union, delivered a petition to the legislature with 15,000 signatures in favor of women's suffrage. When Anthony's NAWSA headquarters warned California suffragists to separate themselves from the temperance issue to avoid trouble from the liquor lobby, the California women laughed, as most of them were WCTU officers.

Equal suffrage victory in Colorado in 1893 gave them new impetus to try again. State senators protested an amendment enfranchising women, questioning its constitutionality. So suffrage allies introduced a resolution in March 1895 amending the state constitution simply by striking the word "male" from the voting clause. Amendment 13 would be on the ballot on November 3, 1896. During the spring, activists supervised a massive petition campaign, gathering some 40,000 signatures of male and female supporters. Ellen Sargent, whose husband Senator Aaron Sargent had in 1878 introduced what would eventually become the Nineteenth Amendment, steered the campaign in northern California. She hailed the "educational value of the petition work," saying, "It gave opportunity for the distribution of a vast amount of literature" and for the opportunity to educate "large numbers of people." By its very size, the canvassing also rebutted the charge that women did not really want the vote.

Although maintaining a non-partisan posture – Anthony believed that the movement should take endorsements from any party but affiliate with none – suffragists reached out to all of California's myriad parties. Republicans quickly endorsed the initiative, followed by the Populists, the Prohibition Party, and the Social Labor Party. Democrats remained opposed, toppling suffrage hopes for united establishment support. Later in the campaign, Populists teamed up with Democrats to sacrifice women in hope of defeating Republicans.

In southern California, suffragists reached out to a diverse coalition of activists – temperance, clubwomen, working class, and populists. The big tent in southern California was mostly white and Protestant – Mexican American and Chinese voters were not recruited. But it did include some African American activists, such as Naomi Anderson, a NAWSA official from Kansas, who found support from the Afro-American

Women's League, and Sarah Overton, a black leader in San Jose. For the first time, the movement reached out to working-class women, who were tapped to speak at factories. Amid a nationwide economic depression, with frequent strikes and protests by workers and farmers, this proved a winning strategy.

Innovations were many. The Los Angeles Wage Earners' Suffragist League, whose members included women of trade union families, held the city's first open air meetings, sang songs in city parks, and distributed doughnuts packaged with Votes for Women ribbons. In San Francisco, the College Equal Suffrage League excelled at advertising, its college graduates and professional women touring in autos, speaking on streets, addressing factory workers. One of the most iconic posters of the American suffrage movement emerged from their efforts. It said, "Women Vote for President and for all other officers in all elections on the same terms as Wyoming, Colorado, Utah and Idaho." Its last line: "Why Not in California?"

But in northern California, where the electorate was far larger, business owners feared the costs of labor reforms suffragists were promoting, and German and Irish immigrants shared their conservative views of female activism. Bay Area voters that year also chose William McKinley over William Jennings Bryant. Analysts concluded that they had voted for social order over anarchy on the presidential ballot and for status quo over radical reform on the suffrage initiative. It did not help that the Southern Pacific Railroad published virulent anti-suffrage publications, alleging that women reformers would drive up costs of doing business.

In every county where suffragists had formed precinct clubs and visited every voter and distributed leaflets, the amendment passed. There were mass meetings in every county with a town of more than 200 residents. In 1896, from early April in San Diego until late June in Humboldt County, suffragists held more than 190 meetings, including forty-six conventions in county seats that lasted two days each. In other precincts, leaders had trouble recruiting staffers, because of what one San Francisco worker called a "deadly apathy" among women who saw no need of the ballot. Plans to organize in each precinct had to be abandoned.

Precinct work in all districts might not have been enough to overcome the liquor lobby. Anticipating the onslaught, suffrage speakers often emphasized that female voters in Wyoming had not agitated for prohibition in twenty-seven years. It did not quiet the storm. Ten days before the election, the Wholesale Liquor Dealers' League met in San Francisco, vowing "to take such steps as … necessary" to protect their interests. Earlier in the campaign, the lobby had pressured the political parties not to support the measure, threatening a loss of campaign funds. Now, on the eve of the election, the League issued a letter to every saloon owner, grocer, and pharmacist in the state saying, "It is to your interest and ours to vote against the woman-suffrage amendment. We urge you to work and vote against it and do all you can to defeat it." On Election Day, liquor interests escorted hundreds of men from San Francisco's slums. Each had been instructed how to mark an "X" against the suffrage amendment. Each had been told if the amendment passed, liquor would never be sold in the city again.

Amendment 6 was defeated, 137,099 to 110,355, or 55 percent to 45 percent. Every county in southern California had approved the amendment, with the largest, Los Angeles County, providing the largest vote for the amendment, 4,600 in favor. Defeat came in San Francisco and Alameda Counties in northern California, for a combined total of 27,399 against the amendment. Anthony called on California women to renew the fight again in a few years. For now, many California women deserted suffrage organizations in favor of civic causes, eager to pursue their reforms without the toxic associations of the political movement.

Eventually the strategy suggested to Anthony in 1884 would bear fruit. As in many contemporary movements for social change, small steps in the states led to larger ones in the nation. Repeated campaigns, even losing ones, conditioned the public to soften toward an idea, once deemed radical, later viewed as unthreatening. But the great victories in the states – in California, Illinois, and New York – would come in the next century, after suffragists had adopted new, more modern styles of campaigning. Now, as the century came to an end, the first generation of leaders, veterans of Seneca Falls and Syracuse, of battles for abolition and over the Fourteenth and Fifteenth Amendments, were fading from the scene.

Lucy Stone had died in 1893, virtually her last act to strategize about the Colorado campaign. Elizabeth Cady Stanton, a popular speaker on divorce, marriage, and childrearing, had by the mid-1890s been written out of the very suffrage movement she founded. Her bestselling *Woman's Bible*, published in 1895, criticized religious leaders for teaching women to be subservient to men's commands. Over Susan B. Anthony's objections, NAWSA had condemned the book. Stanton had also upset the establishment by sending a congratulations note to Frederick Douglass on his second marriage, to white suffragist Helen Pitts. Aware that many feared her note would suggest that suffragists were embracing interracial marriage, Stanton instead teased Douglass about his new "mixed-marriage" between a voter and a non-voter. "If a good man from Maryland sees fit to marry a disfranchised woman from New York," Stanton wrote, "full liberty of choice in such relations should be conceded." Anthony had begged her not to send the letter, fearing the move would renew charges that suffragists were free love advocates. Stanton had already left the movement, leaving Anthony at the helm. Stanton died in 1902, Anthony in 1906. In their wake came a new generation of leaders – Anna Howard Shaw, an ordained minister whose speaking abilities outflanked her organizational talents, Alice Paul, a Quaker reformer who rallied militants, and Carrie Chapman Catt, a keen strategist whose observation of defeats in the states now inclined her to adopt a new strategy.

In state after state, Catt concluded, allies who had pledged support never delivered. More, the liquor lobby's muscle only added to suffragists' angst. Angered by the influx of "ignorant foreigners" likely to vote before women could, she and other suffrage leaders looked toward the South, embracing educational voting requirements designed to discriminate against black voters who had not been schooled. The southern strategy would ultimately fail, but not before hurtling the movement into what historians call the doldrums, a period of scant progress toward women's suffrage. With its blatant attempt to promote the ballot for white women at the expense of black men, this nativist turn was in keeping with its times, part of a cultural debate about the nature of American democracy, and the color of its electorate.

6

The Coloring of the Electorate

The last thirty years of the nineteenth century are sometimes called the Gilded Age, an expression coined by humorist Mark Twain as a measure of derision for a generation of upper-class Americans blinded by the excesses of their own wealth. But it was also a time of enormous turmoil for the soul of a nation founded by Anglo-Saxons. Unprecedented levels of immigration – by the turn of the century 14 percent of the U.S. population was foreign-born – had provoked a public debate over whether these new Americans would dilute the country's homogeneity. Southerners had unleashed a wave of mob lynching of African Americans, seeking to rob them of life, liberty, and the rights won after the Civil War. Newspapers had pounded a drum for war with Spain to liberate Cuba, and at its conclusion the United States for the first time became an imperial power, with territories in Hawaii, Guam, Puerto Rico, and the Philippines. Soon, the U.S. Supreme Court and Congress grappled with questions of citizenship, if not nationhood. Who was an American? Who should be allowed to vote?

As the nation's borders expanded, so too did these questions of nationality, citizenship, and suffrage. On the East Coast, an influx of immigrants from Italy and Eastern Europe stirred xenophobia, provoking new employment bans against Jews and Italians. In the South, the Great Migration of nearly six million African Americans began as black Americans left rural poverty seeking work and opportunity in the North, Midwest, and West. In the Midwest, states had once encouraged

And Yet They Persisted: How American Women Won the Right to Vote, First Edition. Johanna Neuman.
© 2020 John Wiley & Sons, Inc. Published 2020 by John Wiley & Sons, Inc.
Companion website: www.wiley.com/go/Neuman

workers to resettle their sparsely populated region by offering the vote to non-citizens, or at least those who pledged their intent to become citizens. Now state after state repealed so-called "alien suffrage," instead extending the amount of time in residency required to become a voter. In the Southwest, the Treaty of Guadalupe-Hidalgo, which ended the Mexican–American War in 1848, gave all Mexicans living within the newly ceded territory (parts of what are now Arizona, California, Colorado, Nevada, New Mexico, Utah, and Wyoming) citizenship, but not voting rights. As one Texan put it, "They are foreigners who claim American citizenship but who are as ignorant of things American as the mule." Some white Americans felt threatened by immigrants from Europe as well as Asia and South America, and by newly empowered African Americans who were changing the color of the nation's electorate. It was a time of nativism, and empire.

After the 1890 Census, the federal government proclaimed that the nation's borders were all roughed in. The Gold Rush of the mid-century, Horace Greeley's injunction to "Go West, Young Man," all had come and gone. There was no more room to expand. Three years later, historian Frederick Jackson Turner wondered what this "closing of the American frontier" would mean for the dynamism of the national character. He postulated that the soul of the country had already shed longtime customs of Europe – in its embrace of technological innovation and democratic ideals over rigid hierarchies and autocratic rule. Within five years, the United States was embroiled in the war with Spain, launched in the name of bringing democracy to Cuba, which would end with a new American empire of foreign territories.

The Spanish–American War

"It was a splendid little war, begun with the highest motives, carried on with magnificent intelligence and spirit, favored by that Fortune which loves the brave." So wrote U.S. Secretary of State John Hay to Theodore Roosevelt at the conclusion of the Spanish–American War, a conflict between the United States and Spain over the fate of Cuba and other vestiges of Spain's dwindling empire. Roosevelt, assistant secretary of the U.S. Navy when the war began, had emerged as a military hero for his conquest of San Juan Hill in Cuba. The 1st United States Volunteer Cavalry that he commanded, called the Rough Riders by admiring journalists, had attracted cowboys, ranchers, miners, and college athletes. Fighting alongside the regular army and the Rough Riders were members of the 24th Infantry and the 9th and 10th Cavalry, all African Americans, dubbed Buffalo Soldiers. The heroism of the entire force in the bloodiest fight in the conflict made headlines across the country and cemented Roosevelt's political star. It also validated the decision by African Americans to participate in a war for American victory abroad while they were being denied the very rights of citizenship at home. Twenty-six black American soldiers died that day, and Quarter Master Sgt. Edward L. Baker Jr., wounded by shrapnel, was awarded the Medal of Honor.

Perhaps Hay thought the war was "splendid" because, at least in Cuba, it lasted weeks. For months beforehand, a newspaper war between William Randolph Hearst's *Journal* and Joseph Pulitzer's *World* had whipped up war frenzy with exaggerated headlines about Spanish abuses against Cubans battling for their independence. The public was regularly assaulted by images from Cuba of starving women and children and rebels fighting for self-determination, much as American colonists had more than a century before. When the battleship *Maine* was blown up in Havana Harbor, huge headlines proclaimed it the work of the Spanish (this was never proven) and a Hearst headline proclaimed, "How do you like the *Journal*'s war?"

Citizens of Hawaii, Guam, Puerto Rico, and the Philippines would react in various ways to this new claim by the United States to rule their countries. In the Treaty of Paris that ended the war, Cuba was the only of Spain's imperial holdings to win outright independence. Hawaii, a former kingdom whose monarch had been toppled by white American businessmen, was annexed – against its will – by a McKinley administration looking for strategic assets from which to wage its Pacific wars. Women in Hawaii did not win the vote until 1920, despite the fact that virtually every officeholder on the islands sought to enfranchise them earlier. Filipino nationalists fought a three-year insurgent war – an estimated 4,000 Americans and 20,000 Filipinos died – for independence from U.S. rule. Rebels lost, and the country did not win sovereignty until July 4, 1946 – nearly a decade after Filipino men had gone to the polls and overwhelmingly embraced women's suffrage.

At a time of vast immigration and the closing of the nation's borders, conquering populations of different color or religion was seen as a civilizing mission, an obligation, in Rudyard Kipling's words, a manifest destiny, to export the values and habits of American democracy to a wider world. Even Massachusetts Senator George Hoar, one of the few Republicans to vote against the war resolution, thought the cause was just, "the most honorable single war in all history." The conflict rallied Americans in their first reunited effort since the Civil War had divided them, a national cause for a new imperial power.

For members of the American Anti-Imperialist League, such as William Lloyd Garrison Jr., son of the famed abolitionist, this taking of colonies tarnished the American experiment. Some even wondered if perhaps the assumption of sovereignty over another nation violated the U.S. Constitution. Issuing a protest, the League said robbing Filipinos of self-governance was the height of hypocrisy, since Americans had proved so inept at governing, both in big city corruption up north and Jim Crow discrimination down south. "While colored men are denied the suffrage in defiance of the Fifteenth Amendment, while lynchers go unwhipped of justice, ... while Tammany threatens New York ... it is not for us to insist that the Filipinos must do what after centuries of experience we failed to do," he wrote.

The Black Man's Burden Association in Chicago protested these supremacist instincts as well as the continuing harassment and murder of blacks at home. One week after the explosion of the USS *Maine*, white vigilantes burned down the home of Frazier Baker, a schoolteacher and the postmaster of Lake City, South Carolina. The mob shot and killed Baker and his 1-year-old daughter Julia because, as South Carolina's Senator Ben Tillman said, the "proud people" of Lake City refused to get "their mail from a n—r." Baker's wife Lavina and five other children survived by fleeing the house. "Remember the Maine is the white man's watch word," commented one African American newspaper, the *Lexington Standard*. "Remember the murder of postmaster Baker at Lake City should be the Negro's." Within the African American community, a growing number believed imperialism was designed to rob "the manhood of the darker races." For one of America's new possessions, the former kingdom of Hawaii, the result of this imperialist war was not to rob men of color of their political rights, but a woman of color, in fact the Queen.

Losing Women's Suffrage in Hawaii and Puerto Rico

The Kingdom of Hawaii became its own nation in 1795, after King Hamehameha corralled all the islands into one country and established a dynasty that lasted almost a century. In 1819, the first group of American Protestant missionaries arrived from Boston, converting many Hawaiians to Christianity. The missionary presence ended many of the *kapus*, or taboos, that guided Hawaiian life, many restrictive of women's behavior, such as the belief that women could not eat with men, and that they were forbidden to eat certain foods. Other traditions that were soon abandoned in the name of Christianity included chiefs killing offenders as human sacrifices to the gods and the island's native sexual mores, accepted as part of marriages to multiple partners. To traders, the islands had long been a lure, and in 1887 they engineered a bloodless revolution that changed the country's constitution, extending the vote to white settlers as well as natives. In 1893, a group of white American businessmen led by Sanford B. Dole (his cousin ran the pineapple company) and U.S. State Department envoy John Stevens overthrew Queen Lili'uokalani, the first queen and last monarch of Hawaii (Fig. 6.1). She dedicated the rest of her life to trying to reclaim the throne.

Figure 6.1 Queen Lili'uokalani was the last sovereign of Hawaii, before the United States annexed the country as its fiftieth state. Angered by attempts to annex them by treaty, native Hawaiians, many women, staged rallies and circulated a petition to Congress. The Queen traveled to Washington, DC and persuaded senators to defeat the treaty. Amid a coloring of the American electorate, some senators had worried that adding Hawaii to the United States would "corrupt the homogeneity of the nation." But even before the royal delegation returned home, congressional leaders, eager to obtain Hawaii's strategic assets in the coming fight with Spain, plotted to absorb Hawaii by joint resolution. This move was a setback for Hawaiian women, who in the early days of the kingdom had enjoyed not only an equal role in the lower house of the legislature but also seats in the House of Nobles. 1891 photograph by James J. Williams, *Honolulu Star-Bulletin*, November 12, 1917, *Source:* Public Domain.

Dole appealed to President Benjamin Harrison to sign a treaty of annexation, putting Hawaii on the road to statehood. But when Grover Cleveland, an opponent of annexation, was inaugurated, he ordered an investigation that found Dole and his allies had acted improperly. Investigator James Blount was sent to Hawaii, where after an inquiry he ordered that American flags be lowered from government buildings and that the Queen be restored to her throne. In a demonstration of unfettered audacity, Dole refused to relinquish power, arguing the United States had no right to interfere in another nation's affairs.

Four years later, after William McKinley was inaugurated, the new president signed a treaty of annexation with the white government. Native Hawaiians, angered by the overthrow of their sovereign by foreigners, staged protest rallies and circulated mass petitions. The *Hui Hawaii Aloha Aina*, the Hawaiian Patriotic League, and its female counterpart, the *Hui Hawaii Aloha Aina o Na Wahine*, collected signatures on two petitions – one signed by women, the other by men. More than half the population – 21,269 native Hawaiians – signed the 556-page "Petition Against Annexation." Its arrival in Washington, along with Queen Lili'oukalani, won the day. Senators defeated the treaty, which required a two-thirds vote, in part because of her persuasive powers. Reflecting an era of "manic xenophobia," likely many senators worried that the political absorption of Hawaii, with its dark-skinned natives, would "corrupt the homogeneity of the nation." But even before the royal delegation returned home, congressional leaders, eager to secure Hawaii for its strategic assets for the anticipated fight with Spain, plotted to annex Hawaii by joint resolution, requiring only a majority vote.

In the early days of the Hawaiian kingdom, women from the ruling elite had enjoyed not only an equal role in the lower house of the legislature but also seats in the House of Nobles. Now, stripped of their cultural standing, Hawaii's women watched as their political interests were misrepresented and hijacked by a procession of American agents from white congressional overseers to white leaders of the women's suffrage movement. Congress decreed that Hawaiian women would be excluded from voting or from serving in the Hawaiian Senate or House of Representatives. Unlike other territories, whose legislatures had been granted the power by Congress to enact their own provisional constitutionals, Hawaii would have its new constitution written by an all-male Congress. Susan B. Anthony protested, saying, "I have been overflowing with wrath ever since the proposal was made to engraft our half-barbaric form of government on Hawaii." In fact, male settlers such as Dole had divested Hawaiian women of their rights some decades before, by imposing male rule. Now they were being disfranchised not because of their gender but because of their race. "There are about seven

Hawaiian women to one white woman here," explained one American male. "This would give a big majority of undesirable votes." Like Dole, Anthony professed to speak for the women of Hawaii, but her "Hawaiian Appeal" was generated in New York, not Honolulu. In fact, the only appeal women of Hawaii themselves had made to Congress was not to be annexed to the United States, to be restored to their independence.

White female do-gooders who presumed to speak for them often abrogated the voices of Hawaii's women. Here it was not the male patriarchy but the white maternal orthodoxy that blocked their self-expression. In 1918, Almira (Myra) Hollander Pittman, whose Boston-born husband Benjamin K. F. Pittman was a descendant of the Hawaiian chief of Hilo, testified before Congress about their visit to the islands and the aspirations of Hawaiian women for the vote. She reported that during the days of the monarchy "women took great interest and could be effectively active in politics." One congressman asked her if the natives she met were educated and spoke English. "They were all very well educated," she said. "They speak our language as well as we do and many of them better than many of us." Despite appeals by legislators in both parties to let the Hawaiian legislature decide the issue, women in Hawaii did not get the vote until 1920, when the Nineteenth Amendment was ratified. As the *Pacific Commercial Advertiser* announced on its front page of November 3, "For the first time in the history of Hawaii women voted yesterday at a regular election in these Islands. Thus Queen Kaahumanu's dream of a century ago [to void the *kapus* that severely restricted women's rights] has come to pass." According to the newspaper, women "turned out early ... and showed keen interest in their newly acquired rights."

The situation in Puerto Rico was far murkier. In 1904, the U.S. Supreme Court considered the question of whether Puerto Ricans were citizens of the United States. Isabel Gonzalez had arrived at Ellis Island in New York in the summer of 1902, a single woman who was pregnant. Viewing her as immoral, "likely to become a public charge," immigration officials rejected her admission, detaining her as an immigrant alien. Gonzalez, whose fiancé had arrived before her to find factory work in Staten Island, planned to join him. At a hearing to discuss her case, Isabel's brother and uncle joined her to testify that she had family in New York who would be "able, willing and legally bound to support" her. Immigration officials were not impressed. Lawyers for Isabel Gonzalez appealed to the Supreme Court. In *Gonzalez v. Williams*, a unanimous court issued a narrow ruling that Puerto Ricans were not immigrant aliens, leaving for another day the question of whether they were U.S. citizens. In 1917, Congress enacted a bill granting Puerto Ricans U.S. citizenship. To this day, residents in Puerto Rico remain in legal limbo.

Like residents of Washington, DC, U.S. citizens in Guam and Puerto Rico elect representatives to Congress who have the power to vote only in committees, not on the House or Senate floor. Unlike Americans in DC, who vote in presidential elections, residents of these territories vote in presidential primaries, and send delegations to national party conventions. But nowhere, on any of the U.S. territories, do its citizens cast votes in the general election for president.

Race, Gender, and Suffrage

For many white men, fighting Spain to liberate Cuba and acquire new territorial possessions was an act of chivalry, a way to recover their sense of manliness amid the growing influence of women in public life. The temperance movement, the abolitionist campaign, the new openings for women in local political offices – all led to what social critics called the feminization of politics and an attendant masculinity crisis. Advocating "the strenuous life," Theodore Roosevelt preached that "the highest form of success ... comes not to the man who desires mere easy peace, but to the man who does not shrink from danger." In the 1890 Census records, Roosevelt saw that whites were declining in their fertility while immigrants were increasing in theirs. Race suicide of the upper classes, he believed, threatened to warp the fabric of the nation. Calling the issue "grave cause for anxiety," he urged white women to preserve the race, eschewing birth control to protect "white civilization."

For African American men, the war posed an existential dilemma of whether to fight for a country that did not join them in fighting against lynching, intimidation, and discrimination against black American citizens. There was much commentary in black newspapers about the issue, on both sides. As the Indianapolis *Freeman* put it at the war's start, "If the government wants our support and services, let us demand and get a guarantee for our safety and protection at home." Countered the *Kansas State Ledger*, "War with Spain means a good deal; we understand that a great amount of the people in Cuba are Negroes, then we hope to see this government stand by them and protect them from all hazards." Once the conflict moved to the Philippines, opinion turned cynical. To some African Americans, the colonization of people of color – complete with reports that U.S. troops had referred to Filipino rebels as "n——s" – was a reminder of their own subjection. As the Omaha *Progress* said, "Since it is inevitable that black American soldiers must bear arms against a people of their own hue, [who fight] for the right of self-government ... let them fight, if for nothing more than to show ... the country of their birth that they are not cowards." The *Lexington*

Standard said it would not blame revolutionary leader Emilio Aguinaldo for resisting American sovereignty. "The more Aguinaldo reads the reports of how the colored people are being cut up for souvenirs in Georgia and hanged and shot to death in the other states, the more determined he is never to put himself under the protections of such a country," said the newspaper. "And who in the h – l can blame him?"

The era's xenophobia had stirred fear among black men that hard won voting rights would be rolled back. Already, Congress had made repeated efforts to repeal the Fourteenth and Fifteenth Amendments that enfranchised black men after the Civil War. As Rep. Thomas Hardwick of Georgia alleged, these amendments were passed "against the will of the majority of all the people in the Union, by trickery and treachery in the North and by force and violence in the South." African American women, who had long guarded the black male franchise as a community asset, took a lead in calling out the effort. Gertrude Bustill Mossell, an editor at the black newspaper *New York Age*, came from a prominent African American family. Her great-grandfather, Cyrus Bustill, had served as a baker for George Washington's Continental Army. After the war, he opened a bakery in Philadelphia and co-founded the Free African Society, the nation's first benevolent society for African Americans. Now, Mossell warned that repeal efforts by southern lawmakers were an ill-concealed attempt to restore white supremacy without spilling blood. "These men want the Fifteenth Amendment repealed," she said. "They want to … rule without the disgrace of shooting the Negro."

Throughout the Old Confederacy, states enacted laws meant to keep blacks from the ballot, coupling administrative obstacles with the intimation of violence and death for any black man who dared overcome them. The South was not alone in imposing poll taxes and literacy requirements on men of color. In 1866, the state of Oregon had enacted a poll tax on "every 'negro, Chinaman, Kanaka [Native Hawaiian], or mulatto' in the state." The provision, part of an assault on interracial marriage, also reflected the waves of change that were roiling the economies of West Coast states. After the Gold Rush of 1849, Chinese immigrants had come to California, Oregon, and Washington to build the first transcontinental railroad. Fearing the Chinese immigrant population would grow, Congress in 1875 restricted the immigration of Chinese women, slurring them as prostitutes "believed to be serious threats to white values, lives and futures." Citing the "racial inferiority of the Chinese," Congress declared them "a menace to republican institutions and the existence there of Christian civilization." California Governor Leland Stanford agreed, saying, "Asia, with her numberless millions, sends to our shores the dregs of her population." Feeling these nativist winds from the West, in 1882 Congress enacted the Chinese

Exclusion Act, suspending Chinese immigration for ten years and barring Chinese immigrants from U.S. citizenship. Unlike their white counterparts, enfranchised in 1920, Chinese women would not be eligible to vote until 1943, when Congress repealed the Chinese Exclusion Act.

Andrew Jackson's Indian Removal Policy, which had inspired an early petition drive by women seeking to overrule a government decision, had plundered much territory from Native tribes for southern farmers. His "Trail of Tears" sent Indians on a long death march to Oklahoma. Now, with Americans clamoring for still more land, Congress in 1887 enacted the Dawes Act, intended to abolish the communal land ownership of Native American tribes. Under the guise of ending Indian poverty, the U.S. government offered an allotment of land to any Native American who would agree to leave his tribe and farm his land separately. If the Indians did not partake of the offer, the federal government would confiscate the land and sell surplus parcels to railroads, mining companies or white ranchers. Few Native Americans, who revere the earth as an ancestral grandmother, accepted these terms. Worse, the Indian Office allotments tended to preserve irrigable land for whites. Those who protested – such as the nine elderly men on the Yuma reservation who refused to accept their land allotments – were jailed. In 1893, amid the worst economic depression in the nation's history, an estimated 100,000 settlers claimed plots of these lands in the Oklahoma Land Rush, in what was called the Cherokee Strip. The extent of the ethnic cleansing was manifest in the rhetoric. Theodore Roosevelt called the policy "a mighty pulverizing machine to break up the tribal mass." The problem with the Indians, said the author of the bill, Senator Henry Dawes of Massachusetts, was that "there is not selfishness, which is at the bottom of civilization." Until Native Americans "will consent to give up their lands, and divide them among their citizens so that each can own the land he cultivates, they will not make much progress," he added. By 1934, when President Franklin Roosevelt ended the program, Native Americans had lost two-thirds of their lands, from 138 to 48 million acres in half a century. Native American women would not win the vote until 1924.

White Suffragists' Racist Strategy

For nearly thirty years, suffragists held annual meetings in Washington, DC, emphasizing the movement's commitment to winning approval from Congress for a federal amendment. In 1895, the National American Woman Suffrage Association (NAWSA) convened its convention in Atlanta. Eager to rouse southern votes for the cause, organizers designed the meeting to court local white sympathies. Anthony personally asked Frederick Douglass, the famed African American orator, not to attend. Douglass had been the only man to speak out for women's right to vote at the 1848 Seneca Falls convention. The very women who had applauded his support then were silencing him now. Asked by African American journalist Ida B. Wells why she had snubbed this great friend of women's suffrage, Anthony said she did not want to jeopardize potential support in Georgia. It was a question of political self-interest. More, Anthony confessed to Wells, "when a group of colored women came and asked that I come to them and aid them in forming a branch of the suffrage association among the colored women, I declined to do so, on the ground of that same expediency." During the convention, South Carolina lawmaker Robert Reid Hemphill, who had fought in the Civil War and served in Congress, promised to introduce a constitutional amendment in South Carolina enfranchising women. After his speech, Anthony cued the band to play "Dixie," even then the musical emblem of those who clung to the segregationist narratives of the Confederacy, referred to as the South's Lost Cause.

Within the next decade, the movement's white southern strategy gathered some steam. Women's suffrage amendments were introduced at constitutional conventions in Mississippi in 1890, Louisiana in 1898, Alabama in 1901, and Virginia in 1902. As the Huntsville, Alabama newspaper *Republican* explained, "No matter how modest a constitutional convention is nowadays some female suffragist will find it out and insist on making a speech." Amid the turmoil over voting rights came some modest progress on taxpayer suffrage, with Louisiana and Alabama granting taxpaying women the right to vote on tax issues, although Alabama legislators withdrew their offer the following day. In Mississippi, delegates weighed a proposal to offer the vote to all women who owned or whose husbands owned $300 of real estate. What all of these overtures had in common was that enfranchising women of property would advantage white women. Spurred by Laura Clay of Kentucky and Kate Gordon of Louisiana, white suffrage leaders had adopted a strategy to "bring in the South." The way to win the South, they concluded, was to push for educated suffrage, as it too would disproportionately favor white women. Without legally robbing blacks of the vote – a ploy likely to provoke Congress – the South could restore white supremacy at the ballot box by enfranchising only educated or propertied female citizens, skewering the demographic toward whites. Lobbying Mississippi's congressional delegation, Henry Blackwell, widower of suffragist Lucy Stone, explained it as "a legal way to disenfranchise the Negro."

This new direction fanned the flames of racist and nativist rhetoric. At NAWSA's 1899 convention in Grand Rapids, Michigan, Frances Griffin, an Alabama suffragist, complained about her "Negro boy" gardener who, though illiterate, was eligible to vote. Carrie Chapman Catt, an ascendant star in suffrage organizing who would succeed Anthony as president in 1900, urged that foreigners be stripped of their vote. "Cut off the vote of the slums and give it to woman," she said, complaining of "the ignorant ... foreign vote ... manipulated by corrupt politicians to party advantage." When, in 1887, the Dawes Act offered the vote to any Native American who would leave his tribe and pay taxes on an allotted piece of land, Catt complained to an audience in South Dakota, "The murderous Sioux is given the right to franchise which he is ready and anxious to sell to the highest bidder." So notable was this increase in racist language that it soon smothered other reform efforts that once found favor among suffragists. At NAWSA's 1899 meeting, Anthony quashed efforts by Lottie Wilson Jackson, a black delegate from Michigan, to win support for a resolution condemning Jim Crow laws. Jackson proposed that the association censure railroads requiring African American women "to ride in smoking cars, and that suitable accommodations be provided for them." The resolution set off a heated debate, with the convention opting – apparently with a push from Anthony – to hide its prejudice behind the veneer of a one-cause agenda.

By 1903, NAWSA leaders were making no secret of their white southern strategy. At the annual convention in New Orleans, African American women were disinvited. Rev. Anna Howard Shaw, soon to be president, publicly upbraided southerners for enfranchising former black slaves before white women. "Never before in the history of the world have men made former slaves the political masters of their former mistresses," she thundered. In a statement, NAWSA officially branded itself as a party of "state rights, ... leaving to each State Association to determine the qualifications for membership" and the extent of the suffrage reforms it would seek from its state legislatures. And in her keynote address, Carrie Belle Kearney, a white supremacist, temperance advocate, and the first woman elected, in 1924, to the Mississippi State Senate, applauded the South for its "desperate effort to maintain the political supremacy of Anglo-Saxonism." She lamented that 4.5 million former slaves had already been added to the voting rolls, but argued that if a new "education qualification for the ballot [were] impartially applied to both sexes and races," it would result in "immediate and durable white supremacy, honestly attained."

Anthony was complicit in these forays into racist policy, but she was, perhaps as the movement's elder, not unmindful of coalitions between black and white women that had fueled the movement in earlier days. As convention rhetoric droned on, she left to pay a visit to the Phillis Wheatley Club, perhaps the largest African American woman's club in New Orleans. Named for the African American poet celebrated by General George Washington during the Revolution, the club was dedicated to the uplift of the black community. In 1896, the club had opened a hospital for blacks who could afford to pay for medical care but were often denied entry to white hospitals. Members also sponsored a nurses' training program for black women at New Orleans University. The club's founder and president, Sylvanie [cq] Williams, a respected teacher in the Orleans Parish Public Schools, was stunned when NAWSA barred her from its convention.

On greeting Anthony, Williams presented her with a bouquet of flowers, accompanied by words that betrayed her own bitterness. "Some flowers are fragile and delicate, some strong and hardy, some are carefully guarded and cherished, others are rough treated and trodden under foot," it read. Those treated roughly and stepped on, Williams noted, were black women. "They have a crown of thorns continually upon their brow, yet they are advancing and sometimes you find them further on than you would have expected." She ended by thanking Anthony for speaking to them, helping to restore their belief "in the Fatherhood of God and the Brotherhood of man, and at least for the time being in the sympathy of woman." In response, Anthony urged club members to use the ballot as they had their organization – to improve the fate of their community and address wrongs in the courts.

In the end, the suffrage movement's departure into southern politics achieved little. Not a single southern state of the Old Confederacy enacted women's suffrage, educated or otherwise, and only Texas, Arkansas, and Tennessee were among the thirty-six states that ratified the Nineteenth Amendment after its passage in 1920. As one lawmaker in Mississippi explained, there was no need to "cower behind petticoats," using "lovely women" to restore white supremacy. The wily politicos of the South had devised other strategies – presumably this was a reference to poll taxes, literacy requirements, and mob lynching – to achieve that end without sullying the purity of women with the coarseness of politics. Sexism vied with racism for their allegiance. If white power could be achieved without empowering women, more's the better. For black women, the assault on their activism was but the latest example of white suffragists throwing them under the bus whenever politically expedient, in this case to curry favor with white southerners. What was more damaging was the inference that black women were not worthy as voters because they were not respectable as women. This canard stemmed from slave days, when white slaveholders disparaged the morality of black women to rationalize their own sexual plundering. Now it was being used to deny them the vote.

African American Women Launch Own Campaigns

For African American women, the snub by white feminists was hurtful, but not a surprise. Years earlier, Helen A. Cook, president of the Washington Woman's League, an African American club with several hundred members, wrote an open letter to Susan B. Anthony. Published in the *Washington Post* on February 19, 1898, Cook chastised Anthony for supporting white suffrage after the Civil War rather than universal suffrage. One week later Charlotte Forten Grimke, a black suffragist from Philadelphia, wrote of her agreement. "While Afro-American women appreciate the value of woman suffrage quite as keenly as other women do, they will never cease to rejoice that their fathers and brothers, and sons and husbands" were enfranchised. Many African American women viewed the ballot as a tool for the betterment of their people, part of the "racial uplift" that was their mission.

Since passage of the Fourteenth Amendment in 1868, black women had treated the enfranchisement of black men as a sacred community asset. At one polling place in Macon, Georgia in 1872, women arrived at the polls as "part of their religion to keep their husbands and brothers straight in politics." Straight meant away from the Democrat Party of slavery and toward the Republican Party of Lincoln. In South Carolina, black women came to the polls with sticks to mete out punishment for those who veered toward the party of slavery, threatening to withhold sex from husbands who voted wrong, or evict them altogether. Later, when Illinois enacted school suffrage in 1891, African American women in Chicago used a local school board election to counter talk of repealing the Fourteenth and Fifteenth Amendments. Lucy Flower, a Republican candidate for trustee of the University of Illinois, sought their support in 1894 by pledging to win scholarships for African American students. Although she had voiced support for educated suffrage, code for whites only, black women in Chicago "threw their full strength into the campaign." Because of their backing, Lucy Flower became the first woman in Illinois elected to statewide office.

Black women also launched crusades against wrongs done to their race. In March 1892, three African American men – Tom Moss, Calvin McDowell, and Will Stewart – were murdered by mob. They had defended their People's Grocery, a gathering place for blacks, from white vandals furious at the economic encroachment on their business. While in jail, they were abducted and fatally shot. McDowell's eyes were gouged. In his last words, Moss said, "Tell my people to go west. There is no justice for them here." A native of Memphis, and childhood friend of Tom Moss, suffragist Mary Church Terrell was horrified on hearing the news. She sought out the preeminent black leader in Washington – acclaimed orator Frederick Douglass – and the two went to the White House. There, they asked President Benjamin Harrison to condemn lynching in his annual address to Congress. He refused, the first of many presidents to look the other way. Not until 2005 did the Senate apologize for taking no action against lynching "when action was most needed."

A columnist and co-owner of a black newspaper, *Memphis Free Speech*, Ida B. Wells (Fig. 6.2) was also enraged, incensed that white violence had claimed another black family man, whose wife was her good friend. Born a slave six months before Lincoln issued his Emancipation Proclamation on January 1, 1863, Wells was born a fighter. She attended Shaw College, a school for newly freed slaves, and later Fisk University. In 1884, traveling by train from Memphis to Nashville, the conductor ordered her to move from her first-class seat to the car for African Americans. She sued the Chesapeake & Ohio Railroad, won a $500 settlement in circuit court, only to see her moral victory erased by the Tennessee Supreme Court. "I felt so disappointed because I had hoped such great things from my suit for my people," she said. "O God, is there no … justice in this land for us?"

Now she turned to journalism to find justice for victims of racial injustice. She began a systematic investigation into the frequency and cruelty of lynching, disproving the white claim that targeted black men had raped white women, and the corollary claim that only men were lynched. She found instances of women and children murdered by mobs, and noted that only one third of the slain black men were even accused of rape, much less found guilty. Traveling the South to gather statistics about lynching took some courage, exposing her to great risks. She prized herself on interviewing as well as quoting white newspaper accounts.

As her editorial against the People's Grocery lynching was being set in type in May of 1892, she left for Philadelphia. She had been invited to give a speech on the right to vote by black suffragist Frances Ellen Watkins Harper. While she was gone, a mob of white supremacists burned her newspaper to the ground, her staff barely escaping the flames. Warned she would be lynched if she returned, Wells relocated to New York. There T. Thomas Fortune, owner of the influential *New York Age*, published her report on the front page, across seven columns. He printed 10,000 copies of "the first inside story of Negro lynching," which included names, dates, and places. Among her findings was that some accused black men had been conducting illicit relations with white women, presumably consensual. This finding was sure to stoke fury among southerners keen to preserve the myth of white female purity. "Nobody in this section of the country believes the old thread-bare lie that Negro men rape white women," she wrote. "If Southern white men

Figure 6.2 Ida B. Wells was one of the most dynamic figures in the women's suffrage movement, black or white. Born into slavery in 1862, as a journalist in Memphis she became a crusader against the lynching of African Americans, drawing on support from wealthy black women after segregationists burned down her newspaper. She was a founder, in 1907, of the National Association for the Advancement of Colored People (NAACP). Rebuffed by white suffrage leaders, she defied Alice Paul's edict that blacks not march in the 1913 suffrage parade in Washington, DC, waiting on the sidewalk until the Illinois delegation came within sight, then joining the procession. She also formed the first black suffrage society, the Alpha Club of Chicago, which was instrumental in winning the vote for women in Illinois in 1913 and in backing Oscar De Priest as the city's first elected black alderman in 1915. She was married to Ferdinand Barnett, and even as she raised four children she continued her writing. Photograph by Mary Garrity, circa 1893, *Source:* Public Domain.

are not careful, they will over-reach themselves," she warned, and would damage "the moral reputation of their women." So incendiary was this allegation that a group of black New Yorkers asked her to "put the soft pedal" to the charges and the *Times* labeled her "a slanderous and nasty-minded mulatress."

Wells wanted to publish a booklet on her findings, to be distributed nationally. Without the funds herself, she reached out to a group of elite African American women. On October 5, 1892, in New York's Lyric Hall, 250 black women came to honor Ida B. Wells and raise funds for a report that would rouse a national crusade against lynching called "Southern Horror: Lynch Law in All Its Phases." One scholar called donors "a who's who of the black Eastern establishment." Josephine St. Pierre Ruffin, a suffragist of French and African descent, was there from Boston. Dr. Susan McKinney, the third African American to earn a medical degree, came from Brooklyn. Sarah Garnet, the first black school principal, represented New York. They raised $500 (about $13,000 in today's dollars). Wells called it "the greatest demonstration ever attempted by race women for one of their own."

In the North, alarmed by the concerted efforts of southern states to rob black men of the right to vote and cut short their lives, middle-class African American women gravitated to social clubs in enormous numbers, participating in programs designed to improve standards of living and provide racial uplift. As one wit said, they congregated after being segregated.

Josephine St. Pierre Ruffin was the well-educated daughter of a French African father from Martinique and a white mother from Cornwall, England. She traveled often in white company. During the Civil War, she worked for the U.S. Sanitary Commission to raise funds and provide aid for soldiers in the field. In 1869, with Lucy Stone and Julia Ward Howe, she had founded the American Woman Suffrage Association. After her husband's death in 1886, she had turned her organizational talents and financial inheritance into *The Woman's Era*, the first newspaper published by and for African American women. With features such as "Social Etiquette," "Health and Beauty from Exercise," and "Eminent Women," the newspaper was popular. But Ruffin also gave space to covering women's suffrage victory in Colorado and profiling leaders such as Harriet Tubman, the former slave who repeatedly returned to the South to lead other slaves to freedom on the so-called Underground Railroad.

Ruffin was a member of the mostly white New England Woman's Press Association and the New England Woman's Club. By 1892, she hoped to widen the circle of influence, forming a Woman's Era Club of prominent African American Bostonians. The club adopted the slogan, "To help to make the world better." In the early 1890s, she polled the readers of *The Woman's Era* about the need for a national organization of black clubwomen, to positive response. When, in 1895, a little known Missouri journalist, John Jacks, attacked Ida B. Wells for her anti-lynching campaign, he alleged that black women had "no sense of virtue." This was a familiar white smear against black women, that they were not as virtuous as white women. Ruffin called for a national conference in Boston, to address "vital questions concerning our moral, mental, physical and financial growth and well-being." On July 29, delegates arrived from forty-two black women's clubs in fourteen states – including the Ida B. Wells Club of Chicago – for the three-day session at Berkeley Hall. Margaret Murray Washington, third wife of Booker T. Washington, spoke of the need to help those still struggling. Ella Smith, the first black woman to earn a masters degree from Wellesley, talked of the value of higher education. Author Anna Julia Cooper, who would later receive her PhD in history from the Sorbonne in Paris, argued for more organizing. Victoria Earle Matthews, born into slavery in 1861, would later start a settlement house for young African American girls in Manhattan's Upper West Side. Now she urged women to preserve the writings of and about African Americans. Not all the speakers were women – or black. They included William Lloyd Garrison Jr., a lawyer whose father was the famed abolitionist and who now spoke on the importance of the vote.

But it was Ruffin who captured the rationale, the urgency, behind the meeting. In recent years, leaders of major organizations of female benevolence had turned their back on African American women. In a recent interview while in London, Frances Willard of the Woman Christian Temperance Union had disparaged black male voters, saying, "It is not fair that a plantation Negro who can neither read or write should be entrusted with the ballot." Black women suffered through depictions of their men as corrupt and themselves as promiscuous. There was a sexual undertone to the critique, as if whites stereotyped blacks as illicit. As one Memphis newspaper editor put it, "When immorality is almost universal among the women of a race; its doom is sealed." Angered and frustrated, Ruffin now responded. "Year after year, Southern women have protested against the admission of colored women into any organization on the ground of the immorality of these women," she said. She lamented that "the charge was never crushed," adding, "It is 'mete, right and our bounded duty' to stand forth and declare ourselves and principles, to teach an ignorant and suspicious world that our aims and interests are identical with those of all good aspiring women."

At the conclusion of the conference, delegates voted to make permanent their collective will, forming the National Federation of Afro-American Women. Across the country, black women also joined together to fight for the vote – in venues as disparate as the St. Louis Suffrage Club, the Colored Women's Club of Los Angeles, the Colored Woman's Republican Club of Denver, the New Era Club of Boston, the Women's Loyal Union of Tennessee, and the Colored Women's Progressive Franchise Association in the District of Columbia. Often, when the issue was on the ballot, in Idaho, Montana, North Dakota, Nevada, Arizona, Oklahoma or New Mexico, they formed new clubs, what Frances Watkins Harper called "the threshold of woman's era." So many black social clubs formed that in 1896, the National Federation of Afro-American Women merged with the National Association of Colored Women's Clubs, begun by another black suffragist, Mary Church Terrell. By 1916 this umbrella organization included 300 black women's clubs from around the nation, with a combined membership of nearly 100,000. Founded by Terrell, Ruffin, Francis Ellen Watkins Harper, Wells, and others, the club took as its slogan "Lifting as We Climb." At the launch in Boston, Ruffin asked women "to break the silence, not by noisy protestations of what we are not, but by a dignified showing of what we are."

In 1900, Ruffin arrived in Milwaukee for the General Federation of Women's Clubs, the most influential of the movements for female benevolence. She appeared as a delegate for two largely white organizations, the New England Woman's Press Association and the New England Woman's Club, as well as the African American Woman's Era Club, sometimes known as the New Era Club. Federation officials at first appeared to accept all three of Ruffin's affiliations, but reaction from its southern members was fierce. The Kentucky State Federation worried that admitting Ruffin would create "a precedent for the admission of colored clubs generally." Amid the storm of protests, the board refused to seat Ruffin as a delegate for the Woman's Era Club. One affiliate, the Medford Women's Club of Massachusetts, was so offended by the board's "unjust and illegal" action it withdrew from the Federation. As for Ruffin, she departed for Boston, later writing in the Chicago *Tribune* that female reformers needed to rise above "the baser motives of society" to achieve real change. Her Woman's Era Club issued a statement that black women should from now on "confine themselves to their clubs and the large field of work open to them there."

And so they did. Clubs around the country opened kindergartens, an idea imported from Germany, lobbied for public parks, pioneered programs to train African American women and girls in the professions, and lectured on the importance of keeping a clean home. Eager to distance themselves from sexualized views that stereotyped black women as promiscuous and lacking in hygiene, some embraced what historian Evelyn Brooks Higginbotham called "the politics of respectability," combatting with propriety the myth that black women were licentious. Ruffin often talked about the need for "moral education and physical development." Mary Church Terrell (Fig. 6.3), one of the first black women to graduate from Oberlin and the first black woman in the country appointed to a school board, this in Washington, DC, often urged temperance in all areas of life, calling for "purer homes, better homes." She disparaged how often "whole families are huddled together in a single apartment without regard to age or sex," warning that "evil in the home must be corrected."

Figure 6.3 Mary Church Terrell, one of the first black women to graduate from Oberlin and the first black woman in the country appointed to a school board, this in Washington, DC, was the first president of the National Association of Colored Women. Concerned about the "politics of respectability," she often urged black women to practice temperance in all areas of life, calling for "purer homes, better homes." She picketed the White House in 1917, lectured internationally in several languages, and fought back against the racism within the National American Woman Suffrage Association. "I want you to stand up not only for children and animals but also for negroes [cq]," she told delegates at NAWSA's convention in 1904. "You will never get suffrage until the sense of justice had been so developed in men that they will give fair play to the colored race." *Source:* Getty Images Library of Congress.

As president of the National Association of Colored Women (NACW), Terrell now applied for membership in the National Council of Women, the nation's largest sectarian organization of women's advocates, on grounds of "enlightened motherhood." Established in 1888, the organization promised to "freely band ourselves together into a federation of all races, creeds, and traditions, to further the application of the Golden Rule to society, custom, and law." In the name "of justice and humanity," she urged the National Council to recognize that their mission was "to do all in your power both by precept and example to make the future of my race as bright and as promising as should be that of every child born on this American soil." The daughter of two former slaves of biracial ancestry, Terrell was a spellbinding speaker. Having studied for two years in Europe, she won rousing applause at the International Congress of Women, held in Berlin in 1904, by delivering her speech first in German and then repeating it in French.

To Terrell's delight, the National Council agreed, admitting the NACW to its tent in November 1900. But three years later, swaying to the racist drumbeat of the times, the council refused to hear the reports of African American clubs. Sylvanie Williams sent a report anyway on the Phillis Wheatley Club, urging the executive committee to read the report "in justice [to] ten thousand intelligent colored women."

As Carrie Chapman Catt began to publicly criticize black men for selling their votes to big city bosses for political favors, Terrell fought back. "My sisters of the dominant race," she said at the 1904 convention, "stand up not only for the oppressed sex, but also for the oppressed race." Delegates that year also debated the dangers of child and animal abuse. Defying their newly stated standard of a one-issue agenda, white suffragists urged legislation for the protection of these innocent creatures, so vulnerable to cruelty. This was too much for Terrell, a lifetime member of NAWSA. "I want you to stand up not only for children and animals but also for negroes [cq]," she said. "You will never get suffrage until the sense of justice had been so developed in men that they will give fair play to the colored race."

If the Spanish–American War of 1898 offered a stage for men – white men seeking to restore their vigor, black men seeking to prove their patriotism – for many women, the war broached questions of national priorities. Some voiced concerns that a nation preoccupied with a civilizing mission abroad would neglect female rights at home. They did not talk, as Terrell had suggested, of giving "fair play to the colored race." To overcome male resistance, to convince men that it was in their interests to share political power with women, to demonstrate to them that the vote would neither harden women nor emasculate men, suffrage leaders now summoned the greatest cross-class coalition in movement history, turning their attention to disciplined organization from the ground up, and to public relations campaigns in the nation's newspapers. Some called it the selling of suffrage.

7

The Tactical Turn in Women's Suffrage

In February 1907, Clara Silver and Mary Duffy testified at the state capitol in Albany, New York, "the first … time women of the industrial class had appeared before a legislative committee to plead their own cause." The day before, anti-suffragists had testified that granting women the vote would only empower the radicals and socialists among them. Representing the Buttonhole Workers Union, Silver countered so effectively, reporters said, that she silenced the critics. "We working women are often told that we should stay at home and then everything would be all right," Silver said. "But we can't." Recounting the final illness that took her husband, "a diamond setter, a fine workman," she explained that returning to a job was the only way she could keep a roof overhead and family intact. "I had to go back to my trade to keep the family together," she said. "Gentlemen, we need every help to fight the battle of life. To be left out by the state just sets up a prejudice against us."

Both women were members of the Equality League of Self-Supporting Women spearheaded by Harriot Stanton Blatch (Fig. 7.1), youngest daughter of suffrage matriarch Elizabeth Cady Stanton. After twenty years of living in England as the wife of a British businessman, Blatch had returned to America shocked to find that the movement launched by her mother in 1848 had lapsed into "a rut deep and ever deeper," one that "bored its adherents and repelled its opponents." The campaign's thunder, she noticed, was directed at the same middle-class clubwomen

And Yet They Persisted: How American Women Won the Right to Vote, First Edition. Johanna Neuman.
© 2020 John Wiley & Sons, Inc. Published 2020 by John Wiley & Sons, Inc.
Companion website: www.wiley.com/go/Neuman

Figure 7.1 Harriot Stanton Blatch, youngest daughter of suffrage matriarch Elizabeth Cady Stanton, infused the American suffrage movement with new energy in the early 1900s. After twenty years of living in England as the wife of a British businessman, Blatch had returned to America shocked to find that the movement launched by her mother in 1848 had lapsed into "a rut deep and ever deeper," one that "bored its adherents and repelled its opponents." The campaign's thunder, she noticed, was directed at the same middle-class clubwomen who attended annual conventions every year, listening politely to "the same old arguments." She built one of the broadest cross-class coalitions for social change, attracting teachers and factory workers as well as young professionals and established socialites. And she aimed their advocacy not at the converted but at the vast unexplored territory of public opinion. Bain News Service, *Source:* Library of Congress Prints and Photographs Division.

who attended annual conventions every year, listening politely to "the same old arguments." Now she vowed to infuse the American movement with new energy. She would build a new movement, a cross-class coalition attracting teachers and factory workers as well as young professionals and established socialites. And she would aim their advocacy not at the already converted but at the vast unexplored territory of public opinion.

In England, activists had sparked renewed interest in the campaign through public spectacle. Tapping the talents of the Artists' Suffrage League and the Suffrage Atelier, British activists produced stunning posters, floats, buttons, and broadsheets designed to counter anti-suffrage cartoons and illustrations with vivid and pointed artistry. For the British, this debate by art, facilitated by an expanding newspaper industry, was critical in swaying Parliament. As one poster said, "Our weapon is public opinion." For Blatch, who had witnessed this awakening firsthand in England, the idea of selling suffrage to an American audience was appealing. Showcasing neatly dressed women in choreographed parades would erase the old image of a "shrieking sisterhood" of radicals who had upset gender norms with their calls for free love, divorce reform, and atheism. It would reassure male voters this new electorate would not threaten the polity. And it would establish the working class as a viable component of a broad coalition for change. At the League's first meeting, Linda Gano of the Interborough Women Teachers' Association explained to a reporter why having the vote was instrumental in the fight for equal pay. "We are never going to give up till we do get" equal pay legislation, she said. "There are ten thousand women behind this bill, and now that we know our power, we are a dangerous lot." In this battle for the vote, suffragists in both countries were fighting stereotypes about femininity – and everything they now did would be viewed in that prism.

To draw notice to their cause, a new generation of suffragists like Blatch now deployed all manner of attention-getting schemes. Soapbox speeches, parades, pageants, concerts, sandwich boards, organ grinder concerts, suffrage shops, whistle-stop tours from trains, "Votes for Women" signs on children and pets, automobile tours to reach rural voters, suffrage days at baseball stadiums to reach urban ones, cold calls made to men at work, pamphlets dropped onto the presidential yacht from airplanes piloted by women – no spectacle was too outrageous, no line of propaganda too shocking, as long as a captivated press would give publicity to the cause. For all of them, the target of their advocacy became not political insiders or a small circle of like-minded reformers but the public. And in widening the direction of their campaign from the inside to the outside, in privileging appearance and public engagement, they ushered in what one scholar called "a period of stunning political experimentation as innovative as anything" suffragists had ever attempted before.

This new coalition of diverse interests, with its focus on winning public approval, also provoked conflicts. Class warfare broke out between union suffragists and the wealthy socialites who helped finance their strikes, often over the merits of capitalism versus socialism. Amid violence by British suffragettes who lobbed bombs into buildings, American women wondered if mainstream activism would win, or whether militancy was needed.

The turn toward the tactics of the marketplace also produced a debate over ideology. In the nineteenth century, most suffragists articulated a natural rights rationale, that women merited the vote as equal citizens. Now, many pivoted to a more pragmatic assertion that women would improve politics through their morality. Borrowing from the memes of the Republican Motherhood, they campaigned on a pledge that women would reform the political system with their "municipal housekeeping," extending the boundaries of the home to the public square. To sell suffrage, its leaders again distanced themselves from African American activists, rationalizing that their inclusion would alienate white male voters whose support they were courting. Much like women of color in other countries – particularly India's suffragettes, who combatted both British imperialism and their own Indian national identity – black suffragists in the United States continued their own fight for the vote, often in tandem with a campaign against racism. Finally, this renewed energy at the national level sparked new campaigns to win the vote in the states. And local activists, still smarting over earlier losses, pointedly asked national suffrage stars to stay away.

These new tactics had given the movement a sense of energy and excitement, but they also highlighted the difficulties of holding together a broad coalition for social change.

Class Coalition, Class Conflicts

The shirtwaist blouse – inspired by a man's shirt, worn tucked into a skirt – was advertised in the late 1890s as an expression of female independence, a rebuttal to the Victorian Era's restrictive styles. Sales reflected the popularity of both the blouse and the pitch, exemplified by the Gibson Girl, with her upswept hair and attitude of cheeky independence. With more than 500 plants in New York and at least 35,000 employees, business owners eyeing their profit sheets shoe-horned workers into airless factories with few fire exits, working them in twelve-hour shifts, six days a week. The shirt was a fashion sensation. Business was booming.

But grievances about wages and conditions, as well as the American Federation of Labor's resistance to including women in its ranks, prompted reformers in Boston to establish the Women's Trade Union League (WTUL). By 1904, there were also branches in Chicago and New York. Together, they fought for an eight-hour workday, a ban on night work for women, abolition of child labor, and a minimum wage. In New York, several women boasting enormous family fortunes joined the WTUL board. They were part of a Progressive Era movement eager to right the injustices of income inequality and government corruption. "We can't live our lives without doing something to help from the title and the violence, eager to reassure male power brokers that if granted the vote, they would not threaten the political order. They would be suffragists, not suffragettes, respecting the gender code of ladylike behavior. Still, no matter how they described their activism, their new tactics provoked male resistance at almost every street corner where they now appeared. By their very assertion of voice in a public debate, they threatened male dominance.

The first import from Britain was the soapbox speech, conducted on the streets, often at lunchtime. Like Lucy Stone and other suffragists from the nineteenth century, these twentieth-century activists faced considerable backlash from men outraged that they were speaking in public – seeing in the posture a threat to home and family. Frances Perkins, then a New York social worker and later the first female member of a presidential Cabinet, this in Franklin Delano Roosevelt's administration, explained how it worked. Traveling in pairs – one woman to speak, the other to distribute literature – suffragists often chose to stand in front of a saloon where "you were always sure of a crowd" of sometimes rowdy men. "You took your box – a good strong grocery box of some sort, because they had wooden boxes … in those days," Perkins recalled. Without loud speakers, "you had to do it all with your own voice." Reaction was rough. "You would get jeered at. You would get heckled. You would get asked impertinent questions, but I don't recall ever having been insulted or treated to obscene language." Laura Ellsworth Seiler, a college student at Cornell University, did. "Sometimes, depending on the neighborhood, stones would be thrown into the crowd," she recalled. "Things would be thrown from the roof." It was all part of a strategy of interesting those who had never before considered the idea. "We believed that you had to get the people who weren't in the least interested in suffrage," said Seiler, who worked for Blatch's Women's Political Union. The "whole idea was that you must keep suffrage every minute before the public so that it got used to the idea and talks about it, whether they agree or disagree."

All over the country, soapbox speakers began appearing on street corners, selling suffrage even as they redefined the role of women in American political society. "Up to that time, no one in Montana … had heard of a respectable young woman making a public street corner speech," recalled Belle Fligelman Winestine, who later worked for Montana's Jeannette Rankin, the first woman elected to Congress. Belle said she was "terrified as I took my place on what was supposed to be a busy Helena street corner. Suddenly, it seemed, there was not a soul in sight. But I had something to say, so I just started talking to the world. First one person stopped to listen, then another, "and soon I had a large audience, all listening attentively – partly, I suppose, because they had never heard a woman speaking on the street."

them," explained Anne Morgan, whose father J. P. Morgan was said to be the richest man on Wall Street. "Of course the consumer must be protected, but when you hear of a woman who presses forty dozen skirts for $8 a week, something must be very wrong. And fifty-two hours a week seems little enough to ask." Anne Morgan was one of the few wealthy labor reformers not driven by suffrage activism, but by a kind of entitled philanthropy. "I believe in the true aristocracy," she once said, "which realizes that it has inherited something magnificent, with the obligation to carry it on."

Amid this new era of reform, and like the Lowell Mill Girls before them, on November 23, 1909, thousands of workers from hundreds of factories in New York put down their tools, collected their hats and belongings, and walked off the job. Many were young Italian and Jewish girls whose families had migrated to America from Italy, Russia or Eastern Europe as part of the wave of 23 million immigrants who arrived in the United States between 1880 and 1920. Employed by a burgeoning textile industry exploiting a new fashion trend, they were willing to risk police beatings and difficult jail terms for better wages and conditions. Called the Uprising of the Twenty Thousand, this first major strike by female workers would become a landmark in American labor history. But it was also the opening chapter in a new effort by suffrage leaders to demonstrate that women of all classes wanted the vote.

Alva Vanderbilt Belmont had long recognized that supporting the striking factory workers might swell suffrage ranks with an infusion of new, young women to the suffrage cause. The inheritor of not one but two Gilded Age fortunes – from the Vanderbilts and from the Belmonts – she would spend the rest of her life and much of her fortune supporting women's suffrage. Now, with Morgan, she paid salaries so striking women could support their families and covered bail when strikers were arrested for picketing. Newspaper reporters who spied them coming downtown in their fancy cars and fancy clothes dubbed these social celebrities "the mink brigade." Once, Belmont sat up until 3 a.m. in the Jefferson Market Courthouse to bail out four workers arrested on the picket line. Informed that bail was set at $100 each, Belmont said she had no cash but could offer the collateral of her home at 477 Madison Avenue. The specter of a wealthy matron offering her East Side mansion for bail money was laughable, newspaper fodder across the country. But the strikers were released.

During the strike, which lasted for four months, picketers were often harassed. The Association of Waist and Dress Manufacturers explained that they hired prostitutes to assault the picketers because it would not do for hired "gentlemen" to be seen beating women in public. Strike leader Clara Lemlich suffered six broken ribs during seventeen arrests and was later blacklisted. A Jewish immigrant, she early saw the connection between labor activism and the vote. "If Mayor McClellan knew that we girls have a vote, do you suppose he would have laughed at us when we marched to City Hall during the shirtwaist strike? Oh no. He would have been very courteous to us," she said. "And the police, they would not have been dragging us to the station house without the slightest provocation." The strike was finally settled in February 1910. Strikers won a fifty-two-hour week, four holidays with pay per year, and no retaliation against union members – but no new provisions to improve safety conditions. At a Hippodrome gathering sponsored by Belmont, 8,000 factory workers, union organizers, college sympathizers, and members of the mink brigade all celebrated the victory in a massive hall lit by the still-rare sight of indoor electricity and festooned with banners demanding, "Votes for Women," "Equal Pay for Equal Work," and "Give Women the Protection of the Vote."

Within two years, the cheers of victory had turned to grief and working-class activists seethed with anger at their wealthy benefactors. In November 1911, in one of the deadliest industrial accidents in New York history, 146 garment workers were killed in a fire at the Triangle Shirtwaist Factory, many leaping to their deaths from a building where the exits had been sealed to prevent employee theft. At a memorial at the Metropolitan Opera House, labor organizer Rose Schneiderman accused capitalists of having blood on their hands. "We have tried you good people of the public and have found you wanting … This is not the first time girls have been burned alive in the city," she said. "Every year thousands of us are maimed. The life of men and women is so cheap and property is so sacred. There are so many of us for one job it matters little if 146 of us are burned to death."

Tensions had already been festering between the wealthy and the trade unionists, many of them socialists. The Socialist Labor Party, committed to a class struggle to defeat the bourgeoisie, had distanced itself from the women's movement, with its army of middle-class clubwomen. At its 1907 meeting in Stuttgart, Germany, the Second International issued guidelines to socialists around the world. "The Socialist women shall not carry on this struggle for complete equality of the right of vote in alliance with middle class women suffragists," declared the International. Equal suffrage was one of socialism's "fundamental and most important reforms." But so was toppling the capitalist system that created the middle class. Theresa S. Malkiel, in her *Diary of a Shirtwaist Striker,* wrote of her suspicion that wealthy sponsors had only supported the strike to advance their own interests in suffrage. "I shouldn't wonder their conscience pricks them a bit – they must be ashamed of being fortune's children while so many of the girls have never known what a

good day means," she wrote. Aghast at the economic differenc[e] separated strikers from the chief beneficiaries of capitalism's ex[cess] Malkiel spoke at a grueling, five-hour meeting by labor leaders t[o dis-] cuss whether to continue cooperating with wealthy suffragists.

Now, even moderate voices within labor circles thought the b[allot] too important to working-class women to be entrusted to leisure-c[lass] women. To union leader Leonora O'Reilly, it was clear the wealthy [suf-] fragists "really don't speak our language." At the end of the meetin[g,] union members voted to end the alliance that had brought much pu[b-] licity and money to the cause. This improbable coalition would yet yiel[d] benefits. For now, it splintered.

Gender and Militancy

British activists were making headlines, in Britain and America, for new innovations in public advocacy – as well as new militant tactics that defied gender decorum. Under the banner of "Deeds, Not Words," as leader Emmeline Pankhurst explained, "We threw away all our conventional methods of what was 'ladylike' and 'good form' and we applied to our methods the one test question, will it help?" Beginning in 1905, these militants threw rocks at 10 Downing Street, set fire to pillar boxes, smashed windows in Knightsbridge's luxurious shops, treated golf courses with acid, and cut telegraph wires. They heckled and attacked MPs, including Winston Churchill. They set off a bomb at the Theatre Royal in Dublin, started a fire at the Orchid House in Kew Gardens, and bombed Lloyd George's country house. Imprisoned at the infamous Holloway Prison, many protested their incarceration with hunger strikes. The brutality of forcing liquids down their throats by tube, and a medical protest against the practice, sparked renewed publicity and continued militancy. In 1913, suffrage activist Emily Davison threw herself at King George V's horse at the Epsom Derby, whether an attempt to die for the cause or to attach a suffrage banner to the horse's bridle never determined. What is clear is that British activists were breaking all the rules of ladylike behavior, if only to win the establishment's attention. As British novelist Winifred Holtby put it, "Militant political action … had broken down hitherto unimaginable taboos."

Labeling them troublemakers, British journalist Charles Hands in 1906 dismissed the militants as mere suffragettes, diminutive "-ettes" hardly worthy of notice in a political drama. Activists in London embraced the label, eager to distinguish themselves from the constitutionalists of the National Union of Women's Suffrage Societies, and to turn derision into a badge of honor. In America, by contrast, activists distanced themselves

In the big cities, female suffragists were often greeted by a sea of fedora-hatted men listening to a solitary woman on a box or on the back seat of a parked automobile. The newspaper photos of their encounters – the female speaker surrounded by a surge of some hostile male listeners – suggest how effective the tactic was. Mabel Vernon gathered one such large lunchtime audience to a soapbox speech in Chicago, demonstrating with a booming voice what she always taught new recruits, "Don't be afraid to open your mouths and yell." When she visited New York, Pankhurst stood on a car to deliver a speech on Wall Street. A mob of messenger boys stormed the car's footboard and hurled epithets at Pankhurst, drowning out her voice. Sympathetic merchants formed a flying wedge so her car and its passengers – Pankhurst, Harriot Stanton Blatch, and Anna Howard Shaw – could flee. They showed themselves unafraid of the fray, willing to step into the ring if that's where the votes were.

Of all the tactics suffragists now brought to the public square, part of a renewed Votes for Women campaign, none was as effective, or as controversial, as the suffrage parades through the public streets. The parades were a visual display of suffrage's new cross-class coalition – working-class women, shop girls, teachers and librarians, actresses and academics, lawyers, doctors, college students and wealthy matrons. The message was multi-layered – women were no longer confined to their homes, or to their domestic roles. They were dressed in white – Macy's was the official headquarters for suffrage paraphernalia – with sashes declaring their affiliation. At Blatch's direction, they marched by delegation, "head erect and shoulders back," demonstrating the serious discipline needed for voting. There was column after column of women, "a mass of gleaming white," declaring their interest in the ballot.

For some activists, the tactic posed a great dilemma. Worried that her first steps onto the grubby streets of New York would mark her as a streetwalker, Elizabeth Callender Stevens, who had been recruited to lead the New Jersey Equal Franchise Society, resigned. Over the pleas of her husband, Richard Stevens, who begged her to reconsider, she insisted, "Men ... do not have respect for women who will walk through the public streets in this manner ... It is so undignified and so unwomanly ... It will do no end of harm." Defending these tactics against critics within the movement, *The Woman Voter*, a monthly suffragist journal published by the Woman Suffrage Party in New York, explained these tactics of bravado were necessary to persuade the public. "The public is not a reasoning public," said the journal. "It is blind, deaf and ignorant.... It demands to be shocked before it will listen. Any and all things which will arrests its attempt and compel thought have their place in our propaganda."

Alva Belmont had held back, in the 1911 parade riding in one of her automobiles alongside marchers. But in 1912, Blatch – keen to present a homogeneous portrait of disciplined female citizens – discouraged the practice. "Riding in a car did not demonstrate courage. It did not show discipline," she said. "Women were to march on their own two feet out on the streets of America's greatest city; they were to march year by year, better and better." So Belmont agreed to head a delegation of her own suffrage organization, the Political Equality Association. She also invited the association's Harlem chapter, the first time a unit of black suffragists was formally welcomed to a parade organized by white suffrage leaders. The Harlem association turned out "in all its strength." One newspaper called Belmont's decision to risk social stigma by marching on the streets an "epic in the history of womanhood." Journalist Marie Manning said Belmont's appearance forced politicians to take notice. "The greatest shove ever given to the … movement will always be that lady's appearance at the head of a suffrage parade in New York City," she wrote. Of Belmont, wrote the *New York Times*, "She had the appearance of a brave soldier facing fire, looking straight ahead."

Soon, women staged parades and pageants all over the country. Even NAWSA, whose leaders earlier resisted the parade as too extreme, now joined the processions. With Anna Howard Shaw in the presidency, the organization authorized a parade to be conducted in Washington, DC, on the eve of Woodrow Wilson's inauguration as president in 1913. Shaw tapped a young Quaker activist, fresh from serving in Pankhurst's organization in England, to lead the effort. Alice Paul, who had been arrested seven times in Britain for her protest activities, jailed three times, and subjected to force feeding, was eager to apply some of the lessons she had learned on the picket lines – and in the jailhouses – to the American cause. When Shaw asked her to run the parade, she unknowingly set the tripwire on a chapter of suffrage history that would prize confrontation over conciliation and expose the prejudice against African Americans that had long characterized the movement.

The 1913 Procession

Woodrow Wilson arrived at Washington's majestic Union Station the day before his first inauguration, full of anticipation. In the 1912 election, he had defeated not one but two U.S. presidents – the incumbent, William Howard Taft, and the previous White House occupant, Theodore Roosevelt. The candidate of the Bull Moose party ticket, Roosevelt had split the Republic vote with Taft. The long shot Wilson's victory was so overwhelming – more than a two million margin over Roosevelt in the them," explained Anne Morgan, whose father J. P. Morgan was said to be the richest man on Wall Street. "Of course the consumer must be protected, but when you hear of a woman who presses forty dozen skirts for $8 a week, something must be very wrong. And fifty-two hours a week seems little enough to ask." Anne Morgan was one of the few wealthy labor reformers not driven by suffrage activism, but by a kind of entitled philanthropy. "I believe in the true aristocracy," she once said, "which realizes that it has inherited something magnificent, with the obligation to carry it on."

Amid this new era of reform, and like the Lowell Mill Girls before them, on November 23, 1909, thousands of workers from hundreds of factories in New York put down their tools, collected their hats and belongings, and walked off the job. Many were young Italian and Jewish girls whose families had migrated to America from Italy, Russia or Eastern Europe as part of the wave of 23 million immigrants who arrived in the United States between 1880 and 1920. Employed by a burgeoning textile industry exploiting a new fashion trend, they were willing to risk police beatings and difficult jail terms for better wages and conditions. Called the Uprising of the Twenty Thousand, this first major strike by female workers would become a landmark in American labor history. But it was also the opening chapter in a new effort by suffrage leaders to demonstrate that women of all classes wanted the vote.

Alva Vanderbilt Belmont had long recognized that supporting the striking factory workers might swell suffrage ranks with an infusion of new, young women to the suffrage cause. The inheritor of not one but two Gilded Age fortunes – from the Vanderbilts and from the Belmonts – she would spend the rest of her life and much of her fortune supporting women's suffrage. Now, with Morgan, she paid salaries so striking women could support their families and covered bail when strikers were arrested for picketing. Newspaper reporters who spied them coming downtown in their fancy cars and fancy clothes dubbed these social celebrities "the mink brigade." Once, Belmont sat up until 3 a.m. in the Jefferson Market Courthouse to bail out four workers arrested on the picket line. Informed that bail was set at $100 each, Belmont said she had no cash but could offer the collateral of her home at 477 Madison Avenue. The specter of a wealthy matron offering her East Side mansion for bail money was laughable, newspaper fodder across the country. But the strikers were released.

During the strike, which lasted for four months, picketers were often harassed. The Association of Waist and Dress Manufacturers explained that they hired prostitutes to assault the picketers because it would not do for hired "gentlemen" to be seen beating women in public. Strike leader Clara Lemlich suffered six broken ribs during seventeen arrests and was later blacklisted. A Jewish immigrant, she early saw the connection between labor activism and the vote. "If Mayor McClellan knew that we girls have a vote, do you suppose he would have laughed at us when we marched to City Hall during the shirtwaist strike? Oh no. He would have been very courteous to us," she said. "And the police, they would not have been dragging us to the station house without the slightest provocation." The strike was finally settled in February 1910. Strikers won a fifty-two-hour week, four holidays with pay per year, and no retaliation against union members – but no new provisions to improve safety conditions. At a Hippodrome gathering sponsored by Belmont, 8,000 factory workers, union organizers, college sympathizers, and members of the mink brigade all celebrated the victory in a massive hall lit by the still-rare sight of indoor electricity and festooned with banners demanding, "Votes for Women," "Equal Pay for Equal Work," and "Give Women the Protection of the Vote."

Within two years, the cheers of victory had turned to grief and working-class activists seethed with anger at their wealthy benefactors. In November 1911, in one of the deadliest industrial accidents in New York history, 146 garment workers were killed in a fire at the Triangle Shirtwaist Factory, many leaping to their deaths from a building where the exits had been sealed to prevent employee theft. At a memorial at the Metropolitan Opera House, labor organizer Rose Schneiderman accused capitalists of having blood on their hands. "We have tried you good people of the public and have found you wanting ... This is not the first time girls have been burned alive in the city," she said. "Every year thousands of us are maimed. The life of men and women is so cheap and property is so sacred. There are so many of us for one job it matters little if 146 of us are burned to death."

Tensions had already been festering between the wealthy and the trade unionists, many of them socialists. The Socialist Labor Party, committed to a class struggle to defeat the bourgeoisie, had distanced itself from the women's movement, with its army of middle-class clubwomen. At its 1907 meeting in Stuttgart, Germany, the Second International issued guidelines to socialists around the world. "The Socialist women shall not carry on this struggle for complete equality of the right of vote in alliance with middle class women suffragists," declared the International. Equal suffrage was one of socialism's "fundamental and most important reforms." But so was toppling the capitalist system that created the middle class. Theresa S. Malkiel, in her *Diary of a Shirtwaist Striker*, wrote of her suspicion that wealthy sponsors had only supported the strike to advance their own interests in suffrage. "I shouldn't wonder their conscience pricks them a bit – they must be ashamed of being fortune's children while so many of the girls have never known what a good day means," she wrote. Aghast at the economic differences that separated strikers from the chief beneficiaries of capitalism's excesses, Malkiel spoke at a grueling, five-hour meeting by labor leaders to discuss whether to continue cooperating with wealthy suffragists.

Now, even moderate voices within labor circles thought the ballot too important to working-class women to be entrusted to leisure-class women. To union leader Leonora O'Reilly, it was clear the wealthy suffragists "really don't speak our language." At the end of the meeting, union members voted to end the alliance that had brought much publicity and money to the cause. This improbable coalition would yet yield benefits. For now, it splintered.

Gender and Militancy

British activists were making headlines, in Britain and America, for new innovations in public advocacy – as well as new militant tactics that defied gender decorum. Under the banner of "Deeds, Not Words," as leader Emmeline Pankhurst explained, "We threw away all our conventional methods of what was 'ladylike' and 'good form' and we applied to our methods the one test question, will it help?" Beginning in 1905, these militants threw rocks at 10 Downing Street, set fire to pillar boxes, smashed windows in Knightsbridge's luxurious shops, treated golf courses with acid, and cut telegraph wires. They heckled and attacked MPs, including Winston Churchill. They set off a bomb at the Theatre Royal in Dublin, started a fire at the Orchid House in Kew Gardens, and bombed Lloyd George's country house. Imprisoned at the infamous Holloway Prison, many protested their incarceration with hunger strikes. The brutality of forcing liquids down their throats by tube, and a medical protest against the practice, sparked renewed publicity and continued militancy. In 1913, suffrage activist Emily Davison threw herself at King George V's horse at the Epsom Derby, whether an attempt to die for the cause or to attach a suffrage banner to the horse's bridle never determined. What is clear is that British activists were breaking all the rules of ladylike behavior, if only to win the establishment's attention. As British novelist Winifred Holtby put it, "Militant political action ... had broken down hitherto unimaginable taboos."

Labeling them troublemakers, British journalist Charles Hands in 1906 dismissed the militants as mere suffragettes, diminutive "-ettes" hardly worthy of notice in a political drama. Activists in London embraced the label, eager to distinguish themselves from the constitutionalists of the National Union of Women's Suffrage Societies, and to turn derision into a badge of honor. In America, by contrast, activists distanced themselves from the title and the violence, eager to reassure male power brokers that if granted the vote, they would not threaten the political order. They would be suffragists, not suffragettes, respecting the gender code of ladylike behavior. Still, no matter how they described their activism, their new tactics provoked male resistance at almost every street corner where they now appeared. By their very assertion of voice in a public debate, they threatened male dominance.

The first import from Britain was the soapbox speech, conducted on the streets, often at lunchtime. Like Lucy Stone and other suffragists from the nineteenth century, these twentieth-century activists faced considerable backlash from men outraged that they were speaking in public – seeing in the posture a threat to home and family. Frances Perkins, then a New York social worker and later the first female member of a presidential Cabinet, this in Franklin Delano Roosevelt's administration, explained how it worked. Traveling in pairs – one woman to speak, the other to distribute literature – suffragists often chose to stand in front of a saloon, where "you were always sure of a crowd" of sometimes rowdy men. "You took your box – a good strong grocery box of some sort, because they had wooden boxes … in those days," Perkins recalled. Without loudspeakers, "you had to do it all with your own voice." Reaction was rough. "You would get jeered at. You would get heckled. You would get asked impertinent questions, but I don't recall ever having been insulted or treated to obscene language." Laura Ellsworth Seiler, a college student at Cornell University, did. "Sometimes, depending on the neighborhood, stones would be thrown into the crowd," she recalled. "Things would be thrown from the roof." It was all part of a strategy of interesting those who had never before considered the idea. "We believed that you had to get the people who weren't in the least interested in suffrage," said Seiler, who worked for Blatch's Women's Political Union. The "whole idea was that you must keep suffrage every minute before the public so that it gets used to the idea and talks about it, whether they agree or disagree."

All over the country, soapbox speakers began appearing on street corners, selling suffrage even as they redefined the role of women in American political society. "Up to that time, no one in Montana … had heard of a respectable young woman making a public street corner speech," recalled Belle Fligelman Winestine, who later worked for Montana's Jeannette Rankin, the first woman elected to Congress. Belle said she was "terrified as I took my place on what was supposed to be a busy Helena street corner. Suddenly, it seemed, there was not a soul in sight. But I had something to say, so I just started talking to the world." First one person stopped to listen, then another, "and soon I had a big audience, all listening attentively – partly, I suppose, because they had never heard a woman speaking on the street."

In the big cities, female suffragists were often greeted by a sea of fedora-hatted men listening to a solitary woman on a box or on the back seat of a parked automobile. The newspaper photos of their encounters – the female speaker surrounded by a surge of some hostile male listeners – suggest how effective the tactic was. Mabel Vernon gathered one such large lunchtime audience to a soapbox speech in Chicago, demonstrating with a booming voice what she always taught new recruits, "Don't be afraid to open your mouths and yell." When she visited New York, Pankhurst stood on a car to deliver a speech on Wall Street. A mob of messenger boys stormed the car's footboard and hurled epithets at Pankhurst, drowning out her voice. Sympathetic merchants formed a flying wedge so her car and its passengers – Pankhurst, Harriot Stanton Blatch, and Anna Howard Shaw – could flee. They showed themselves unafraid of the fray, willing to step into the ring if that's where the votes were.

Of all the tactics suffragists now brought to the public square, part of a renewed Votes for Women campaign, none was as effective, or as controversial, as the suffrage parades through the public streets. The parades were a visual display of suffrage's new cross-class coalition – working-class women, shop girls, teachers and librarians, actresses and academics, lawyers, doctors, college students and wealthy matrons. The message was multi-layered – women were no longer confined to their homes, or to their domestic roles. They were dressed in white – Macy's was the official headquarters for suffrage paraphernalia – with sashes declaring their affiliation. At Blatch's direction, they marched by delegation, "head erect and shoulders back," demonstrating the serious discipline needed for voting. There was column after column of women, "a mass of gleaming white," declaring their interest in the ballot.

For some activists, the tactic posed a great dilemma. Worried that her first steps onto the grubby streets of New York would mark her as a streetwalker, Elizabeth Callender Stevens, who had been recruited to lead the New Jersey Equal Franchise Society, resigned. Over the pleas of her husband, Richard Stevens, who begged her to reconsider, she insisted, "Men ... do not have respect for women who will walk through the public streets in this manner ... It is so undignified and so unwomanly ... It will do no end of harm." Defending these tactics against critics within the movement, *The Woman Voter*, a monthly suffragist journal published by the Woman Suffrage Party in New York, explained these tactics of bravado were necessary to persuade the public. "The public is not a reasoning public," said the journal. "It is blind, deaf and ignorant.... It demands to be shocked before it will listen. Any and all things which will arrests its attempt and compel thought have their place in our propaganda."

Alva Belmont had held back, in the 1911 parade riding in one of her automobiles alongside marchers. But in 1912, Blatch – keen to present a homogeneous portrait of disciplined female citizens – discouraged the practice. "Riding in a car did not demonstrate courage. It did not show discipline," she said. "Women were to march on their own two feet out on the streets of America's greatest city; they were to march year by year, better and better." So Belmont agreed to head a delegation of her own suffrage organization, the Political Equality Association. She also invited the association's Harlem chapter, the first time a unit of black suffragists was formally welcomed to a parade organized by white suffrage leaders. The Harlem association turned out "in all its strength." One newspaper called Belmont's decision to risk social stigma by marching on the streets an "epic in the history of womanhood." Journalist Marie Manning said Belmont's appearance forced politicians to take notice. "The greatest shove ever given to the … movement will always be that lady's appearance at the head of a suffrage parade in New York City," she wrote. Of Belmont, wrote the *New York Times*, "She had the appearance of a brave soldier facing fire, looking straight ahead."

Soon, women staged parades and pageants all over the country. Even NAWSA, whose leaders earlier resisted the parade as too extreme, now joined the processions. With Anna Howard Shaw in the presidency, the organization authorized a parade to be conducted in Washington, DC, on the eve of Woodrow Wilson's inauguration as president in 1913. Shaw tapped a young Quaker activist, fresh from serving in Pankhurst's organization in England, to lead the effort. Alice Paul, who had been arrested seven times in Britain for her protest activities, jailed three times, and subjected to force feeding, was eager to apply some of the lessons she had learned on the picket lines – and in the jailhouses – to the American cause. When Shaw asked her to run the parade, she unknowingly set the tripwire on a chapter of suffrage history that would prize confrontation over conciliation and expose the prejudice against African Americans that had long characterized the movement.

The 1913 Procession

Woodrow Wilson arrived at Washington's majestic Union Station the day before his first inauguration, full of anticipation. In the 1912 election, he had defeated not one but two U.S. presidents – the incumbent, William Howard Taft, and the previous White House occupant, Theodore Roosevelt. The candidate of the Bull Moose party ticket, Roosevelt had split the Republic vote with Taft. The long shot Wilson's victory was so overwhelming – more than a two million margin over Roosevelt in the popular vote and a landslide 435–88 in the Electoral College vote – that his coattails had also flipped the Senate from Republican hands and bolstered the Democrat majority in the House. Taft finished a distant third, with eight Electoral College votes – the lowest showing for an incumbent president. Now, for the first time since 1895, Democrats controlled all three branches of government.

Now, at 55 years old, Wilson stood on the steps of Union Station, overlooking the city that would be his new domain, one day before his improbable inauguration as the nation's 28th President of the United States. As the Wilsons made their way through "a crush of arriving thousands" at Union Station, few seemed interested in this newcomer. In an exchange that may be more apocryphal than proven, Wilson reportedly asked, "Where are the people?" To which an aide replied, "Over on the Avenue, watching the suffrage parade."

In the days before the parade, there had been a feverish anticipation. The *Washington Post* said the city had gone "suffrage mad." Special trains from Chicago, New York, and elsewhere, decorated with suffrage propaganda, arrived in a whirl of activity at Union Station. As marchers assembled, it became clear that Alice Paul had orchestrated a visual tableau. They would walk in professional affiliation, each group dressed in a different color – actresses in rose, librarians in blue, college women in their academic robes – giving the affair a rainbow cast. There was a contingent of Quakers, and of men newly sympathetic to the cause, along with a mud-caked group of suffrage pilgrims who had marched from New York under the direction of a woman they called General Rosalie Jones. Orders here were much as they had been in the 1912 parade in New York: "To march steadily in a dignified manner, and not to talk or nod or wave to anyone in the crowd." At 3:25 p.m. the procession began.

Known for boring speeches among intellectuals, a rejuvenated suffrage campaign would now sweep the masses into its fold. To achieve such ambitious goals, the 28-year-old Paul had conceived a pageant on the steps of the U.S. Treasury Department that would convey female achievement, beauty, and artistry. An actress portraying Columbia would be at center stage, flanked by others channeling Justice, Liberty, Charity, Peace, and Hope. To buttress the visual impression with a serious message, she had arranged twenty-six floats depicting the countries and the six states that had already granted full suffrage to women. The Liberty Bell in Philadelphia was represented on one float, followed by signage outlining highlights in the first sixty-five years of the woman's rights struggle. Commanding the parade, in a flowing white gown atop a white horse named Gray Dawn, rode Inez Milholland (Fig. 7.2), the movement's impassioned orator and great beauty, a new Joan of Arc. She wore a white suit, flowing cape, and gold tiara, and carried a message

Figure 7.2   Inez Milholland Boissevain was one of the movement's great icons of beauty, courage, and intelligence. For the 1913 suffrage procession in Washington, DC, she rode atop a white horse, a new Joan of Arc for a new era. She wore a white suit, flowing cape, and gold tiara, and carried a message borrowed from the Pankhursts: "Forward Into Light." In her wake came another banner bearing the parade's political message: "We demand an amendment to the United States Constitution enfranchising women of the country." During a 1916 campaign trip to California, she collapsed on stage, her last words, "Mr. President, how long must women wait for liberty?" She died within the month of pernicious anemia. Alice Paul arranged for a memorial at the U.S. Capitol, the first for a woman and for a non-member of Congress. Davis & Eickemeyer, *Source:* Library of Congress Prints and Photographs.

borrowed from the Pankhursts: "Forward Into Light." In her wake came another banner bearing the parade's political message: "We demand an amendment to the United States Constitution enfranchising women of the country" (Fig. 7.3).

"We were creating our own mythology of women on the march, women active, and dramatic," explained suffragist Rebecca Hourwich Reyher. "Alice Paul insisted on it." Police officials had at first suggested she stage her march along Sixteenth Street, with its respectable middle-class homes. But Paul understood symbolism, and worked

Figure 7.3 Arriving at Union Station in Washington, DC the day before his inauguration as president, Woodrow Wilson reportedly asked, "Where are the people?" To which an aide replied, "Over on the Avenue, watching the suffrage parade." The 1913 procession, organized by the 28-year-old Alice Paul, was conceived as a pageant on the steps of the U.S. Treasury Department that would convey female achievement, beauty, and artistry. An actress portraying Columbia would be at center stage, flanked by others channeling Justice, Liberty, Charity, Peace, and Hope. To buttress the visual impression with a serious message, she had arranged twenty-six floats depicting the countries and the six states that had already granted full suffrage to women. The Liberty Bell in Philadelphia was represented on one float, followed by signage outlining highlights in the first sixty-five years of the woman's rights struggle. But the parade was marred by mob violence – mobs of men clogged the parade route, spat on or abused the marchers, and had to be cleared by U.S. army troops – and by Paul's decision to discourage participation by black suffragists. *Source:* Library of Congress Prints and Photographs.

connections to win approval for Pennsylvania Avenue – where the inaugural parade would take place the following day. The Inaugural Committee had banned women from marching on March 4. Paul wanted to make sure to paint a contrast with her parade on March 3. Women were now part of the nation's public face. They would no longer be told to sit quietly at home.

Despite the vast planning and expenditure of talent, time, and money, in the end the parade was marred by the haunting shadow of racial discrimination, and the stubborn menace of gender anger. Southern suffragists had threatened to boycott the march when word spread that two groups of students from Howard University planned to join the parade. In the application, the Delta Sigma Theta Sorority made clear they would not participate only to be segregated. "We do not wish to enter if we must meet with discrimination on account of race affiliation," wrote one young woman. At first Paul hesitated, writing Alice Stone Blackwell, "The prejudice against them is so strong in this section of the country that I believe a large part if not a majority of our white marchers will refuse to participate if negroes in any number formed a part of the parade." She added, "We must have a white procession, or a negro procession, or no procession at all." Eventually she reneged, placing the Howard University students with other college women, segregated not by race but by educational attainment. Likewise when Ida B. Wells, the anti-lynching crusader who had founded the Chicago-based Alpha Club of African American suffragists, asked to march with the Illinois delegation, Paul rejected the idea, fearing white defections. In a heated debate of the sixty-member delegation, Wells pleaded for inclusion. "The southern women have tried to evade the question time and again by giving some excuse or other every time it is brought up," she said. "If the Illinois women do not take a stand now in this great democratic parade, then the colored women are lost." Illinois suffrage leader Grace Wilbur Trout opted to exclude African Americans. Defiant, Wells waited on the sidewalk until the Illinois delegation came into view, then squeezed in between two white friends who had conspired to welcome her, and marched with them the rest of the parade route. Also marching was Mary Church Terrell, former president of the National Association of Colored Women, and the first African American woman named to a school board in a major city, this in Washington, DC.

As the women marched, mobs of men clogged the parade route and spat on or abused the marchers. "They came out gradually," said Jane Burleson, who was walking near the head of the parade. By Fifth Street on Capitol Hill, "we found ourselves up against this horrible howling mob, this jeering mob." Men hurled insults that one woman described as "vulgar, obscene, scurrilous, abusive." The men snatched banners, dragged women to the sidelines, tossed lighted cigarette butts at them, spat on them, tripped and shoved them and made suggestive comments. By day's end, one hundred women had been transported to the hospital. Helen Keller, a revered figure for having learned to function with deafness and blindness, was scheduled to speak that evening at a post-parade rally at Constitution Hall. The Chicago *Tribune* reported that she was "so exhausted and unnerved by the experience" she did not.

Local police – some smug or indifferent, others simply overwhelmed by a crowd said to number 250,000 – did nothing to clear the path of marchers or still the caustic curses of anti-suffragist ruffians. One of Paul's lieutenants, Elizabeth Seldon Rogers, called her brother-in-law, Secretary of War Henry Stimson. Literally, he sent in the cavalry, clearing the streets one block at a time, setting the stage for a congressional investigation into police incompetence and provoking a political showdown over suffrage. The next morning's newspapers told a story of dueling impressions. "Woman's Beauty, Grace and Art Bewilder the Capital," headlined the *Washington Post* in one front-page account. The *New York Times* was similarly impressed, calling the procession "one of the most impressively beautiful spectacles ever staged in the country." Another front-page story, in the Chicago *Daily Tribune*, said, "Mobs at Capital Defy Police; Block Suffrage Parade." For Paul, all the coverage was welcome attention. She was hopeful that male anger at the specter of women marching in the streets for their right to vote would have an impact on public opinion. As the New York *Tribune* observed a few days later, "Capital Mobs Made Converts to Suffrage."

Alice Paul's attempts to exclude African American college students and activists from the suffrage procession in 1913, much like Carrie Chapman Catt's decision to disinvite members of the Phillis Wheatley Club to NAWSA's Convention in New Orleans in 1903, exposed the movement's racist intent. The very appearance of African American women, they worried, would alienate white voters, stoking fear that enfranchising women would change the color of the electorate, and thus threaten the implicit power held by white men.

Amid these new tactics for a new generation, black women launched their own campaigns, designed to convince the public that they were as upstanding as their white colleagues. Mary Burnett Talbert, the only black woman in her class at Oberlin College, spoke at a 1915 conference in Washington, DC, titled "Votes for Women: A Symposium by Leading Thinkers of Colored Women." If white women did not welcome them into suffrage, she argued, black women would have to organize their own. Like Talbert, Adella Hunt Logan believed it was imperative that black women organize themselves, since white suffragists were clearly not going to welcome them into the mainstream movement. The fourth of eight children of a mixed-race mother and a wealthy white farmer who had served as a Confederate soldier during the Civil War, she was educated at Bass Academy and at Atlanta University, an all-black college. Later, Logan became a faculty member of the Tuskegee

Institute, teaching English, serving as the school's first librarian, and leading monthly discussions on suffrage at the Tuskegee Woman's Club. The product of white, black, and Native American ancestry, Logan was so fair she could pass for white. Sitting in the back of the room, she often attended NAWSA meetings so that she could report back to black women, keeping them in the loop on how "the superior sister" did things. She concluded that a number of black women could have conducted the meetings "more intelligently."

As suffrage moved into a new century, African American women began to campaign for the vote in their local communities. The St. Louis Suffrage Club in Missouri, the Colored Women's Republican Club in Denver, the Colored Women's Progressive Franchise Association in Washington, DC – all marshaled the African American vote for suffrage in their areas. In Chicago, Ida B. Wells-Barnett started the all-black Alpha Suffrage Club in 1911. Within three years, she had attracted 200 members who joined forces and convinced male voters to elect Oscar De Priest, Chicago's first black alderman.

When a new Congress convened on April 7, 1913, Alice Paul organized a new parade. This time, 531 suffragists marched down Pennsylvania Avenue toward the Capitol, two from each state and one from each congressional district, seeking a constitutional amendment. The police chief made sure there were 300 officers on hand to protect the marchers, who were greeted on the Capitol steps by congressmen from the nine states that had already enfranchised women. It was all very civil. But the response to their appeal for Congress to enact a constitutional right for women to vote was the same as it had been every year since the idea was first introduced twenty-six years earlier.

So anemic was Congress's reaction to the appeal that in 1914, two members of NAWSA's Congressional Committee proposed a new idea designed to push the issue before the states. Ruth Hanna McCormick, daughter of famed political savant Mark Hanna, who had engineered William McKinley's rise in politics, and Antoinette Funk, a lawyer once jailed for making an unauthorized suffrage speech on the streets of Minor, South Dakota, were promoting the new amendment. Named for its sponsors – Senator John Franklin Shafroth and Representative Alexander Mitchell Palmer – the amendment required states to hold a referendum on women's suffrage at the request of 8 percent of the state's voters. The Shafroth-Palmer bill was passed by the Senate Woman Suffrage Committee but never received a vote on the Senate floor. Amid this stalemate in Congress, the selling of suffrage would have to continue. This time, suffrage leaders again looked to the states. But by this time, local leaders had their own ideas of how to organize the campaigns, and did not always want their help.

New Victories in the States

As the twentieth century dawned, activists in the state of Washington were frustrated by difficulties in winning suffrage, none more vexing than the repeated lawsuits filed by men seeking to overturn their victories. In 1871, Susan B. Antony had traveled to the territory, only to have the legislature reject her calls for a suffrage bill. In 1886, the territory of Washington had extended voting rights "to all American citizens, male and female." But the territory's Supreme Court nixed the idea the next year, saying in response to a lawsuit that the legislation had been inappropriately titled. In 1888, the legislature re-enacted the suffrage law, this time with appropriate title. By this time, the state Supreme Court had intervened in another case, saying the federal government had intended to put the word "male" before "citizenship" in Washington's application for statehood. So as efforts began anew in 1910 to win voter approval for a change in the constitution, local leaders Emma Smith DeVoe and May Arkwright Hutton devised a new strategy of disciplined organization.

Unlike national leaders, they would not emphasize public rallies or street parades. They would conduct a quiet, almost a stealth campaign. First they organized the state down to the local level, attracting suffrage supporters in every town, calling on activists to influence at the personal level, convincing husbands, sons, and brothers to go to the polls. They also won support from some of the state's populist reformers – the Grange and the Farmers Union among them. On Election Day, November 8, 1910, they were rewarded with a nearly 2-to-1 margin. The law was restricted to female citizens who could read and speak English, thus excluding Chinese immigrants and Native Americans. And victory had come in yet another lightly populated western state, weakening its effectiveness as a tool of political persuasion. Still, suffrage leaders were ecstatic. Alice Paul sewed the fourth star on her suffrage flag of purple, green, and gold. All of them cast their eyes to the upcoming battle in California.

In California, the disappointing defeat in 1896 had made local suffragists leery of national suffrage leaders. Anthony had instructed local activists that the best way to ensure victory was to win endorsement of all parties, protecting suffragists from accusations of partisanship. In 1896, local activists had dutifully won endorsements from the Republicans, the Populists, the Prohibitionists, and one quarter of the state's Democrats, and still they lost. There had been other miscalculations – Anthony urged the Woman's Christian Temperance Union, arguably the strongest suffrage organization in the state, to stay away, for fear of alienating German and Italian immigrants fond of drink. Instead, at a time of protests and strikes, economic depression, and political anarchy, many male voters in the Bay Area saw women's suffrage as part of an unwelcome social revolution. At least in San Francisco and Alameda Counties, the state's industrial center, these voters wanted no part of it.

Sifting through the results, local leaders also noticed that in every county where suffragists had formed precinct clubs and visited every voter and distributed leaflets, the amendment passed. So for the new campaign in 1911, they drilled down to the precinct level, canvassing likely voters in personal encounters, distributing one million pieces of campaign literature. They also embraced all kinds of new public relations tactics – parades and rallies, and new electric billboards – aimed at reaching every voter from San Diego to Sacramento. Ads and press releases featured waitresses, laundry workers, fruit pickers, and teachers. Some blacks and Mexicans joined the effort. Chinese immigrants did not, as suffragists feared a backlash.

There was a class component to the pitch. The California Federation of Women's Clubs had, since its founding in 1900, embraced a popular brand of middle-class activism – building a network of municipal playgrounds, commissioning public art, and leading "good government" reform efforts. Now its civic-minded members appealed to supporters, saying the vote would make them even more effective. In Los Angeles, Charlotta Spears Bass wrote pro-suffrage editorials in the state's largest African American newspaper, the *California Eagle*. At union halls, meanwhile, copies of Maud Younger's pamphlet, "Why Wage-Earning Women Should Vote," were distributed. In San Francisco, the Wage Earners' Suffrage League designed one float for a parade drawn by six black horses, covered with victory streamers. In San Diego, workers designed wagons bearing signs that said "Votes for Women" as well as "Equal Pay for Equal Work." Eager to tap into populist support, activists even targeted farming and rural areas. On Election Day, they were rewarded.

Mindfully, suffragists had sent 1,066 poll watchers, both men and women, to the polls in San Francisco, and their observations netted 3,000 fraudulent ballots. With only the Bay Area votes counted, city newspapers declared the referendum defeated. But as more votes came in it became clear that the outreach to small towns and rural areas had paid off. The referendum offering women the right to vote in all federal, state, and local elections won by a tiny margin of 3,587 votes, one per precinct – but the effect was dramatic, increasing to 1.3 million the number of female voters eligible to cast ballots in the 1912 presidential election.

That year in Illinois, Grace Wilbur Trout, newly elected president of the Illinois Equal Suffrage Association, teamed up with Ruth Hanna

McCormick, heir to Mark Hanna's political acumen, to win suffrage. Focused on organization, Trout made sure there was one chapter of the state organization in each senatorial district. She tracked the suffrage history of each lawmaker. "There were many Senatorial districts in which there was no suffrage organization of any kind, and as the time was short, competent women were immediately appointed in such districts to see that their respective legislators were properly interviewed, and to be ready to have letters and telegrams sent to Springfield when called for," she said.

They met with Governor Edward Dunne, who agreed to support the measure on one condition. He wanted only one initiative on the ballot that year, and it was not theirs. So he pledged to work with them to win women's suffrage not from voters but from the legislature. All that the legislature was empowered to do was grant women municipal and presidential suffrage, not state suffrage. Winning women's suffrage by legislative decision had always been the tougher route. But after three months of behind the scenes effort, the Senate passed the bill 29–15 in May, clearing the two-thirds vote requirement. The House posed a stiffer challenge, but Trout engineered a seat near the House door, "to prevent any friendly legislators from leaving during roll call, and to prevent" anti-suffrage activists "from violating the law and entering the House during the session." The House tally was 83–58, six votes above the required majority. Illinois became the first state east of the Mississippi to grant women presidential suffrage. At the signing ceremony, Dunne invited no women of color, despite their vocal, active campaigns. Still, the strategy had doubled, to two million, the number of women enfranchised to vote for president by their states.

In 1915, New Yorkers went to the polls to vote on a suffrage initiative, defeating the measure, 42.5 percent to 57.5 percent. Furious at the defeat, Harriot Stanton Blatch blamed immigrant men, steeped in their Old World customs of patriarchy, uneducated in the ways of American democratic ideals. "No women in the world are so humiliated in asking for the vote as the American woman. The English, the French, the German women all appeal to the men of their own nationality," she complained in an interview with the *New York Times*. "The American woman appeals to men of twenty-six nationalities, not including the Indian." Her comments were interpreted as singling out the Jewish immigrant vote. "In New York ... we have the biggest German city in the nation, the biggest Jewish city to convert from its Germanic and Hebraic attitude toward women," she had said before the election.

There is no question that New York was a polyglot city. In 1910 some 37 percent of its population was Jewish and 31 percent Roman Catholic – a concern to activists as the Catholic Church, while technically neutral, was known to be hostile to women's suffrage. Of these Catholics, 13 percent were either first- or second-generation Irish, and another 13 percent were first- or second-generation Italian. So complete was this infusion of immigrant energy into the city that by 1920 a majority of Manhattan's population was foreign born or had foreign-born parents.

Agitation for and against women's suffrage was evident in the ethnic press. In the runup to the election, the National Progressive Women's Suffrage Union targeted garment workers on the Lower East Side, holding open air meetings, staging demonstrations that attracted both crowd and press attention, distributing millions of pamphlets and flyers, many in Yiddish, German, and Italian. Most of the Yiddish newspapers endorsed the initiative. But *America* and the *Catholic Mind*, two Catholic newspapers, disparaged women's suffrage as an "ungodly" sex rebellion "set aflame at the time of the so-called Protestant Reformation." Taking up their charge, Joseph V. McKee, a teacher who represented the Bronx in the New York Assembly beginning in 1918, alleged in one article that women's suffrage was a threat to the home, an "opening wedge" for the destruction of the family and for socialism. Amid these public and private pressures, working-class immigrants were easy marks for stereotyping.

Two years later, voters in New York enfranchised women overwhelmingly – this time with a margin of more than 100,000 votes. Vira Boarman Whitehouse was widely credited with the win. Orchestrating a disciplined statewide campaign, she had rolled up huge majorities in the city and almost reached majority in the more rural counties upstate. New York would now send to Washington the largest pro-suffrage delegation in Congress, forty-three men whose voters had opted to include women in politics. Many in the suffrage movement, sure that New York's congressmen would now be pressured to vote as their constituents had, hailed this moment as the tipping point for a federal amendment. In fact, it took another two years. By 1919, when Congress passed the Nineteenth Amendment, women were already eligible to vote for president in thirty of the forty-eight states. The state-by-state approach to winning suffrage – so painstaking in its slow victories, so heartbreaking in its many disappointments – had finally produced results. The states had served as incubators for social change.

Given these victories, there was much talk, in print culture of the day, about the so-called New Woman. The fictional character, described by American novelist Henry James as feminist, educated, and independent, portrayed by Norwegian playwright Henrik Ibsen as defying the boundaries of a male-patrolled society, appealed to the modern sensibilities of the times. The New Woman first appeared on the scene in the 1890s, when a bicycle craze swept the country. With its patented Dunlop tires that rode smoothly over paved roads and its implicit invitation to tour the world without a chaperon, the bicycle, as Susan B. Anthony suggested, had "done more to emancipate women than anything else in the world." Amid the advent of the New Woman, men faced a dilemma. Some doubled down, barricading the gates of power ever more firmly, performing feats of virility – and war – to demonstrate their virtue. Others, and at first they were but a few, responded by embracing woman's right to vote. The arrival of these new male suffragists provoked a debate over gender, even within their ranks, and over the role of American women and men in a newly modern era.

8

Male Suffragists and the Limits of Self-Interest

In October 1912, presidential candidate Woodrow Wilson made a campaign appearance at the Brooklyn Academy of Music, where he vowed to break up the nation's monopolies. Maud Malone, a suffragist and socialist known for her gadfly tactics, shouted, "What about woman suffrage? The men have a monopoly." Amid laughter, Wilson insisted that suffrage was a state issue, and, as he was running for national office, not one he would comment on. When Malone persisted, she was arrested for creating a public disturbance. Despite the tendency of Woodrow Wilson and most politicians to duck at the very mention of the subject, there had always been men who had stood with women in this fight for the right.

In the colonial period, James Sullivan, a member of the Massachusetts General Court, urged John Adams, one of the drafters of the Declaration of Independence, to promote universal suffrage, including women, in the new nation's contract with its citizens. In the antebellum era, the missionary and Native American defender Jeremiah Evarts encouraged women to become political actors, and abolitionist William Lloyd Garrison boycotted the World Anti-Slavery Convention in London after British hosts excluded the seven female members of his American Anti-Slavery Society. During the era of women's rights conventions before the Civil War, Frederick Douglass single-handedly salvaged Elizabeth Cady Stanton's plank at the Seneca Falls convention calling for women's suffrage. Afterwards, at the last meeting of the American Equal Rights

And Yet They Persisted: How American Women Won the Right to Vote, First Edition. Johanna Neuman.
© 2020 John Wiley & Sons, Inc. Published 2020 by John Wiley & Sons, Inc.
Companion website: www.wiley.com/go/Neuman

Association, when Stanton and Susan B. Anthony were criticized for campaigning against the Fifteenth Amendment, African American civil rights leader Robert Purvis stood with them, saying, in their account, that "he would rather that his son never be enfranchised, unless his daughter could be also, that, as she bore the double curse of sex and color, on every principle of justice she should first be protected." And when African American women were campaigning for the vote, W. E. B. Du Bois published their appeals in the NAACP's journal, *The Crisis*, which he edited, even as he parried charges by white suffragists that African American men were hostile to the vote for women.

But for all the interest of men in earlier generations, for all their high motives and good intentions, it was not until 1908 that American men began to organize for women's right to vote. The reasons that propelled them to coalesce under the banner of the Men's League for Woman Suffrage, the impact they had on the Votes for Women campaign, and the ways in which their activism complicated the movement's trajectory are instructive. Derided by the newspapers of the day as "mere men," heckled by onlookers as "gay deceivers," virtually ignored by suffrage leaders after the Nineteenth Amendment, they served as witnesses for a modernizing movement. Their motives were diverse. Some were radicals seeking to topple gender and political stereotypes, in some cases sexual adventurers lusting after suffragists. Others, with a genuine passion for progressive causes, were good-government types looking to add women to their circle of reformers. No matter their motives, they normalized the idea of women participating in the political world. By their very activism these men conditioned the public to see women – and men – beyond the gendered construct of the domestic sphere and in light of the interest politics that animated their times.

The Feminization of American Politics

For most of the nineteenth century, political parades were a key to male identity. Rallies gave men of varied backgrounds a sense of belonging. Cheering, wearing buttons to show loyalty to party candidates, marching in militaristic parades – these perks conditioned them to vote their tribe on Election Day. Especially after expansion of the white working-class electorate under President Andrew Jackson, these rituals also cemented a sense of masculinity. While men bonded through these rituals of politics, women created their own organizations – voluntary, charitable, and reform associations – aimed at influencing politics from afar.

During the Civil War, women on both sides entered the public square in acts of charity and protest. In the North, black and white women organized for the U.S. Sanitary Commission, a private relief organization created by the federal government to treat wounded soldiers before the advent of military medics. By war's end they had raised $25 million. In the process, they honed organizational skills that would prove beneficial in coming political contests. Meanwhile in the South, women starving from the exodus of men for the Army organized letter-writing campaigns to the Confederacy's capitol of Richmond. These missives propelled President Jefferson Davis and his Cabinet to grant early release to soldiers who were much needed in combat and increase food allotments to civilians. Adopting tactics men used in petitioning their government, employing the wail of a sex betrayed by the failure of chivalry, they forced the Confederacy to sideline the interests of war to attend to their needs.

After the war, under the umbrella of "municipal housekeeping," women in both North and South joined causes outside the home, seeking temperance, suffrage, sanitation, workplace, and governmental reforms. By the early twentieth century, men and women had seemed to switch roles. Noting that the women's social pressure was as successful as their electoral clout, men gravitated to the special interest politics pioneered by clubwomen. Concluding that their reforms required the muscle of the state, women renewed their campaign to win the vote. As women won suffrage victories in the states, male turnout started to erode. Women's suffrage had become the first political challenge of the modern age, and effort to persuade men to share power. Instead, men now turned to sports – and war – in what one historian called "a virility impulse." As Theodore Roosevelt and his Rough Riders rode off for a quixotic, imperialist adventure to save Cuba from the Spanish Empire, their brigades looked like a masculine rebuttal to this feminization of American politics.

Signs of gender malaise were evident in the popular culture. Cartoons appeared in which bedraggled men tried to feed crying babies from barren cupboards or wash clothes amid an overflow of bubbles while their wives went off to vote. Broadsides continued the attack. "Woman suffrage denatures both men and women; it masculinizes women and feminizes men," explained one flyer produced by the Southern Woman's League for Rejection of the Susan B. Anthony Amendment. Urging state legislators to reject the Nineteenth Amendment, the flyer added, "A Vote for Federal Suffrage is a Vote for Organized Female Nagging Forever." Men in power recoiled. "I do not believe that there is a red-blooded man in the world who in his heart really believes in woman suffrage," said Senator James Thomas Heflin of Alabama. "I think every man who favors it ought to be made to wear a dress. The suffragette and a little henpecked fellow crawling along beside her; that is her husband."

Amid this masculinity crisis, Oswald Garrison Villard, editor of the *Nation* and the *New York Evening Post*, son of suffragist Fanny Garrison Villard, and grandson of abolitionist William Lloyd Garrison, wrote a letter. In his missive to NAWSA President Anna Howard Shaw, he suggested forming "a men's club favoring equal suffrage," much like the one that had formed in London a few months before. They would function as a cadre of 100 silent soldiers, their chief role to "impress the public and legislators." Mindful of how zealously some female suffragists guarded their power, Shaw hesitated. As Fanny Villard may have anticipated when she first discussed the idea with her son, Shaw eventually agreed, especially if Villard recruited prominent men so busy with their business enterprises that all they could give was "their names, and the *influence* [emphasis hers] which goes with them."

Villard reached out to Rabbi Stephen S. Wise, an early advocate for women's suffrage. The Hungarian-born Wise, a descendant of rabbis, had declined an offer to head the congregation at the city's most influential synagogue, Emanu-El. As he explained, he wanted to change the status quo, not preside over it. Forming a Free Synagogue, he used Sunday lectures at Carnegie Hall to address a secular audience. About suffrage, he was outspoken. "As long as women are shut out from citizenship and the exercise of the ballot, which is the symbol of citizenship, ours is no democracy," he said, but "a manocracy" where men could use "brute power to shut women out from the right of equal citizenship."

The two progressives agreed to "share the ignominy, provided someone turned up who would do the work." That someone, their first secretary, turned out to be Max Eastman (Fig. 8.1), a charming if starry-eyed personality who by his own account had earlier discussed the idea of a men's league with a reporter for the *New York Herald*. Influenced by his sister, Crystal Eastman, by his girlfriend, Inez Milholland, by Ida Rauh, a lawyer who became his first wife, all suffragists, and by what he described as "the general mood of America," he agreed.

From a prestigious family, Villard intuitively felt the group should recruit men of distinction, whose class credentials might persuade reluctant lawmakers that women's suffrage would not topple gender norms. He gave Eastman letters of introduction to twelve men of "civic importance." In reaching out to men of prominence – he called them "civic wonders" – Eastman encountered some resistance. Hector S. Tyndale, claiming to be a suffrage supporter, practically threw Eastman out of his office, saying he'd "be damned if he'd see [the cause] made ridiculous." His next visit was more successful. Charles Culp Burlingham, president of the New York Bar Association, a reformer sometimes called "the first citizen of New York," was all in. Burlingham, whose wife was an anti-suffragist, told Eastman he supported the cause because he hungered

Figure 8.1 Max Eastman was the first secretary of the Men's League for Woman Suffrage, charged with recruiting its first 100 members. He believed that feminism "would make it possible for the first time for men to be free," and "demolish traditional, monogamous marriage." Calling women's suffrage "the great fight for freedom in my lifetime," he gave speeches and wrote articles but rarely marched for the cause. The editor of *The Masses*, a magazine espousing socialist ideas, Eastman was later charged with anti-American activities during World War I, and, seen here with his colleagues, acquitted. From left, sister Crystal Eastman, Arthur Young, Max Eastman, Morris Hillquit, Merrill Rogers Jr., and Floyd Dell. Photo Quest, *Source:* Getty Images Courtesy of Photo 12.

for a partner of lively mind, believing "women ought to try to be more intelligent than they are, if only for the sake of their husbands."

In subsequent mailings to prospective members, Eastman made two promises, "the importance of which I had learned in my visits to the original twelve." One was that there would be no public announcement until 100 men had signed up, offering the comfort of a crowd even as it suggested the likelihood of social ostracism. The instinct to gather 100 men before going public may have stemmed from the nineteenth-century stigma of suffrage as the campaign of a radical few. In fact, after one recruit leaked Eastman's letter to the anti-suffrage *New York Times*, the newspaper broke the shocking news that men might support the cause of women's suffrage. Another newspaper headlined in mockery, "Did Their Wives Insist?" At least one of Eastman's recruits bolted, suggesting that public support of suffrage for women was still threatening to the establishment. Dr. John Brannan was a trustee of the Bellevue and Allied Hospitals' board of directors and may have feared repercussions if he remained a member. Later, after the controversy cooled, he quietly rejoined the League, and in fact became an outspoken supporter.

Eastman's second assurance in recruiting was that "no member would be called upon to do anything. The main function of the league would be to exist." This assurance of non-engagement was extraordinary for a cause seeking social change, and may have been another indication of how controversial it was for men to band together to support women's suffrage. But in an environment of great press competition – New York boasted twenty-nine daily newspapers at the time – a stealth campaign was simply not possible. By the time the Men's League held its first meeting at the City Club in late November, press interest vanquished all thoughts of a silent brigade of men symbolically bolstering the cause. "Female suffrage got a decided boost yesterday at a meeting at the City Club, when an organization of men was formed whose object it will be to stand sponsor in all suffrage movements," reported Brooklyn *Daily Eagle*. Derision quickly followed among men for whom the idea of a male suffragist seemed unimaginable. "Men's Leagues for Woman Suffrage are chiefly favored by bachelors," explained the *Eagle* in "an inevitable reflection" by its editors.

Despite Eastman's assurances of inactivity, or of Shaw's hopes that the men would keep a low public profile and merely influence lawmakers with their names, the pledge to go public was embedded in the organization's 1910 constitution, which promised "to express approval of the movement of women to attain the full suffrage in this country, and to aid them in their efforts toward that end by public appearances, … by the circulation of literature, the holding of meetings, and in such other ways as may from time to time seem desirable."

Motives

The members of the Men's League were hardly monolithic in their motivations. Among them were dreamers and pragmatists, egos that bruised easily and souls able to laugh off derision. Some wanted women to have the vote to improve the heart of the polity; others because they thought it would improve the minds of women. Some, like Eastman, joined the Men's League to "demolish traditional, monogamous marriage" and tear down the Victorian Era's sexual constraints, others to uphold the traditions of gender decorum while extending the rights of the ballot to the gentler sex. Some meant to honor family connections of reformist zeal, others to challenge the industrial capitalism that was the bane of so many moderns. For all of them, as Eastman suggested, women's suffrage was part of the era's drumbeat for reform, the latest milestone in what seemed like an arc of linear progress toward egalitarianism, representing "the big fight for freedom in my time."

For Greenwich Village radicals who joined the League, the ballot was but one piece of a larger socialist vision that would end female dependence on men, freeing them from the burden of economic and sexual responsibility. Floyd Dell, a socialist known as a ladies' man, argued that capitalism was corrupt because it encouraged wives and children to be dependent on men for support. Feminism, he argued, "would make it possible for the first time for men to be free." In a speech delivered at Poughkeepsie in 1910 that was reprised as a bestselling pamphlet, "Is Woman Suffrage Important?" Eastman agreed that the vote for women would liberate all citizens from gender stereotype. "When we have abolished that double standard of morality which allows the 'ideal woman' to be ignorant and silly, we shall see the disappearance of that double standard which allows her husband to be profligate and self centered," he said. "When we have less innocence and more virtue in women, we shall have less vice and more virtue in men."

As the League grew in membership and gained traction with middle-class and wealthy men, Eastman and other "bohemian sex radicals of Greenwich Village" left the fold. They had been attracted to a movement for social change. When anti-suffragists accused activists of being proxy for free love, socialism, and Bolshevik revolution, these early Men's League members cheered. But when the cause turned resolutely pragmatic, taken over by earnest reformers interested in clean streets and good government, pursuing the vote for women not because they were equal citizens but because they were adept at municipal housekeeping, they left. As Eastman acknowledged, by 1912 "the suffrage movement was getting too fashionable to appeal to that in me which desires to suffer a little in some high cause."

And fashionable it had become. The League's letterhead, which listed twenty-seven names at its inception in 1910, by 1915 featured sixty-seven men willing to publicly declare their support and lend their names and their time. Villard and Wise stayed the course, as did Tiffany vice president George Kunz, architect William A. Delano, editors George McClelland Harvey of *Harper's Weekly* and Hamilton Holt of *The Independent*, and the Rev. John P. Peters of St. Michael's Episcopal Church. So many Columbia University professors joined the organization – philosopher John Dewey, historian Vladimir Simkhovitch, pathologist Simon Flexner, historian

Charles Beard, law professor George Kirchwey, economist Henry Rogers Seager, and literature professor William P. Trent – that the League might well have served as a satellite office for the Faculty Club.

Many of these men knew each other through the City Club, founded in 1892 to "aid in securing permanent good government for the City of New York through the election and the appointment of honest and able municipal officers and the establishment of a clear and stable system of laws." Here the connective tissue of reform took hold. Richard Welling, a lawyer and Harvard classmate of Theodore Roosevelt's, had launched many a club campaign to improve the city's water supply, end police graft, and change election laws to derail bribery. With Burlingham and lawyer Charles H. Strong, he now joined the Men's League. So did other professionals of their acquaintance, men they had met during the City Club's reform efforts, including the League' s first president, banker George Foster Peabody. This network of reformers – Metropolitan Museum of Art curator William Ivins, Republican Congressman Herbert Parsons, businessman William Jay Schieffelin, and muckraker Lincoln Steffens – saw the vote for women as an extension of, and a benefit to, their other causes.

The very diversity of their reform causes suggested the breadth of the Progressive Era umbrella that also included women's suffrage. Several were passionate about racial inequality, calling for an end to economic and civic disadvantage and to lynching of black men. John Milholland, the son of an Irish immigrant, and Villard, grandson of abolitionist William Lloyd Garrison, were founders of the NAACP, at its birth in 1909 an interracial organization. William Jay Schieffelin, a wealthy businessman and descendant of John Jay whose ancestors were Lincoln Republicans, served as chairman of the board of the Tuskegee Institute, and of the Hampton Institute, a college for African Americans.

The most sizable constituency within the Men's League flew under the banner of municipal reform. Despite the City Club's "chastity rule," which banned its members from accepting a city or state position for at least a year after their reform efforts had created new jobs, quite a few tested their ideals inside the government's tent. Calvin Tompkins, a building manufacturer who headed the Municipal Art Society, was named Commissioner of the Docks after William Gaynor, a former Supreme Court justice elected mayor in 1910, turned against Tammany Hall. After reformer John Purroy Mitchel was elected mayor in 1914 with help from the Women's Fusion League for Good Government, he appointed Dr. Henry Moskowitz as chairman of the city's Civil Service Commission. Frederick C. Howe, whose wife Marie Jenney Howe, a Unitarian minister, had started the unorthodox Heterodoxy Club for women, served as Woodrow Wilson's Commissioner of Immigration at Ellis Island from 1914 onward. "I want woman suffrage because it will also free men," he wrote in *Collier's* in March 1912. "I want woman suffrage for what it will do for woman, for what it will do for men, for what it will do for the muddle we have made of politics ... I cannot myself be happy in a world where there is so much poverty, so much hunger, so much suffering that can so easily be cured." In their eyes, the fight for women's suffrage was not, as one observer put it, a conflict between men and women, but between progressives and the rest. As one newspaper explained, "This is no contest of women against men. The average man is not tyrannical, he is only prejudiced. This is a contest of the women and men who are ruled by reason against the women and men who are ruled by custom."

There was also a large contingency of members who saw themselves as husbands supporting their wives' causes. In their eyes, manhood was less about defending exclusive access to the political process than about expanding the definition of citizenship. Whether they were drawn to the campaign because of their wives' activism or attracted to their wives because of their support for progressive ideals is difficult to say. Either way, their endorsement suggested a shift in attitude among men. As NAWSA press agent Ida Husted Harper observed, the moniker "suffrage husband" had become "a title of distinction."

Playwright George Middleton became a member of the Men's League after he married Fola La Follette, daughter of Wisconsin progressive Senator Robert "Fighting Bob" La Follette. The couple made news after she had asked to keep her given name on marriage, and he championed her right to do so. "When I defended Fola's right to do as she wished, a teapot tempest spilled over," he recalled. "Editorials, interviews, and what not followed, for we were accused of starting another of those feminists' demands which were 'breaking up the home.'" He gave speeches solo "at street corners and store meetings on Fifth Avenue during the lunch hour." He preferred to appear with his wife, who drew crowds. Her verbal gifts, her training as an actress, and her background as the daughter of a prominent politician gave her a presence that delighted him. Once, preceding her at an event in Catskill, New York, he recalled, "I died on my feet. Never have I felt so lifeless an audience." Handing her the podium, he marveled how his wife melted "all the ice I left."

Henry Wise Miller, another League member, likewise campaigned with his wife. Alice Duer Miller had shocked her family by enrolling in Barnard, the new college for women. Despite her father's financial ruin amid a banking collapse, she vowed to attend college even if she had to pay her own expenses by tutoring other students. As the news spread in her social circle, it "shocked society and alienated her friends." Caroline Schermerhorn Astor, the doyen of High Society, paid a call on Alice's mother to say, "What a pity, that lovely girl going to college." Alice later won acclaim as a writer, and it was her facility on her feet that most impressed her husband. "There was a perfection in what she said from the platform and in the press," he wrote. Miller too was called on by mainstream organizations to share the podium as a suffrage husband. "One of the stunts of the suffrage campaign was a husband and wife speaking as a team," he recalled. He thought the tactical result "as good as anything we have had since the Boston Tea Party ... a model of propaganda, combining in nice proportion premeditated violence with an appeal to reason."

George Creel, who later became director of President Wilson's wartime propaganda arm, the Committee on Public Information, was not a suffrage husband. Far from it, he had to negotiate an arrangement with his wife, actress Blanche Bates, to devote time to the cause. "My wife and I worked out a financial arrangement," he recalled. "When – and if – I made enough money to take care of my share of household expenses for the year, the rest of the time would be mine" to spend on progressive reform campaigns, including suffrage. Although he described his wife as "a vociferous anti," he admired greatly her independent career as an actress. More, he ascribed his enthusiasm for the cause to "the deep conviction that my mother outweighed any man when it came to brains and character," although she too had "held firmly to the Southern insistence that woman's place was in the home." Against this backdrop of domestic indifference or even hostility, Creel enunciated a passionate appeal for the vote. "Equal Suffrage is part and parcel of the great big struggle for equal justice and real democracy," he wrote to new members in his role as the Men's League's publicity director. "It is as much the man's fight as the woman's."

Ever mindful of the potential of the media to spread malicious canards, Creel organized a committee of ten men to respond to all anti-suffrage material in the newspapers. "It will be the member's duty to read the anti-suffrage letters and editorials in the ... papers assigned to him and either answer them himself or, if necessary, have some member of the Publicity Committee ... do so," Creel explained. He also reached out to well-known authors across the country to write articles. Creel wrote William Allen White, the respected owner of the Emporia *Gazette* in Kansas, in the fall of 1915, suggesting that suffrage campaigns in New York, Pennsylvania, Massachusetts, and New Jersey "could have no greater boost than an article" from him in the Saturday *Evening Post*. During the campaign, male and female suffragists tried every tactic in the new arsenal – holding outdoor meetings, concerts, parades, staging hikes and torchlight processions, soliciting votes from bankers, firemen, lawyers, railroad workers, streetcar operators, longshoremen, and barbers. "All of us are working night and day, and unless things go wrong at the last minute, I think we are going to carry in New York and Massachusetts," Creel wrote. (They did not.) "For heaven's sake, come to the front with a sane article that will bring some facts into this eastern nightmare of falsehood."

More than other male suffragists who were businessmen, good government reformers or academics, Creel was a propagandist with a great feel for the art of politics. In January 1915, when Congress defeated a federal women's suffrage amendment 204 to 174, Creel urged his circle of male correspondents to "get after" the thirty-one congressmen in the New York delegation's forty-man roster who voted no, letting them know there would be a political price to pay at the polls. Not one to mince words, he said, "I'd like to see them burned alive."

Impact on Campaign

Despite Shaw's early suggestion that the men influence with their names only, soon they became visible – offering League members as speakers, holding fundraising pageants, marching in parades, canvassing voters, raising funds, organizing rebuttals to anti-suffrage editorials, and even serving as poll watchers on Election Day – all in coordination with female suffrage leaders. By 1912, one thousand men marched in the New York suffrage parade, 20,000 men had signed up for a national Men's League, and there were thirty Leagues around the country. The Men's League for Woman Suffrage in Chicago was the first to organize, and its first mass rally in early 1909 featured Jane Addams, founder of Hull House; Maud Wood Park, noted suffragist from Boston; and Catharine Waugh McCulloch, a lawyer and the first woman justice of the peace elected in Illinois, speaking in a hall where "the house was packed." In Iowa, a delegation of the local Men's League traveled to the capitol in Des Moines to appeal for a joint resolution on women's suffrage. And the Men's League in Connecticut hosted British suffragette Emmeline Pankhurst as a featured speaker. Leagues sprouted at colleges, including one at Harvard University, formed by John Reed, whom Eastman had converted to the cause. Yale and Dartmouth soon followed.

Arguably nothing the Men's League ever did achieved the notoriety – or swelled the ranks of male suffragists – as much as the 1912 parade. Harriot Stanton Blatch had set out to organize a street parade "the like of which New York never knew before." Eager to defuse criticism that women had dallied the previous year, evidence of their unsuitability for the ballot, Blatch insisted the 1912 parade began promptly at 5 p.m. Remember that "the public will judge, illogically of course, but no less strictly, your qualification as a voter by your promptness," she said. The parade was held only a few weeks after the sinking of the RMS *Titanic,* which had sparked a nationwide debate about the chivalry of men, such as John Jacob Astor IV, who went down with the ship so that rescuers could save "women and children first." Identifying himself as "Mere Man," one letter-writer to the Baltimore *Sun* asked, "Would the suffragette have stood on that deck for women's rights or for women's privileges?" As a result of the criticism, Blatch was under some pressure to postpone the parade, but she remained convinced a parade representing women in many fields of endeavor would sway the public. "Men and women are moved by seeing marching groups of people and by hearing music far more than by listening to the most careful argument," she said. She underestimated the attention, and influence, the male marchers received.

In 1911, only eighty-nine members of the Men's League had marched in the parade. "The crowd generally assumed that we were not there of our own free will," commented Villard. As the *New York Sun* reported, there were three thousand female marchers – architects, typists, aviators, explorers, nurses, physicians, actresses, factory workers, cooks, painters, writers, milliners, hairdressers, librarians, and the like. But "the only jeers to be heard came, and came in plenty, when the eighty-nine mere men of the Men's League for Woman Suffrage hove into view." One year later, more than one thousand men joined the parade along New York's Fifth Avenue, and the derision they encountered suggested the threat they posed to the stability of gender relations, reflected too in the hyperbolic alarms raised by the antis. The anti-suffrage *New York Times* reported that one band, "as if to give courage to the less courageous of the mere men marchers … broke into a lusty marching tune as the men swung from Thirteenth Street into Fifth Avenue." It is doubtful the drum and fife corps drowned out heckling from onlookers: "Tramp, tramp, tramp, the girls are marching." Questioning their motives, the *Times* noted that some had participated in the parade to curry favor with female customers, especially female tailors.

In his diary, Rabbi Stephen Wise (Fig. 8.2) wrote of the mockery he encountered that day. "For a few moments, I was very warm and took off my hat, whereupon someone shouted, 'Look at the longhaired Susan.' Some of the other delightful exclamations that greeted us were: 'Who's taking care of the baby? … Oh, Flossy dear, aren't they cute? Look at the Mollycoddles.'" George Middleton recalled hecklers crying, "Take that handkerchief out of your cuff," "Oh you gay deceiver," and "You forgot to shave this morning." Wise found the event uplifting, because while both male and female "rowdies" had shouted insults, "the most hopeful

Figure 8.2 Rabbi Stephen S. Wise was a Hungarian-born descendant of rabbis, a reformer, lecturer, and one of the first activists to join the Men's League for Woman Suffrage. In his diary, Wise wrote of the mockery he encountered in 1912 when he marched in a women's suffrage parade. "For a few moments, I was very warm and took off my hat, whereupon someone shouted, 'Look at the longhaired Susan.' Some of the other delightful exclamations that greeted us were: 'Who's taking care of the baby? … Oh, Flossy dear, aren't they cute? Look at the Mollycoddles.'" Wise found the event uplifting, because while both male and female "rowdies" had shouted insults, "the most hopeful thing" was the "respect by the intelligent class of people." Participation by men helped normalize the idea of women voting, defusing fears among male voters that the franchise would harden women and emasculate men. *Source:* Library of Congress Prints and Photographs Division.

thing" was the "respect by the intelligent class of people." Others were not as sanguine. One said he felt like an early Christian in the arena. Raymond Brown, whose wife Gertrude Foster Brown was an official in the New York Woman Suffrage Party, reported that they felt isolated. "Tagging after the girls – that's what we were doing; and nobody would let us forget it," he recalled.

Perhaps to the surprise of the male marchers and their female colleagues, the week after the parade, male recruits descended on

League headquarters. Quite a few said they had been "moved by the guying their brethren got in the parade." Likewise, when New York lawyer William Benedict learned his Union League Club had voted to oppose the franchise, he resigned, donating his dues instead to the Woman Suffrage Party. "About this time of year I should have been paying my annual dues to the Union League Club had I not resigned on account of its action on the equal suffrage question," he wrote the New York Woman Suffrage Party. "I accordingly take pleasure in sending you a check for the amount of said dues to be used as you may think best in furthering the cause."

The advent of the male suffragists only emboldened men on the other side. In 1913, the Man Suffrage Association Opposed to Political Suffrage for Women formed in New York, headed by Everett P. Wheeler, a lawyer and one of the founders of the American Bar Association. He said he had toyed with the idea of naming the group the "Society for the Prevention of Cruelty to Women," but later shortened the title to the Man Suffrage Association. By whatever name, the association was proactive – issuing briefs, legal arguments, and speeches. Its pamphlet, "The Case Against Woman Suffrage," ran to eighty pages. In December 1913, Wheeler pressed the case in testimony before the Rules Committee against a proposal to create a congressional committee on women's suffrage.

James Lees Laidlaw, a member of the League and husband of Harriet Laidlaw, a New York suffrage leader, had already testified before the committee, dismissing the outdated views of these male anti-suffragists who would rob women of their rights to participate in democracy. Also testifying for the idea was Charles Beard, another League member, a Columbia University historian and husband of fellow historian Mary Ritter Beard. The vote, he noted, would benefit the woman, "sharpen her intellect, force upon her an interest in the social and economic conditions which are determining her own destiny … and finally give her that self-respect and self-sufficiency which prevent her from being content with the alternate adoration and contempt of the opposite sex." If any committee members needed an explanation of the extent of male contempt toward women, Wheeler provided it. Holding up a photo of NAWSA President Anna Howard Shaw, he said, "When I saw this person here shake her clenched fist and declare 'We demand our rights,' I said to myself, 'clenched fists mean fight.' The manhood of this nation has been trained to respect and revere womanhood, and I claim that for American manhood today, but if we are challenged to fight this movement there will be blows to give as well as take." Later still, after women's suffrage was enacted in New York in 1917, Wheeler changed the group's name to the American Constitutional League, dedicated to opposing the Nineteenth Amendment. Publishing an anti-suffrage newspaper, the *Woman Patriot*, the League formed chapters in fifteen states, lobbied against ratification, and worked "to protect the federal Constitution from further invasion." The League also took the ratification fight to the U.S. Supreme Court, with Wheeler, William Marbury, and George Arnold Frick arguing that the Nineteenth Amendment had not been legally ratified. In 1922, the court unanimously disagreed.

Normalizing Women's Suffrage

Many of the women who marched in the 1912 parade never forgot the strength they derived from men in the procession. "It took so much more courage for a man to come out for woman's suffrage than it did for a woman," recalled Laura Ellsworth Siler, a junior at Cornell University marching in her first parade. Many singled out the League's president, James Lees Laidlaw, an outdoorsman equally at home in the men's clubs of Manhattan and in the Sierra Nevada mountains of California, for making them braver. "It meant much for him to do this, for he was in the very forefront and faced the derision of the men in his own clubs, as they sat in their windows and watched us go by," recalled Charles Strong. Harriet Laidlaw agreed, writing a friend, "all Mr. Laidlaw's banking firm were against him in it." Frances Perkins, a social worker who later became Franklin Roosevelt's Secretary of Labor, the first female Cabinet officer in U.S. history, agreed. "I recall him so plainly and am heartened by it still, as he joked and encouraged us on East 10th Street as we waited to 'fall in' in the great suffrage parade," she said. "I can never be thankful enough for the courage he gave to many of us – young and doubtful – when he took up the suffrage movement on his own." Laidlaw was the only man honored on a suffrage plaque at the state capitol in Albany, but suffrage leaders rarely mentioned him, or any male supporter, in their memoirs and biographies.

The Men's League's greatest contribution, however, may have been to buck up the men. As Laidlaw, by then president of both the New York and the national organizations, replied when asked why the League joined the parade, "We are marching to give political support to the women and moral support to the men." Soon the League would be called on to do more than offer moral support to the men. Events conspired to require political support.

As West Virginia part-time legislature debated a women's suffrage amendment in 1916, opponents threatened to rob Senator Raymond Dodson of his day job if he did not abandon his support for the franchise. Dodson worked as an attorney for the United Fuel Gas Company, where his boss, Harry Wallace, objected to the idea of women in politics. Word reached Laidlaw, who rallied male supporters in New York and elsewhere to save the senator. The Men's League issued a press release meant to "arouse indignation." Dodson served out his term. Four years later, as Dodson prepared to vote for ratification of the Nineteenth Amendment, opponents again tried to unseat him, this time by claiming he had moved out of his district. Again Laidlaw successfully rallied the troops.

For many men, the very presence of male suffragists was an assault on their perception of manhood, and they responded with ridicule. Belfort Bax, a social critic, disparaged women for using sex to manipulate men into supporting the cause, while at the same time insulting men for falling for the ploy. "Any success women may achieve in their 'anti-man' crusade is entirely due to the help given them by 'rats' from the camp of men themselves," he wrote. Newspaper columns and the halls of power were full of outcries against the idea of emancipating women. One man wrote the Illinois Senate that man-hating suffragists would ruin the family. He called women "the sex which has accomplished absolutely nothing, except being the passive and often unwilling and hostile instruments by which humanity is created." One New York state senator said he feared that if they won the vote, women would lose their "feminine qualities," sullied by the dirty world of cigar smoke and politics. For other men, masculinity was associated with feats of virility, and suffrage activism with its opposite, weak-kneed effeminacy. On observing a mass rally conducted by the Men's League for Women's Suffrage in England, one American reporter expressed surprise that the League's speaker, "instead of being an anaemic, henpecked appearing old gentleman with furtive eye and drooping whiskers," was "a robust young fellow of 25 or thereabouts who looks as if he might have been drafted by the 'cause' from the football field."

The question of what the male suffragist looked like, or how he behaved, preoccupied these new male suffragists. Looking for ways to expand suffrage support, James Lees Laidlaw suggested members wear a blue button of courtesy, signaling to anti-suffrage women on streetcars that, as one newspaper put it, "the days of chivalry were not over when it came to giving a woman a seat in a crowded car." His appeal was not to anti-suffragist males but to their wives and daughters, women who could counter the arguments made at home by their husbands and fathers by reporting on these offers of courtesy from male suffragists.

The anti-suffrage *Brooklyn Life* was quick to pounce on this contortion of gender messages. In an article titled "Ostentatious Gallantry," the magazine pierced the hypocrisy of preaching equality while offering privilege. "Gentlemen never make a special feature of courtesy and consideration for women," said the magazine. "They do not have to. It is second nature with them and the last thing they would think of bragging about." Calling the League "that knightly organization," *Brooklyn Life* belittled the men, suggesting male suffragists ask women for help carrying their luggage. "It seems to us that this would be much more consonant with the aim and purpose of the league," said the magazine, "which is to drag women into politics before a majority of them has signified the slightest desire for political equality."

In November 1912, Harriet Laidlaw planned a torchlight parade to celebrate recent victories in California and Washington, and again conflicts arose about the appropriate vogue for male marchers. Robert C. Beadle (Fig. 8.3), secretary for the Men's League, complained that

Figure 8.3 Robert C. Beadle, the Men's League secretary, poses here with other suffragists outside the headquarters of the Woman's Suffrage Party of Manhattan. Newspaper critics often dismissed them as bachelors hoping to meet attractive female activists, but many male suffragists campaigned with their wives. George Middleton was married to suffragist Fola La Follette, daughter of Wisconsin progressive Senator Robert "Fighting Bob" La Follette, and the two often spoke together at suffrage rallies. Once, preceding her at an event in Catskill, New York, he recalled, "I died on my feet. Never have I felt so lifeless an audience." Handing her the podium, he marveled how his wife melted "all the ice I left." Bain News Service, *Source:* Library of Congress Prints and Photographs Division.

suffragists had requested a male parade marshal who wasn't "too hand-
some," raising again the issue of what a male suffragist was supposed to
look like. He suggested one candidate who might do, as he was bald,
and this, Beadle said sarcastically, "might do something to remove the
impression that all men suffragists have long hair." Perhaps he was referring to the "long-haired" taunts that rained down on male reformers, or
perhaps to a narrative that male suffragists were sexually adventurous.
Either way, concern suggested that anti-suffrage sentiment was soaring,
even as suffrage was gaining. Mocking this "most pretentious celebration
ever attempted," the New York *Telegram* reserved its greatest sarcasm for
the men, suggesting they were only chasing women. "Don't think that
Mere Man will be left standing on the sidewalk, balancing himself on
one foot and then on the other, while lovely women go marching by,"
sneered the paper. "Any man is at liberty to enter the ranks, provided
he obtains an ordinary chrysanthemum for the buttonhole of his coat."
Sarcastically, the paper added, "What up to date man, with red blood
in his veins and with a discerning eye for the beautiful, can resist the
captivating glances of a suffragette?"

This tussle over gender expectations often produced other ironies.
In 1915, as male suffragists formed a new Men's Committee to work for
the women's suffrage ballot initiative in New York, they had a difficult
time finding a place to meet. First they tried the Lotos Club, a venue
they abandoned when it was discovered that the club barred women,
including the many female reporters who covered suffrage. They
moved to the Manhattan Club, only to discover that it too did not admit
women. It was as if, reported the New York *Tribune*, these men, many of
them club members, were putting up a WANTED sign advertising for "a
refuge for men suffragists where women may be admitted to meetings;
apply at once. Gilbert E. Roe, [treasurer], 65 Liberty St." The men were
rescued from social embarrassment when Laidlaw's family banking firm
offered a meeting place that welcomed female reporters.

Though many had other motives – of sexual conquest or liberation, or
bragging rights in their radical circles – for many of the men who joined
the movement in the 1910s, suffragism was part of their progressivism.
Taking their lead from female suffrage groups, sharing podiums with
their wives, marching at the back of suffrage parades, they demonstrated
a new kind of masculinity. Response from male hecklers was pointed
precisely because these men posed a threat to the male order. But they
were no less typical of men of their times than the Rough Riders of
Teddy Roosevelt's San Juan or the Wild West cowboy shows of Buffalo
Bill Cody. Progressivism was for them as much about reforming manhood as asserting it. The Progressive Era was a time of wide debate over
social change, and the campaign for women's suffrage was part of that.

These men joined not a women's cause but a progressive campaign, although one that for all its presumed enlightenment shunned participation by African Americans. Seeing their allegiance to white privilege, W. E. B. Du Bois, a black suffragist, never joined the League and took a guarded view about the likely results of enfranchising women. "There is not the slightest reason for supposing that white women under ordinary circumstances are going to be any more intelligent, liberal or humane toward the black, the poor and the unfortunate than white men are," he wrote. "On the contrary, considering what subjection of a race, a class or a sex must mean, there will undoubtedly manifest itself among women voters at first more prejudice and petty meanness toward Negroes than we have now." Du Bois supported the cause of women's suffrage not because he thought women were more moral than men but because he thought it would spark public debate "on the fundamentals of democracy," a discussion that would accrue to the benefit of the disenfranchised of color, both male and female. If there was indifference among black voters on the issue of women's suffrage, he suggested, it was probably because of "the reactionary attitude of most white women toward our problems." Still, he concluded, "every argument for Negro suffrage is an argument for woman suffrage; every argument for woman suffrage is an argument for Negro suffrage; both are great movements in democracy."

The discussion was further complicated by a crisis facing white manhood. Theodore Roosevelt, who had recovered from a childhood of sickliness by embracing a cult of vigor, now promoted a return to large, white families. The age of the bachelor, some called it, had led to a lower birthrate among native-born whites and caused a backlash against the New Woman, who was better educated, more independent, and more often employed than an earlier generation. As immigrants bulging with satchels and clinging children surged through Ellis Island, Roosevelt expressed fear that these cultural currents would lead to white race suicide. Later, as the nominee of the Progressive Party in 1912, the first presidential candidate nominated by a woman, Hull House reformer Jane Addams, he endorsed the cause. For now, convinced that a woman's first duty was to the nation's demographic future, he argued that women would get the vote when a majority of them insisted on it. Until then, he said, the nation had other priorities, not least of them, the manly business of war.

In a series of columns published in the New York *Tribune* from 1914 to 1917, titled "Are Women People?" Alice Duer Miller, a suffragist who delighted in writing satire, poked fun at male resistance to female emancipation. Commenting on a school board's decision to fire a woman engineer with an exemplary record because of her gender, or the speaker who claimed that girls who study algebra lose their ability to procreate, or U.S. laws requiring women to renounce their American citizenship on marrying foreigners, she was as knowing as she was amusing. She was at her most biting in promoting suffrage. In one column, "Why We Oppose Votes for Men," she made her case. "Men are too emotional to vote," she observed. "Their conduct at baseball games and political conventions shows this, while their innate tendency to appeal to force renders them peculiarly unfit for the task of government."

In fact, the approach of America's participation in World War I divided many members of the Men's League for Woman Suffrage. The intersection of their many causes had coexisted in times of peace. Once war came, many went their separate ways, their other causes taking precedence. Oswald Garrison Villard, who had initiated the League nearly a decade before, wrote the White House, urging President Wilson to disarm and to turn his attention to fighting "the barbaric system of lynching which prevails in various parts of this country." Banker George Peabody, the League's first president, cofounded an Emergency Peace Federation, proposing to "Keep America Out of War and Its Intended Consequences." Max Eastman likewise joined the American Union Against Militarism, urging Wilson to be true to his campaign promise, "He Kept Us Out of War." But their early confidante in male suffrage advocacy, Rabbi Stephen Wise, wrote Wilson that the time had come to answer destiny's call, and join the struggle against lawlessness, for America to become a champion of world democracy. And George Creel, one of the most aggressive tacticians in the League, resigned in April 1917 to become head of Wilson's new U.S. Committee on Public Information, the propaganda arm charged with selling the war to the American public. For most, their suffrage activism took a back seat to issues of war and peace.

As American troops left for Europe to join the trench war horrors of World War I, female suffragists faced a similar dilemma – weighing the perils of pursuing their own political interests at a time of national rallying around the flag. In hopes of winning the vote after the war, Carrie Chapman Catt abandoned her peace activism and volunteered the millions of women in NAWSA's suffrage army for war service. Vowing not to abandon activism during the conflict – a mistake she felt Elizabeth Cady Stanton and Susan B. Anthony had made in pausing their advocacy during the Civil War – Alice Paul meanwhile organized pickets at the White House. Debate raged about whether they were pragmatists or opportunists, patriots or traitors. The tactical decisions moderates and militants made in these critical years would impact the course of the suffrage movement when the world was at war, and long afterward.

9

Campaigning in Wartime

On February 2, 1917, as war fever gripped the nation's capital, President Wilson and First Lady Edith Galt Wilson invited two people to dinner at the White House: Secretary of the Navy Josephus Daniels, whose expertise was critical as Wilson prepared for a war he did not want to fight, and Carrie Chapman Catt, president of the National American Woman Suffrage Association. No record exists of what was said, or what was promised, but if there was a grand bargain for women's suffrage, it likely took place here. All that is known, in Catt's own telling, is that whenever she thereafter sought the president's help for suffrage, he provided it. At the very least, there was a tacit understanding around the table, of loyalty for loyalty. Catt would abandon her principles as a pacifist to commit the considerable regional, state, and federal resources of NAWSA's mighty army of two million women to the war effort. In exchange, there was an implicit understanding that Wilson would afterward endorse a constitutional amendment to enfranchise the women of the United States.

The next day, Secretary of State Robert Lansing announced that the United States had broken off diplomatic relations with Germany. Catt called for a meeting of her Executive Council of One Hundred. A few weeks later, delegates from thirty-six states attended, and debate was heated. On a 63–13 vote, these regional leaders decided that if war came, they would abandon NAWSA's "unbroken custom" of avoiding government jobs until women had the vote. Now, they would "organize

And Yet They Persisted: How American Women Won the Right to Vote, First Edition. Johanna Neuman.
© 2020 John Wiley & Sons, Inc. Published 2020 by John Wiley & Sons, Inc.
Companion website: www.wiley.com/go/Neuman

for war service." In a letter to Wilson announcing the decision, Catt decried "the settlement of international difficulties by bloodshed" as "unworthy of the twentieth century." But if the United States was drawn into war, she said, "We stand ready to serve our country with the zeal and consecration which should ever characterize those who cherish high ideals of the duty and obligation of citizenship." In the name of suffrage, NAWSA's members would sell Liberty Bonds, roll bandages, fundraise for Red Cross and work in factories, on farms, and as enumerators in the Census. They would demonstrate the depth of their patriotism, and their worthiness as citizens, in hopes they would be rewarded afterward with the prize that had long eluded them: the vote.

To some, it was a sacrilege, in suffragist Crystal Eastman's words, a "high handed," "undemocratic," and "inexcusable" betrayal. One biographer called the decision "the most widely criticized act of Catt's life." The New York branch of the Woman's Peace Party removed Catt's name as honorary chairman. Members of the rival National Woman's Party, many pacifists, thought it a contradiction to participate in the war effort, even on the home front, when they were excluded from decision-making. "It is impossible to think that [women] should be asked to wage war for the principle of self-government and to protect it and make great sacrifices, most supreme sacrifices, without having some part in the Government," Elizabeth Selden Rogers told Congress that year.

Alice Paul too had considered whether to suspend suffrage activities during war. Certainly that is what Emmeline Pankhurst, who had taught her much about the battle in England, now suggested to her. But Paul, a pacifist with no interest in war, had as a graduate student studied the American suffrage posture during the Civil War. Then, Elizabeth Cady Stanton and Susan B. Anthony had decided to cease their activism while the nation was at war in hopes of being rewarded at war's end. Instead, Republican reformers in Congress decided that it was "the Negro's Hour," that women would have to wait. Now, Paul felt suffragists had a special obligation in wartime to fight for their rights. Retreating "at high national moments," such as the Civil War, had been a strategic mistake, one that only served to diminish their cause. At its convention in March 1917, Women's Party members debated whether to put all suffrage activity on hold until the war ended, or to become a peace party. Neither appealed to Paul. "Those who wish to work for preparedness, those who wish to work for peace, can do so through organizations for such purpose," she said. "Our organization is dedicated only to the enfranchisement of women." Most members agreed, vowing to continue the fight during the war, in hopes of highlighting "our insistent demand that no action on war or another measure be taken without consent of women."

Scholars have long posited that one legacy of World War I was the emancipation of women. Some have gone so far as to credit the war with providing the tipping point for women's suffrage in the United States, one historian calling their volunteer efforts "indispensable to suffrage victory." This chapter suggests instead that men did not grant women the vote because of their war service but because fighting for their cause during wartime had made them better politicians. Promoting an unpopular cause at a time of flag-waving jingoism was a challenge for both moderates and militants within the movement, one that hardened them as political actors. That they later parlayed this knowledge into pressuring lawmakers and collecting chits was key to their victory. In the meantime, moderates and militants within the movement vied for power and public attention. Their dueling strategies and personal animus divided opinion among activists across the country. It was a war within the war.

The Militants and the Moderates

Alice Paul was the oldest child of a family whose tree was lined with Quaker, American, and British pedigree. "I have practically no ancestor who wasn't a Quaker," she once said. "My father and mother were, and their fathers and mothers were." One branch of her family had participated in the Flushing Remonstrance in 1657, one of the earliest appeals for freedom of religion in America. On her mother's side, she claimed connection to William Penn, founder of the American colony named for him, Pennsylvania. Closer in memory, her great grandfather Charles Stokes and his son-in-law William Parry were Quakers who supported temperance and abolition in the nineteenth century. For her, the Quaker teachings of gender equality and individual conscience were less about religion than service in the public square.

While in graduate school in England, Paul had been drawn to the militant British suffrage movement. Raised in the tradition of giving silent witness to protest, she resonated to the Pankhurst dicta of "Deeds, Not Words." On the streets, she sold copies of the organization's newspaper, *Votes for Women*, made speeches to lunchtime crowds, marched in parades, heckled Winston Churchill, broke stained-glass windows at the Lord Mayor's banquet in the Guild Hall, was imprisoned and force fed at Holloway Jail. As she explained to her mother Tracie, who often read of Paul's activities in the Pennsylvania newspapers, "It was simply a policy of passive resistance & as a Quaker thee ought to approve of that."

After her last arrest, which forced her to prison for a month, she returned to the United States in January 1910, greeted by her family and a handful of reporters. Over the next few months, the 25-year-old Paul gave speeches in which she defended window smashing, compared British suffragettes to American abolitionists, and upbraided Quakers for forgetting "the spirit of democracy." A graduate of Swarthmore, for two years she worked on her doctoral dissertation at the University of Pennsylvania, "Outline of the Legal Position of Women in Pennsylvania 1911." She found time to help activists plan a suffrage parade in Philadelphia. By the time she arrived in Washington, DC to head NAWSA's Congressional Committee, she had concluded that state-by-state efforts to win the vote were too laborious. Convinced the public would respond to spectacle, she vowed to apply visual rhetoric – which had so electrified the suffrage scene in London – to the streets of Washington, DC. Her 1913 pre-Inaugural parade, filled with color and controversy, had thrilled suffrage workers, who gave her a standing ovation at their next convention. But Paul's independence and radicalism horrified suffrage leaders, who booted her from NAWSA.

With Lucy Burns, her associate from their days as the two most prominent Americans in the British suffrage movement, she now formed a new organization, the Congressional Union for Woman Suffrage. Unlike NAWSA, which continued to seek votes both in the states and in Congress, the new society would pursue a singular goal – adoption of a constitutional amendment to the U.S. Constitution. These newly militant suffrage advocates would target Democrats, the party controlling the White House, the Senate, and the House, holding them politically responsible for the failure to act. They would publish a newspaper, *The Suffragist,* known for the beauty of its iconic covers, many designed by political cartoonist Nina Allender, and the lashing bite of its editorials. In everything they did, they would add drama to a movement slogging its way through a maze of state capitols toward Washington, DC.

With both NAWSA and the new Congressional Union lobbying Congress, things began to stir on Capitol Hill. By 1913, a Senate committee voted on women's suffrage for the first time since 1896. Two years later, the House of Representatives voted on the issue for the first time ever. When Wilson traveled to Capitol Hill to deliver his State of the Union address in 1916, members of the Congressional Union finagled tickets in the gallery. Once he began to speak, they unfurled a "Votes for Women" banner over the railing. They and their flag were quickly escorted out. The tactic infuriated Catt, as her lobbyists took flak from congressmen upset by this rupture of decorum. "Nothing about our work was more unpleasant than the need of explaining that we did not agree as to method with the other women working for the same end," said Maude Wood Park, NAWSA's lobbyist. As they heard from congressmen: "Why don't you stop them? ... Why don't you women get together? You can't expect us to vote for you if you can't agree among yourselves."

News of the friction between Catt and Paul broke into print, and younger suffragists urged them to reconcile. At the request of novelist and playwright Zona Gale, Catt met face-to-face with Paul at the Willard Hotel in Washington, DC in December of 1915. Catt became president of NAWSA in 1900, taking the reins from Susan B. Anthony, but left in 1904, to take care of her ailing husband. After the rocky ten-year tenure of Anna Howard Shaw, who was considered a brilliant orator but a weak administrator, Catt had returned. Mindful of the legacy behind her – the pioneering efforts of Anthony, Lucy Stone, and Elizabeth Cady Stanton – she insisted on organizational rigor and a strategic alliance with President Wilson. The wind at her back was an army of millions. Paul, by contrast, was a small player, her party attracting no more than 50,000 at its most robust. Still, her tactics of agitating and protesting were drawing publicity and sparking controversy. While Catt wanted to build bridges to politicians, Paul seemed to want to burn them down.

Between them was a gap of twenty-six years, a generational divide that no doubt influenced their fraught relationship. Catt was schooled in a history of disappointment. After so many losing state campaigns, she was wary of promises from unreliable politicians and fickle voters. Paul had the confidence of youth, sure of the nobility of the fight. Catt was a polished speaker, convinced oratory would sway minds. Paul adhered to the power of symbolic speech. As she began her American activism in 1913, the 28-year-old Paul thought a federal amendment was within her grasp. The 54-year-old Catt worried that she would not live to see a constitutional guarantee of the franchise. "I have always felt that I *enlisted for life* when I went into this movement," Catt had once told Paul, adding, "When you have more experience, you'll know that it's a much longer fight than you have any idea of." To Paul, it sounded as if Catt thought suffrage was unattainable. She had been fighting for a long time.

In college in the 1870s – to overcome her father's lukewarm view of women pursuing education – Carrie Lane paid her own way by washing dishes, working in the school library at Iowa State Agricultural College, and teaching at rural schools on school breaks. Joining the Crescent Literary Society, she toppled a ban on women speaking during meetings, started an all women's debate club, and urged female participation in military drills. Valedictorian of her class, she worked as a law clerk before becoming a schoolteacher and the first female superintendent in Mason City, Iowa. After marriage to newspaper editor Leo Chapman, the couple moved to California. One year later Leo had died of typhoid fever. Carrie stayed in San Francisco, becoming the first female newspaper reporter there. Four years later, she married George Catt, an engineer who encouraged her suffrage activities, allowing her to spend many months on the road each year. She steered NAWSA for one term, resigning in 1904 to take care of George, who died the following year. Now, after steering the New York suffrage campaign, she had returned to the helm. And this time she intended to win.

At the meeting, Catt proposed that the Congressional Union became an affiliate of NAWSA, and offered frequent communication with the main organization. But Catt also demanded that Paul renounce her campaign against Democrats and avoid working in states when NAWSA was conducting ballot initiatives. There was no wiggle room. As likely anticipated by Catt and her team, Paul rejected the terms. At meeting's end, in Paul's telling, Catt turned to her and said, "All I wish to say is 'I will fight you to the last ditch.'" By all accounts, the two never spoke privately again, conversing awkwardly if at all on podiums they shared. Mostly, they communicated through the rival campaigns they now waged for suffrage.

The 1916 Election

By 1916, ten states had enacted suffrage, most in the West. With Illinois' passage of presidential suffrage, nearly one-fifth – 91 of 531 – of Electoral College votes were held by suffrage states. If women were not yet equal citizens in the eyes of the law, they were already factors in the nation's politics. At the Republican National Convention in Chicago in June 1916, and at the Democratic National Convention in St. Louis two weeks later, both parties wrestled with the question of women's suffrage, only to hide behind the fortress of states rights, the original constitutional compromise. The Republican Party platform said it "favors the extension of the suffrage to women, but recognizing the right of each State to settle this question for itself." The Democratic plank, written by Wilson, recommended "the extension of the franchise to the women of the country by the States upon the same terms as men."

Frustrated, Catt called an emergency meeting of NAWSA to announce her "Winning Plan." She had first outlined the plan a few months earlier in a meeting of her executive council, made up of national officers and presidents of state organizations. The plan, approved in a solemn recording of signatures, was a strategically coordinated, multi-pronged attack on winning a federal amendment while keeping up pressure to post more wins in the states. Using a huge map of the United States hung on a wall of a basement room in an Atlantic City hotel, she pointed to four regions of the country. Each would have a different strategy. For those states in the West and in Illinois where women could vote, she asked NAWSA chapters to lobby for resolutions from their state legislatures seeking congressional action on a constitutional amendment. In states such as New York where popular opinion seemed to be tilting toward suffrage, she urged chapters to get legislators to place a suffrage initiative on the ballot. In states where public opinion seemed less certain, she urged chapters to seek presidential suffrage only, something legislators could grant without a ballot referendum. And for southern states, she wanted NAWSA affiliates to try for primary or municipal suffrage, which tracked with state rights. That too could be granted by legislative fiat.

Facing a choice of working in the states or at the federal level, Catt said, "We must do both and we must do them together." She would fund the initiative with the more than $1 million bequest left to NAWSA by Miriam Leslie, widow of a prominent New York publisher. The family had contested Leslie's will, and there had been court battles, but now Catt distributed $200,000 in salaries and earmarked $400,000 to the organization's newspaper, the *Woman Citizen*, formerly the *Woman's Journal*. The rest would go to fund her Winning Plan. She warned that secrecy was of the utmost importance. Everything was to be ready when Congress reconvened in January. Their only hope was to take anti-suffragists, such as the liquor lobby, by surprise. "We care not a gingersnap about anything but that federal amendment," she said. As she explained later, they would use "the political dynamite in the victories gained in the States as a means of blasting through to success at Washington."

Paul too felt it was time for women to flex their new political muscles. In September 1915, she called the first-ever convention of female voters, held at the Panama-Pacific Exposition in San Francisco. An 18,000-foot-long petition was unveiled with 500,000 signatures on a suffrage petition to Congress. Delegate Sara Bard Field drove the petition to Washington, DC, where Paul arranged for her to present the mass document to Congress, and to meet with President Woodrow Wilson. Like Catt, Paul was looking toward January. "We want to make woman suffrage the dominant political issue from the moment Congress reconvenes," she said. "We want to have Congress open in the middle of a veritable suffrage cyclone."

Both camps were technically non-partisan, but Paul believed in holding the party in power – in this case the Democrats – to task for failure to enact a constitutional amendment. If the Democrats failed to deliver, her organization – its name changed from the Congressional Union to the National Woman's Party – would campaign against them, and that included Democrats who had voted for suffrage. "The Woman's Party has no candidates and but one plank, the enfranchisement of the women of America through Federal amendment," Maud

Younger said at the keynote address at Chicago's Blackstone Theater. "With enough women in each state organized to hold the balance of power, the women voters may determine the presidency of the United States." Catt disagreed. Schooled by Susan B. Anthony in the dogma of non-partisanship, she believed that suffrage victory would require allies from both parties. And she thought it particularly shortsighted to focus on the Democratic Party in light of virulent opposition by overwhelmingly Democratic southerners.

As the 1916 campaign began, a sanguine Wilson paid a visit to the NAWSA Convention, speaking to suffrage activists for the first time not at the White House but on their turf. A longtime opponent of a women's suffrage amendment, the year before he had announced that he was voting for women's suffrage in his home state of New Jersey. "I have not come to fight against anybody but with somebody," he said. Noting the progress made since 1848, he predicted "the tide is rising to meet the motion" and the cause would soon be "triumphant." Winning suffrage would require "moving masses," and activists would just have to "wait for them to follow." Anna Howard Shaw, no longer president but still on the organization's board, replied, "We have waited long enough for the vote, we want it now." For her part, Paul privately lobbied Republican presidential candidate Charles Evans Hughes to endorse suffrage – and he became the first major party candidate to do so. (Former President Theodore Roosevelt had done so in 1912, as the candidate of his progressive Bull Moose Party.) She also sent speakers on a tour of already-franchised states, urging female voters to defeat Democrats in the twelve suffrage states – a roster of national speakers that included Harriot Blatch, Sara Bard Field, and Inez Milholland.

Inez Milholland was the epitome of the "New Woman" so lauded in the early twentieth-century cultural lore. She was a Vassar graduate, a working lawyer who filed appeals for convicts on Death Row, and a labor activist who had marched on picket lines with striking garment industry workers. She was also a stunning woman, with her eyes "a deep hue of the jewel called aquamarine" and her spirit like "the lightening." Her oratory was modern, not the thunderous style of Anna Howard Shaw but the epitome of a self-assured, independent mind. She was full of contradictions – an advocate of free love as well as a loving wife to Eugen Boissevain, a socialite as well as a socialist, an heiress with a sense of social justice. When she left New York in early October with her sister Vida on a speaking tour of suffrage states in the West, Inez Milholland Boissevain was 30 years old and quite ill.

Within two weeks, suffering from tonsillitis, she was cancelling appearances. By Salt Lake City, she was tripling her medication. Finally, in the middle of a speech to 1,500 at Blanchard Hall in Los Angeles in late October, she fainted. She had just issued her signature line, "Mr. President, how long must women wait for liberty?" As a reporter for the *Los Angeles Times* described it, "In the middle of an intense sentence she crumpled up like a wilted white rose" and lay on the stage. Alice Paul urged her to rally, especially in time for the final appeal on election eve to enfranchised female voters in Chicago. "Surely she can pull through this," Paul telegraphed. Hospitalized at Los Angeles Good Samaritan Hospital, Inez Milholland died a month later, on November 25, of what is believed to be pernicious anemia.

In the end, Paul's effort to punish Democrats by campaigning against them in 1916 proved elusive. Wilson was re-elected in a close contest, winning 277 electoral votes to Hughes' 254. In Illinois, the only state that counted women's votes separately, analysts reported that a majority of women had voted for Hughes. In California, Wilson won by 3,420 votes out of 928,452 votes cast, and the state's 13 Electoral College votes made the difference.

In the House, Democrats lost sixteen seats, giving the Republicans a 216–214 majority. Despite this, Democrats managed to hold on to control of the House by forming a political alliance with the three Progressives and one Socialist elected to Congress. Still, they had been defeated in Illinois, Indiana, Iowa, Kansas, Louisiana, Maine, Maryland, Michigan, Montana, New Hampshire, New Jersey, New York, Oklahoma, West Virginia, and Wisconsin. How many female voters helped topple incumbents in Illinois, Kansas, and Montana is unknown. But the fear of a new female voting bloc instilled by Paul's campaign was not lost on Democrats. Rep. John E. Raker, a California Democrat and chairman of the Committee on Woman Suffrage, warned southern Democrats accustomed to seniority and committee chairmanships that they "held their positions because women in western states had voted Democratic in 1916." Rep. J. Campbell Cantrill of Kentucky likewise warned his southern colleagues not to commit political suicide by opposing women's suffrage.

In December, Alice Paul arranged a memorial service for her star speaker, Inez Milholland Boissevain, who had given her last breath for the cause. Paul convinced House Speaker Champ Clark, no friend of Wilson's, to let her use Statuary Hall for the ceremony, on Christmas Day, marking the first time the U.S. Capitol had been used to memorialize a woman, and the first time for someone not a member of Congress. Paul banned controversial subjects such as birth control and rights of African American women. Instead, using the National Woman's Party colors, Paul hung banners of purple, white, and gold from marble pillars, with laurel and cedar decorating the dais. Some 1,000 people attended the 4 p.m. service, where Inez was lionized as a martyr for the cause, her last public words – "How long must women wait for liberty?" – now the party's iconic message. The image of Milholland atop a white horse leading suffrage parades became a searing symbol of idealism for many suffragists. As the National Woman's Party newspaper, *The Suffragist*, put it, "The death of Inez Milholland Boissevain has fanned … resentment into a burning flame." Paul had turned her celebrity orator into a martyr for the cause, much as British suffrage leaders did for Emily Wilding Davison, who had died after throwing herself under the King's horse at the 1913 Derby at Epsom Downs. After the memorial, Paul sought a meeting with Wilson.

Picketing the White House

On January 9, a delegation of 300 National Woman's Party (NWP) members took their seats in the East Room. One after the other, they invoked the late Milholland's memory, pleading for presidential relief. Elizabeth Thatcher Kent, wife of California congressman William Kent, read the resolution from the Statuary Hall service, asking Wilson to "intercede to stop such waste of human life and effort" of women who are "exhausting their lives in waiting and appeal." She pleaded, "Will you not be moved to act so that by her death Inez Milholland Boissevain shall have delivered from the sacrifice of her life her countrymen?" Labor activist Maud Younger all but lectured the president, saying it was up to him to decide "whether the life of this brilliant, dearly loved woman whose glorious death we commemorate today shall be the last sacrifice of life demanded of American women in their struggle for self-government."

Wilson turned white with anger, and his manner, said *McCall's Magazine*, became "chilled," "cold," and "icy." He was a son of the South who thought politics was a male purview best left to men. In 1884, while teaching female college students, he had confessed his revulsion on hearing a woman speak in public. He recounted "the chilled scandalized feeling that always overcomes me when I see and hear women speak in public." By 1912, running for president after serving as governor of New Jersey, he confided to a publicity aide that he was "definitely and irreconcilably opposed to woman suffrage." As assistant Frank P. Stockbridge recalled their conversation, "Woman's place was in the home, and the type of woman who took an active part in the suffrage agitation was totally abhorrent to him." To appease female voters in places such as Colorado, which had enfranchised women in 1893, he developed a stock answer that suffrage was a state issue, to be decided by local voters. Now, feeling blindsided by their plea for suffrage when he thought he was simply meeting with the activists to receive a plaque from the

Milholland memorial, he dodged their emotional appeal by citing his role as titular head of the Democratic Party. "I can't as leader of my party do anything that my party doesn't want me to do or take any stand that my party doesn't want me to take," he said. With that, he walked out of the room. Furious, he declared he would never again meet with a delegation of women's suffrage activists.

The women trooped back to headquarters, near the White House at 21 Madison Place on Lafayette Square, for a meeting of the party's advisory board. Harriot Stanton Blatch had joined the NWP the year before, after the failed 1915 suffrage initiative in New York had soured her on conventional methods of activism. Now she and Paul enacted a rehearsed presentation. Blatch reviewed the record, outlining all the tactics by which the party had pursued its goals, calling for new ideas. Paul (Fig. 9.1) put forth a proposal to picket the White House, the first such political protest at the presidential residence in American history. She argued that it would literally confront the president where he lived – and ensure continued publicity even if the United States joined a war already raging in Europe. True to her Quaker roots, she proposed that these protesters were not to speak unless spoken to, serving as silent witnesses to their own grievance. Their signs would speak for them. They were to remain outside the gates, in three-hour shifts, every day of the week except Sundays, no matter the weather, for as long as it took to win congressional approval for a constitutional amendment.

Privately, Paul and Blatch had disagreed over the tactic. Blatch saw picketing as demeaning to women, especially those in the West who already had the right to vote. It was, in her view, a tactic of "weaponless disenfranchised women." She favored more agitation, along the lines of British suffragettes. But now she played the good soldier, endorsing Paul's idea and calling for volunteers to serve as "silent sentinels of liberty and self-government." Dozens of hands went up. Alva Belmont, the party's financial benefactor, no doubt pledged funds for banners, signs, and food. When Inez's father John Milholland learned of the plan at dinner from Sara Bard Field, he gave his blessings. They would start the next day.

On January 10, 1917, with Alice Paul leading the procession, twelve women left party headquarters at 10 a.m. and walked to the east and west gates of the White House. Wearing coats to protect against the frigid air, carrying banners in the party's tricolors, they stood six per entrance, standing three to a side. Ever attentive to the symbolism of words, Paul called them not protesters or pickets but Silent Sentinels, bearing words, often the president's own, to buttress their case against him. One sign said, "Mr. President, What Will You Do for Woman Suffrage?" That the protest was directed at him was not lost on Wilson,

Figure 9.1 When she organized pickets in front of the White House – the first political protests at the presidential residence in American history – Alice Paul was 32 years old, a reformer who learned suffrage tactics in Britain while working for Emmeline Pankhurst's militant suffragettes. She believed in holding the party in power – in this case the Democrats, who controlled the White House, the Senate, and the House – responsible for the failure to enact women's suffrage. Mainstream suffragists tried to distance themselves from her tactics, worried such demonstrations would be seen as unpatriotic at a time when America was preparing to fight in World War I. But Paul, who was descended from Quakers for centuries, believed the pickets were important publicity tools, a policy of passive resistance needed to keep the issue at the forefront even at a time of war. Harris & Ewing, *Source:* Library of Congress Prints and Photographs Division.

who regularly smiled as he tipped his hat toward the picketers. Later, amid "a cruel winter," he instructed guards to invite them in for hot coffee, an offer the picketers declined. They were there to protest, not socialize. Already, Paul had achieved her goal – on the first day, nearly 200 newspapers had taken note, many placing news of the protest on their front pages (Fig. 9.2).

Public opinion was decidedly mixed. The Baltimore *Sun* said the picketing demonstrated "the unfitness of those who take part in it to participate in public affairs." Calling them "selfish and unpatriotic," the

Figure 9.2 Beginning in January 1917, suffragists picketed the White House in shifts of three hours, every day of the week except Sundays, in frigid weather, for almost a year. At first authorities looked the other way, eager not to turn them into martyrs for a cause. Once the nation went to war, authorities began arrests, on charges of obstructing sidewalk traffic. Sent to Occoquan Workhouse, a notoriously filthy Virginia prison, many were beaten and others went on a hunger strike, enduring tube feeding. To maximize publicity, Paul arranged special protests on occasions such as Labor Day or Lincoln's Birthday. Particularly effective was College Day, when female students and graduates from Bryn Mawr, Goucher, Oberlin, Smith, Stanford, Swarthmore, University of Kansas, University of Missouri, University of Pennsylvania, Vassar, Washington College of Law, Wellesley, and Western Reserve walked the line, demonstrating gains women had made since the 1830s, when activists first urged educational opportunities for women. *Source:* Library of Congress Prints and Photographs Division.

paper added, "When they seek to harass and embarrass the President in the face of national dangers and duties such as he confronts at present, with what patience can their claims to citizenship be considered?" Even the *Boston Globe*, a pro-suffrage paper, feared they had "harmed the cause." Some members of the NWP board resigned in protest, and some readers canceled their subscriptions to the party's newspaper. And when, in June, Paul sent out a fundraising letter to supporters, Myrtle Price wrote from Kansas that she was a supporter no more, outraged by the "foolish, childish methods you have used trying to harass our overburdened president." In Congress, Ohio Representative Henry Ivory Emerson called picketing "unbecoming" and Representative Thomas

Harrison of Virginia, a member of the Rules Committee, vowed he would never vote to create a suffrage committee unless pickets were removed from the Congress and the White House.

Catt wrote Paul an open letter, urging her to withdraw the pickets. "The picketing has aroused serious antagonism," Catt wrote. "For the sake of the political freedom of women," she urged Paul to remove her pickets "and with them a cause of hostility in the minds of people who would otherwise be friends of the suffrage movement." Others were thrilled, cheered by the advent of a new wind in suffrage tactics. "I think the picketing is splendid and I will come and do it myself," wrote Elizabeth Seldon Rogers, wife of a prominent New York doctor and sister-in-law of Secretary of War Henry Stimson. Gilson Gardner, the Washington reporter for the Scripps newspaper chain, whose wife Helen was a suffragist, had high praise for the picketers. "During the 18 years I have been a newspaper correspondent in Washington, I have seen no more impressive sight than the spectacle of the pickets surrounding the White House," he wrote, describing "women of all ages, marching in a rain that almost froze as it fell." Many were in their twenties, such as Rose Winslow, a union organizer. Others were in their forties, veterans of a Progressive Era coalition that had tackled political bosses and corrupt city halls across the country. Then there was Mary Nolan, of Jacksonville, Florida, born before the 1848 Seneca Falls convention, who when she joined the picket line was 75 years old.

Over the next 18 months, an estimated two thousand American women served at least one shift as a Silent Sentinel at the White House. To maximize publicity, Paul arranged special protests to mark occasions such as Labor Day or Lincoln's Birthday. Particularly effective was College Day, when female students and graduates from Bryn Mawr, Goucher, Oberlin, Smith, Stanford, Swarthmore, University of Kansas, University of Missouri, University of Pennsylvania, Vassar, Washington College of Law, Wellesley, and Western Reserve walked the lines. Overcoming howling winds and blustery conditions, they walked, including Elsie Hill (Vassar), daughter of Representative Ebenezer Hill of Connecticut, and Eliza Hardy Lord (Western Reserve), first woman dean in the county. Their collective presence demonstrated the gains women had made in education since the time in the 1830s when women's rights activists had first demanded that colleges open their doors to women. It also showcased an assertion of equal citizenship, requiring only the vote to complete the journey. "No one undertaking captured quite so much advertising as did the picketing of the White House," wrote Eleanor Booth Simmons of the New York *Sun*. Many daily newspapers gave the protest front-page coverage. Weeklies followed suit. "Before Alice Paul and the pickets came, days would pass when the word suffrage didn't appear in the dispatches," wrote Simmons. "Since their activities, no word occurs more frequently."

World War I

When Jeannette Rankin (Fig. 9.3) arrived in Washington in early April 1917 at the age of 36 to be sworn in as the first female member of the U.S. Congress, she knew that her first vote might prove her most

Figure 9.3 Jeannette Rankin was a suffragist who helped women win the vote in Montana in 1914. Two years later, at the age of 36, she became the first woman elected to Congress. On her arrival in Washington, DC she was feted by Carrie Chapman Catt, of the mainstream National American Woman Suffrage Association, and Alice Paul of the smaller National Woman's Party. The first vote she would cast as the first female member of Congress was on President Wilson's declaration of war against Germany. Worried that a no vote would hurt suffrage, Catt urged Rankin to vote yes despite her pacifist principles. Paul urged her to vote no. In the end, she did vote no, and newspapers mischaracterized her as crying on the House floor, critics saying it proved that women were too emotional to hold public office. In her official portrait, holding a copy of the *Washington Post* front page that reported her victory, she is seen here as a solitary figure. *Source:* House of Representatives Art Collection.

controversial. Suffragists surged forward to welcome her, in an exuberant display of pride. Privately Catt was appalled that an "unlettered" woman had been elected as the first female member of Congress. Publicly, she called Rankin "the savior of suffrage" and hosted a breakfast in her honor at the Shoreham Hotel, sitting to her right. On Rankin's left sat Alice Paul, who urged her to vote against war. Sandwiched between the pragmatic Catt and the fiery Paul, Rankin was quite literally boxed in. "There will be many times when I will make mistakes," she said. "I need your encouragement and support. I know I will get it."

That evening Woodrow Wilson delivered a Declaration of War Message to a joint session of Congress. His opening line was, "Gentlemen of the Congress." But in fact much pressure fell on Rankin. It was not that her vote would make the difference – the Senate acceded quickly, 82–6, and the House tally four days later was 373–50. But as the first vote of the first woman ever to serve in Congress, her decision was much debated outside the House. Could a woman, not then qualified to serve in the military, send others to die? Her brother Wellington Rankin urged his sister "to vote a man's vote," warning that otherwise she risked backlash from male voters who would see in her opposition the feminization of politics. Friends in the movement pleaded with her to vote for war, fearing otherwise she would hurt chances for suffrage. Paul visited the morning of the vote to tell her "it would be a tragedy for the first woman ever in Congress to vote for war." Harriet Laidlaw, a longtime friend who like Catt had left the Peace Party to volunteer for war service, warned Rankin that a no vote on war could doom suffrage chances. One aide recalled, "I could not imagine her voting for war; neither could I imagine her letting her friends down." Later Rankin said, "The hardest part of the vote was the fact that the suffragists were divided and many of my beloved friends said that you will ruin the suffrage movement if you vote against war."

Reporters covering the 3 a.m. vote exaggerated her demeanor, portraying her, and by extension all women, as too emotional for the business of politics. "The clerk again called her name. She started slightly, passed her hand over her eyes and seemed overcome with emotion," reported the Chicago *Tribune*. When the clerk called for the second time she "hesitated, finally staggered to her feet, and in a choking voice gasped out, 'I want to stand by my country, but I cannot vote for war.'" There was a ban on speeches during a roll call. To a chorus of "Vote! Vote!" she said (gasping, in some accounts), "I vote no."

The vote set off a media furor. The president of the all-male New York Aero Club, formed in 1905, pointed to Rankin's antics as proof that women in office would lead to "semi-emasculation of the electorate." There were also defenders. Asked if Rankin had cried, her colleague

Fiorello LaGuardia replied, "I could not see because of the tears in my own eyes." Months later, during a House hearing on suffrage, a witness cited Rankin's alleged crying as evidence of "woman's inability to support the strains of a war council." Congressman John Raker of California, who had sat within four feet of Rankin on the House floor that night, rebutted the allegation. "That statement that Miss Rankin cried is absolutely false." And back home in Montana, suffragist Grace Erickson praised Rankin for "the sob of a mother's heart. By virtue of the heroic stand of Jeannette Rankin I herein voice our appreciation."

Wilson, in his declaration of war, had placed great weight on the need to fight to make the world "safe for democracy." Paul now made rhetorical use of the phrase on the picket line, using the president's own words to pillory his position on women's suffrage. "President Wilson Is Deceiving the World When He Appears As the Prophet of Democracy," read one banner. "President Wilson Has Opposed Those Who Demand Democracy For This Country," read another. Paul delighted in taunting him. After Wilson's declaration of war speech on April 2, she pulled out one quote soon featured on suffrage banners. "We shall fight for the things which we have always held nearest to our hearts – for democracy, for the right of those who submit to authority to have a voice in their own governments," Wilson had said. Years later, in an oral history interview, Paul said that this skewering of Wilson for his own words – not the picketing – is what made the protesters militant. "This going out and standing there with our beautiful banners wasn't anything very militant," she said. Using Wilson's own words against him, she added, "That's when the militancy really began."

On June 20, representatives from the new Russian government visited the White House. After the abdication of Czar Nicholas II in February, Alexander Kerensky, a socialist, was named Minister of Justice of a new, short-lived revolutionary government. He instituted many reforms, such as freedom of the press and the abolition of ethnic and religious discrimination. He also prepared to introduce universal suffrage. As his envoys approached the White House gates, they saw Paul's Silent Sentinels with a banner that read, "To the Russian Envoys: We the women of America tell you that America is not a democracy. Twenty million American women are denied the right to vote. President Wilson is the chief opponent of their national enfranchisement. Help us make this nation really free. Tell our government it must liberate its people before it can claim free Russia as an ally." So incendiary was the message that lunchtime crowds grabbed the banner and ripped the fabric from its frame. To many, the specter of American citizens seeking to embarrass an American president as he sat down to negotiate with leaders of a foreign country was an act of treason. Several resigned from the NWP, including one member from Pennsylvania who announced, "I am an American before I am a suffragist." To Paul, such departures constituted what one supporter called "a healthy pruning."

Until the war, the Wilson administration had done its best to ignore the picketers at the president's gates, eager not to turn them into martyrs for the cause. Privately, Wilson dismissed them as irritants "bent upon making their cause as obnoxious as possible." Once war was declared, however, public sentiment turned. Sailors ripped at the picketers' signs, schoolboys stole souvenir banners and rowdies shouted, "Send them over to the Kaiser!" When she caught sight of suffragists picketing the White House, Dee Richardson, a soldier's mother, grew so enraged she lunged at Hazel Hunkins, spitting on her banner and sending her scrambling up a fence ledge while shrieking, "You are a dirty yellow traitor."

Within eighteen months, 500 American women had been arrested, and 170 had been jailed for obstructing sidewalk traffic. Mary Church Terrell, former president of the National Association of Colored Women, recalls in her memoirs that sometimes she walked the line with her daughter Phyllis. She said they missed the day when arrests began. Many were jailed at the Occoquan Workhouse in Virginia, a jail so unsanitary that it had been "discarded ten years before as unfit to hold a human being." They resented that they were thrown in with common criminals, not treated as political prisoners. "The sight of two negro girl prisoners combing out each other's lice and dressing their kinky hair in such a way as to discourage permanently a return of the vermin did not produce in us exactly a feeling of recreation," wrote one white suffragist in jail with black prisoners.

Drawn to the NWP, Louisine Havemeyer, one of the biggest collectors of impressionist art in New York, told Alice Paul she would support the cause financially and ceremoniously, but wanted no part of militancy. But Paul knew the value of a celebrity arrest, knew that Havemeyer would garner new publicity for the pickets. So she asked her to come to Washington, DC to participate in an event in which she would burn Woodrow Wilson in effigy in Lafayette Square. Havemeyer said she agreed because "how could I do less" when others had already gone to jail. After five days in jail, the 63-year-old was radicalized. "Sparks of indignation snapped within," she later wrote. "Where was my Uncle Sam? Where was the liberty my fathers fought for? Where the democracy our boys were fighting for?"

On November 14, 1917, in an evening dubbed the Night of Terror, Occoquan's Superintendent W. H. Whittaker ordered guards to club, beat, and torture suffrage prisoners. Dora Lewis, thrown into a cell, hit her head on an iron bed and collapsed. Her cellmate Alice

Cosu suffered a heart attack. Lucy Burns was stripped naked, beaten, her hands chained to cell bars above her head, and left there for the night. Women were thrown into men's cells. "During the time that we were being forced into the cells the guards kept up an uproar, shouting, banging the iron doors, clanging bars, making a terrifying noise," recalled Eunice Dana Brannan. "I could not sleep, having a sense of constant danger."

So violent was the encounter at Occoquan, and so widespread the publicity it received, that it provoked an unexpected backlash against the White House. Representative Charles A. Lindbergh, whose son was the famed young pilot, sent Wilson a detailed description of the mistreatment, urging him to take responsibility. Wilson appointed a physician, Dr. W. Gwynn Gardiner, to investigate conditions at Occoquan. He reported that the prisoners swallowed the feeding tube "willingly." Gilson Gardner, a journalist whose wife Helen was incarcerated at Occoquan, warned Wilson that arresting "women of prominence and refinement," such as Eunice Dana Brannan, daughter of the late New York *Sun* publisher Charles A. Dana and wife of a prominent New York doctor, was an act of "political unwisdom." Vira Whitehouse, president of the New York State Woman Suffrage Party, no fan of picketing, wrote to complain of the ill treatment. Ever decorous, Wilson wrote back saying, "No real harshness of method is being used, these ladies are submitting to the artificial feeding without resistance" and no abuses "have as yet been disclosed."

Dudley Malone had stumped for Wilson on the campaign trail in 1916, telling female voters in California that if they voted for the president, he would "do all he could to help them obtain a national vote." In July 1917, he and two other members of the Men's League for Woman Suffrage – Frederick C. Howe and Amos Pinchot – watched as sixteen picketers were tried, each sentenced to sixty days in the workhouse. Later Malone went to the White House and urged Wilson to free the pickets. When he refused, Malone resigned his lucrative job as collector of the Port Authority in New York. Wilson considered Malone a close ally, telling aide Edward House, "I know of nothing that has gone more to the quick with me or that has seemed to me more tragical than Dudley's conduct, which came upon me like a bolt out of the blue. I was stricken by it as I have been by few things in my life."

On hearing of Malone's gesture, female suffragists were ecstatic. "Although we disagree with you on the question of picketing, every suffragist must be grateful to you for the gallant support you are giving our cause," wrote Whitehouse. Harriet Laidlaw agreed, telling a reporter, "I was thrilled.... I didn't dream any man would do such a chivalrous thing for us. It can't fail to have a splendid effect on the voting men in our referendum this fall." Male suffragists were more suspicious of Malone's motives, noting his role representing them in court. As James Lees Laidlaw told the New York *Sun*, the results of Malone' s action "would depend somewhat on whether he got out and rolled up his sleeves for Votes for Women." Aside from his membership in the Men's League, there is no record that Malone ever did.

Like Wilson, Catt was convinced the pickets were hurting the cause, and she and her allies did everything they could to distance themselves from tactics they viewed as radical. Harriet Laidlaw visited National Woman's Party headquarters, asking leaders to stop the picketing, and stopped in at newsrooms to urge editors not to confuse the efforts of mainstream suffragists with those of these militant protesters. "We have a distinct feeling of shame that the only notable record of ... disloyalty in this heterogeneous melting pot of a nation ... should emanate from the suffragists," said Laidlaw, observing that if Alice Paul had truly "transplanted" British tactics to the United States, she would sign up for war service.

At a parade in New York in advance of the 1917 suffrage referendum, organizers made sure to counter any impression that women were not patriotic. "There was none of the dash and color of the banner parade two years before," recalled one marcher. "The mood was serious ... Dark clothes were worn instead of white." One group of marchers featured women whose sons, husbands or brothers were serving in the military, and when it passed, it "stirred the people to greatest applause." Another contingent saw nurses and Red Cross workers in uniform. A slogan committee insured that the messaging was rigorous, with the effect that "from first banner to last sigh," the parade had all the appearance of "a walking speech." One series of boards, aimed at defusing the shibboleth that women didn't really want the vote, contained the signatures of one million New York women, collected in door-to-door canvassing in each district. Another reported the party raised $7.1 million for the Liberty Loan campaign, demonstrating, wrote the *Times*, "the patriotic contributions of women."

Suffragists did not have the field to themselves. Alice Hill Chittenden, president of the New York State Association Opposed to Woman Suffrage, responded to Wilson's preparedness campaign by raising $46,000 for the Red Cross. Concluding the war was no time for partisanship, she urged male voters to defeat women's suffrage, saying, "The suggestion that [the state] shall offer women the political payment of a vote for war services is a direct slur on woman's patriotism.... "A truly patriotic woman wants no reward for her work."

By contrast, Paul insisted that the goal of continuing to picket at wartime was not to criticize the decision that men had made to go to war but "to remind constantly the president and the people ... that American women are not enfranchised and that we cannot have a true democracy until they are." The party's records suggest the organization may have lost as many as 10,000 members over the decision, but if so, Paul never wavered. She had the financial backing of Alva Belmont, and a magic touch with the newspapers.

Unlike white mainstream suffragists, who saw the war as an opportunity to press for the vote, many black women viewed the conflict in Europe as an opening to gain recognition of African Americans as citizens. They linked the "war to preserve democracy" abroad not to women's suffrage but to black civil rights. African Americans had always served their nation, from the Revolutionary War to the Spanish–American War. Their loyalty was not always recognized. "The race would be patriotic in every instance," said educator Nannie Burroughs, "but must at the same time contend for a democracy at home that will include them."

President Wilson, a southerner with little empathy for the black community, had almost single-handedly resegregated the federal work-force after previous presidents had opened government jobs to African Americans. Soon, the Wilson administration would allow black troops to join the armed forces – about 360,000 served during the war, 200,000 abroad – but insist on segregation. They not only served apart, without commissions, but often in the most menial jobs. In response, African American women formed new organizations, including the Circle for Negro War Relief, with the goal of "promoting the welfare of Negro soldiers and their dependent families." With less of a safety net than white soldiers, club members saw that "the negro soldier's absence will be felt more keenly than ... [that] of any other soldiers in ranks, for ... colored troops represent the most impoverished class in the United States." W. E. B. Du Bois had called for a closing of the ranks, a salute of the black community during a time of war, in hopes that at its end would come a reward of equal citizenship. For many black women, becoming a military nurse conveyed the same claim as that of the black soldier. When forced to work apart, they did so. The National Association of Colored Graduate Nurses fought discrimination in the Red Cross, which barred their service. And when invited to participate in mainstream organizations, they did that too.

When the government organized the Council of National Defense Woman's Committee to achieve food conservation and production of knitted goods, Anna Howard Shaw, former NAWSA president, was named chair. The National Association of Colored Women joined as a member organization. In some states, such as California, black women joined the state's interracial Defense Council. In others, such as Illinois, they organized a separate Committee on Colored Women. In Jacksonville,

Florida, Eartha White organized the Colored Women's Section of the Council of National Defense, to affiliate with Shaw's committee. "Our women ... want the chance to serve the soldier directly and to face with him the dangers of shot and shell," explained the *Savannah Tribune*. "They want the chance to die, if need be."

As the nation returned from war, suffragists lobbied Congress – and a more willing president – to enact the Nineteenth Amendment. In this important marker in the centuries-long fight for the right, they would attempt to parlay their war service – or their war protests – into a constitutional amendment. War had offered a platform, not a guarantee.

10

The Long Road to Ratification

As the new Congress assembled in 1919 after a wave election that changed its leadership from Democrat to Republican, the House enacted the Susan B. Anthony Amendment, now called House Resolution No. 1. Unlike the previous year, when members of the House approved the measure by one vote, this time the vote was 304–89, well above the two-thirds majority required. On June 3, the Senate began its two-day deliberation. James Eli Watson, a Republican senator from Indiana, urged a short debate. The issue, he said, had been discussed "as have but few other questions that have ever engaged the thought and the attention of the American people.... It has been debated on the floors of both bodies and has been discussed throughout the country in every forum where the people are wont to gather to listen to public discussions. What is needed now is action and not speech."

When asked why the vote for women took so long, analysts often talk about the legacy of coverture laws that restricted women's legal, educational, and economic rights, the support suffragists gave to controversial causes such as abolition, temperance, free love and divorce reform that tagged them as figures of controversy, and the stubborn hold of male patriarchy. Sometimes there is debate too about whether suffrage leaders, both moderates and militants, hurt their own cause by privileging the vote for white, educated women. How different this history would look if instead they had campaigned for universal suffrage. But when asked how women finally persuaded men to share the vote,

And Yet They Persisted: How American Women Won the Right to Vote, First Edition. Johanna Neuman.
© 2020 John Wiley & Sons, Inc. Published 2020 by John Wiley & Sons, Inc.
Companion website: www.wiley.com/go/Neuman

the record suggests a different answer: political self-interest. Only when men deduced that their power was best protected by allowing women to enter the polity did the cause prevail. Utah Democrat William Henry King had been a virulent opponent of women's suffrage. In a poignant speech during the Senate's two-day debate, he said, "I am in the unfortunate position of being unable to vote in harmony with my convictions. The mandate of my party and the people of my state requires that I vote for the submission of an amendment to the Constitution providing for woman suffrage." Men like King agreed to share power only after women neutralized business foes and marshaled the muscle of female voters already enfranchised by their states.

By the time the House and the Senate passed the Nineteenth Amendment in 1919, much of the country – twenty-seven of forty-eight states and one territory (Alaska) – had already granted women the vote in some state or federal elections. In presidential elections, 339 of the 531 Electoral College votes needed to win the presidency – well above the 267 required – came from states that had removed the gender barrier to the voting booth. Great swaths of territory remained safely in the hands of the male political establishment – from the Northeast population centers of New Jersey and Pennsylvania to the solid South of the Old Confederacy. But like the tail wagging the dog, the states, where the founders had vested so much power over elections, had become the engines of social change.

As the final debate over the Nineteenth Amendment gripped the Senate floor and as the subsequent campaign for ratification rumbled through the halls of state legislatures, the voices of male superiority and nativist sentiment had a final say in the court of public opinion. Some in the South, notably Mississippi's ardent segregationist James Vardaman, calculated that a vote to empower white women could be used in the region to offset or even prevent any incursion into the polity by African Americans, male or female. And some in the North, led by Everett Wheeler's Man Suffrage Association, mounted a desperate, cross-country lobbying campaign to resist the feminization of politics to the bitter end.

The Congressional Showdown

Even before the end of World War I on November 11, 1918, women's suffrage had become a political football. House Judiciary Committee Chairman Edwin Yates Webb, a North Carolina Democrat, wanted to keep jurisdiction over all women's suffrage issues in his committee, where they were routinely smothered. John Raker of California, chairman of the new Woman Suffrage Committee, wanted sole jurisdiction. House Speaker Champ Clark of Missouri, whose daughter Genevieve had been lobbying him on the issue, resolved the conflict by delaying the issue's consideration until the next session of Congress, when all such bills would be referred to the Suffrage Committee, where they had a hope of passage.

Behind the scenes, Helen Hamilton Gardener, an educated, wealthy, and charming author, was already paving the groundwork. She had befriended her neighbor, House Speaker Clark, by never hounding him with political requests. She also, somehow, had made a friend of First Lady Edith Galt Wilson, who loathed suffragists, especially those picketing the White House, calling them "disgusting creatures." Suffrage lobbyists called Gardener a one-woman "Diplomatic Corps." Now she devised a plan to, finally, win President Wilson's endorsement.

Knowing of Wilson's dislike of confrontation, Gardener suggested to Raker, whose new committee could soon report out a constitutional amendment, that he bring a group of pro-suffrage Democrats to the White House to seek the president's "advice" on how to vote. Responding to the Gardener outreach, Wilson secretary Joseph Tumulty, sympathetic to the issue, arranged the meeting for early January. As head of the Democratic Party, Wilson had always maintained that he could not endorse the measure, as the vote was a matter for the states to decide, not the federal government. Now, for the first time, he told these Democrats he could "frankly and earnestly" advise them to vote for the amendment "as an act of right and justice." It is the first time Wilson had abandoned his state strategy.

The next day, January 10, the House passed the bill, 274–136, with one vote to spare above the needed two-thirds majority required. The House had not voted on the measure since 1915, when the amendment failed by 78 votes. Jeannette Rankin, who had been elected in 1916 as the first woman in Congress, opened debate by asking, "How shall we explain … the meaning of democracy if the same Congress that voted for war to make the world safe for democracy refuses to give this small measure of democracy to the women of our country?" The galleries were packed with supporters – one North Carolina newspaper wryly observed that the day "marked the worst political traffic jam the capitol has seen in many weeks, precipitated by the rush to get on the suffrage band wagon, now that the President has indorsed the federal amendment." Southerners railed against the idea of enfranchising African American women, since "they will ultimately deprive the Southern States of representation." As Tennessee Democrat John Moon explained, "In those Southern States where the colored population outnumbers the white, to double the number of ignorant voters by giving the colored women the right to vote would produce a condition that would be absolutely intolerable." Northerners protested the militancy of Alice Paul's pickets and what Massachusetts Republican William Greene called their "offensive" banners. He might have added their "offensive" departure from gender decorum too.

Now action moved to the Senate. In a letter to NAWSA's congressional chairs in the states, Carrie Chapman Catt demonstrated her belief in the need for disciplined organization. "Please start at once a series of letters and telegrams to your Senators. If they are favorable, get a good many letters off to them from prominent people ... urging that they do everything possible to get an early favorable vote. If they are doubtful, see that a big campaign of letters and telegrams pours in and keep it up. Many House Members told us that they heard nothing from their Districts. They want to hear ... If your Senators are opposed, don't despair; many bitter opponents in the House came around to our side. Start a campaign of letters and telegrams and keep it up.... We won by a single vote in the House; we may be beaten by a single vote in the Senate. Leave no stone unturned."

With Gardener, Catt made a call on Wilson at the White House, asking him to issue a public statement supporting the amendment. After reading his first version, an exasperated Catt suggested that he revise it to make clear he wanted the Senate to act on the amendment during the current session. The delays and sparring on the Hill, the ways in which Congress used women's fundamental right of citizenship as a political game, these habits of Washington's culture were deeply depressing to Catt. "The whole dastardly business of delay, and backing and filling, and hauling and yanking, has rasped CCC sometimes beyond endurance," wrote one colleague. As a result, this was one of her few tactical miscalculations. Offended by the audacity of a president telling them what to do, or perhaps because so many of them genuinely disliked Wilson, the Senate delayed the vote.

Through a hot summer, the two organizations pursued their divergent strategies. At NAWSA, Carrie Chapman Catt made sure a parade of suffrage and petitions flooded the Senate. Her best advocate, Maud Wood Park (Fig. 10.1), and a team of suffragists worked the Hill. Their lobbying methods – meeting with senators, arranging for constituent visits from home, appealing to justice – were so unlike the covert, stealth deal making that characterized the Capitol that one reporter dubbed them "Front Door Lobby." Park kept careful notes on all the members of Congress, tracking their views on suffrage, the pressures from their states, and even the views of their wives and daughters. When Democrats scheduled a vote on the amendment in May, Park knew from her reading of the political winds that suffrage was two votes

Figure 10.1   Maud Wood Park, a Radcliffe graduate who co-founded the College Equal Suffrage League in 1900, was instrumental in winning passage of the Nineteenth Amendment in Congress in 1919. Chief lobbyist for the National American Woman Suffrage Association, she kept detailed index cards on each member of Congress, with their views on suffrage and those of their wives and confidantes in their states who might influence them. From her vantage point, the key pressure on Congress to grant the vote came from victories in the states. "In the beginning, the women who wanted the change were outsiders, trying to storm the political fortresses with no weapons except the appeal of justice to the men inside," she said. "Not until individual states gave votes to women was there any chance for them to work from within the stronghold to open the gates to sister women still outside." *Source:* Public Domain.

short. Democrats came to the same conclusion, delaying the vote until September.

By contrast, the National Woman's Party (NWP) conducted a series of open-air meetings in Lafayette Park to protest the lack of action by the Senate. The first day of the protests proved the hottest on record in Washington history – registering 106 degrees. A large banner read, "We protest against the continued disfranchisement of American women for which the President of the United States is responsible." Although Republicans would take control of the House and the Senate in the midterm elections in November, for now both chambers were in Democratic hands. Blaming Wilson and his Democratic Party for dragging their feet, the massive banner continued, "We demand that the President and his party secure the passage of the suffrage amendment through the Senate in the present session." Police arrested all forty-eight protesters for holding a public meeting in a government park without a permit. They were sentenced to time in the old District workhouse, where several began hunger strikes. On their release, as usual, the NWP hosted a welcome home breakfast for them. Dora Lewis, Gertrude Crocker, Katharine Fisher, Hazel Hunkins, and Julia Emory emerged severely weakened, barely able to walk from the taxi into party headquarters.

As debate neared, Catt arranged a special meeting between President Wilson and women from western states – voters, and constituents, who were already enfranchised. Suffrage House, NAWSA's headquarters on Rhode Island Avenue, saw an influx of supporters from twenty-six states, and much scurrying about to find extra cots for sleeping rooms and porches, "crowded from roof to cellar." At the meeting, Wilson vowed "to assist you in every way in my power … I will do all I can to urge the passage of this amendment by an early vote." Republican Whip Charles Curtis of Kansas confidently predicted the measure would pass, with several votes to spare. But after the chairman of the Rules Committee declared that the Senate would likely recess so senators could go home and campaign, the NWP took to the streets again, this time burning scraps of paper containing the president's "empty words." A cheering crowd of men and women witnessed the burning at the base of the statute of Lafayette, the French aristocrat who fought in both the American and French Revolutions and who once said, "The exercise of natural rights has no limits but such as will ensure their enjoyment to other members of society."

During a five-day debate, senators voiced their fears about the African American votes that threatened southern white male hegemony and their anger at the White House picketing that violated gender decorum. For Democrat Senator James Vardaman of Mississippi, a surprise yes vote on suffrage, racism trumped sexism. "It is going to bring to the ballot box, along with the negro men, a few negro women. I also understand that the negro woman will be more offensive, more difficult to handle at the polls than the negro man … But when I realize that five white women will be added to the electorate where only two or three negro men can possibly be brought to the ballot box, the difficulties are minimized."

As in the House, there was some evidence that victories in the states influenced the Senate outcome. Republican John McCumber of North Dakota said that while he opposed the amendment, his state legislature had passed a new law granting women the right to vote in presidential and local elections – by a wide margin. Conversely, Democrat Joseph Ransdell of Louisiana, a supporter of suffrage, said it was "a source of deep regret" that Louisianans did not agree. In fact the legislature had recently petitioned Congress to oppose the measure. In the end, both men voted yes, one for political expedience, the other for conscience.

As for picketing, Democratic Senator Key Pittman of Nevada accused the Woman's Party of being an adjunct of the Republican Party. Republican Reed Smoot of Utah countered that "the Republican Party is not responsible in any way for the picketing," adding Republicans "have condemned it just as strongly as any Senator upon the other side of the Chamber." Before voting on the amendment, the Senate defeated several amendments, and Maud Wood Park exhaled. One would have limited suffrage to white women (defeated 61–22). Another would have limited the vote to native-born or naturalized citizens (defeated 50–33).

Park believed they were still two votes short, so Catt appealed to Wilson to address the Senate. In a speech to the Senate on September 30, he declared, "We have made partners of the women in this war; shall we admit them only to a partnership of suffering and sacrifice and toil and not to a partnership of privilege and right?" As war's end came into view, he claimed that it "could not have been fought, either by the other nations engaged or by America, if it had not been for the services of the women."

The next day, October 1, the Senate voted, 54 in favor, 34 against, two votes short of the two-thirds required. Wilson's appeal had not changed a single vote. Still, there were some signs of a tilt toward suffrage. Seven yes votes had been cast by men who voted no in 1914. And ten of the new yes votes came from members representing states where suffrage had been approved in 1917. In a rare tactical concurrence, with little more than a month before the elections, Catt and Paul now launched separate campaigns to defeat the two most vulnerable incumbents – Republican John Weeks of Massachusetts and Democrat Willard Saulsbury of Delaware – who had voted no. Both were defeated.

For its part, the NWP began picketing in front of U.S. Capitol, and the Senate Office Building, targeting the thirty-four senators who voted no. "We have removed our pickets from the White House, having won the President over," Alice Paul says. "The House has passed the amendment, hence we are now centering our efforts on the Senate, the last stronghold of the opposition." In midterm elections, the Republican Party gained a slim two-seat majority in the Senate and gained control of the House, picking up twenty-five seats. Voters in three states – Michigan, South Dakota, and Oklahoma – had enacted women's suffrage amendments. That brought the total of Electoral College votes from suffrage states to 267, of 531. One week later, World War I ended, and with it any pretense by suffrage opponents that international issues need take precedence over domestic ones.

On a new attempt in 1919, Senate debate seemed a weary affair, an anti-climax. Suffragists were concerned about an amendment to require ratification by state conventions rather than state legislatures, likely to tilt the outcome to anti-suffrage forces. That amendment was defeated. Soon after, the Senate approved the Nineteenth Amendment on a 56–25 vote.

If ratified by thirty-six of the nation's forty-eight states, the Nineteenth Amendment would – at least on paper – enfranchise nearly 20 million women, cutting men's political power in half. Asked to account for this voluntary ceding of power, lobbyist Maud Wood Park got to the heart of it. "In the beginning, the women who wanted the change were outsiders, trying to storm the political fortresses with no weapons except the appeal of justice to the men inside," she said. "Not until individual states gave votes to women was there any chance for them to work from within the stronghold to open the gates to sister women still outside."

There were no teeth in this constitutional promise of a suffrage guarantee, much as there had been none in the Fifteenth Amendment that included black men in the American electorate. For the black men enfranchised after the Civil War and for the black women granted the vote now, there would have to be a new fight, in a new generation. For now, suffragists had to convince three-fourths of the states to ratify. It would be an epic contest. Businesses would rouse their fiercest opponents to fight. Anti-suffragists would tour the country buttonholing legislators. The effort would exhaust all sides and only survive by the vote of one man in one state who said he was only doing what his mother had told him to.

The Ratification Battle

On June 10, 1919, legislators in Springfield, Illinois, Madison, Wisconsin, and Lansing, Michigan, ratified the amendment, becoming the first states to do so. None of them had much of a fight – the Illinois House approved the measure 132–3, while the Senate vote was unanimous. In Wisconsin, there were only two dissents in the Assembly and one in the House. And in Michigan, the tally was unanimous, in both houses. Throughout the summer, there was a rush to ratify, a jockeying of legislative calendars to earn credit among female voters. In an acknowledgment by lawmakers of a new electoral reality, governors called special sessions. Suffrage was at the top of the legislative agenda, sometimes the only item.

Most of the early ratifications were little contested. Kansas had rejected the idea of women's suffrage in 1867 on a 69 percent to 31 percent vote. Now, fifty-two years later, lawmakers met in Topeka for a special session, ratifying the amendment unanimously as their first order of business. Introducing the bill was Minnie Grinstead, elected only the year before as the first female legislator in state history. Ohio followed close behind, approving 73–6 in the House and 27–3 in the Senate. New York, only two years after enfranchising women, became the sixth state to ratify the amendment, without a dissenting vote. The only controversy during the debate centered on whether Democrats or Republicans had been better friends to the cause.

On June 24, Pennsylvania became the seventh state, and the most surprising of the early ratification states, to validate the amendment, voting 31–6 in the Senate and 153–44 in the General Assembly. Cheers erupted throughout the chamber, mingled with jeers from opponents. Governor William Sproul, instrumental in quieting opponents, welcomed to the podium Lucy Kennedy Miller, president of the Pennsylvania Woman Suffrage Association, the first woman ever to address the state House of Representatives from the speaker's chair. "You have done today the biggest thing you have ever done in your history," Miller said in thanking lawmakers, and praising fair reporters. Catt had worried Pennsylvania would be the hardest to win. Instead, said Miller, "every other Republican state will follow your course." Next came Massachusetts, birthplace of Stone's American Woman Suffrage Association and of the anti-suffrage movement. The vote was 34–5 in the Senate, 185–47 in the House.

On June 28, the same day Wilson signed a peace treaty in Paris ending World War I, Texas became the first southern state to ratify the amendment. The vote was anything but smooth. The Texas House quickly passed the measure, 96–21. But in the Senate, opponents noted that voters in the state had overwhelmingly rejected the idea at the polls and mounted a three-day struggle to defeat the measure on the floor. Among their demands: a statewide referendum on the issue. As Minnie Fisher Cunningham wrote in an account to Catt, "There were constant rumors that two of our signers also favored the Referendum." With a big push from Governor William P. Hobby, publisher of the Houston *Post*, the amendment was ratified by the Texas legislation on a "viva voce vote," no recorded vote needed. Male anti-suffragists soon began a campaign to elect a legislature that would rescind the ratification.

Though still front-page news, ratifications were receding in newsworthiness even as their numbers grew: Iowa on July 2, the House 95–5, the Senate unanimous, the entire process taking less than two hours; Missouri the next day, when the Senate by a vote of 28–3 adopted the House resolution; even Arkansas, a southern state, ratified on July 28, the Senate 29–2, the House 76–19. The Arkansas *Gazette* reported, "Women came to Little Rock from many points in the state and filled the corridors of the statehouse." Carrying yellow banners with the familiar "Votes for Women" slogan, they took pictures in front of the Senate and House chambers, and thanked Governor Charles Brough for calling a special session.

In the first two months after the amendment passed the U.S. Senate, twelve states had ratified it, one third of the total required. Part of Catt's strategy was to keep many states in motion at the same time, diffusing efforts to organize an opposition. The strategy looked promising through the end of the year: Montana, which had sent Rankin to Washington as the nation's first female member of Congress in 1917, seemed to hold no grudge for her anti-war vote. The amendment was ratified, 38–1 in the Senate and unanimously in the House on August 2. That same day, Nebraska saluted with a 94–0 vote in the House on a resolution that had passed the Senate 27–0. Minnesota followed on September 8, where suffragists broke out into a rendition of "The Battle Hymn of the Republic" in the Senate chamber and offered a banquet that evening for the men who had offered them a ballot. "I hope we will bring to the vote a steadfastness of purpose, a fearlessness that you men have not," chided activist Mary Harriman Severance. "We will stand fearless. We have learned sacrifice and service. We come into your parties, women unafraid."

But there were warning signs that winning ratification before the November 1920 election might prove elusive. In late July, the Georgia Senate, by a vote of 39 to 10, refused to ratify, although it would not make the refusal official for another year. Activists were beginning to worry. Alice Paul said ratification would easily win in thirty states. If true, that meant suffragists would need to corral the remaining six from northern states such as Maryland, New Hampshire, and Vermont, and southern ones such as Georgia, Alabama, and Virginia.

In New Hampshire, suffragists had lobbied for a special session in August, but a strong force of anti-suffragists – everyone from women opposed to the franchise to the liquor lobby that feared female voters would outlaw manufacture of alcohol – stilled the governor's hand. After Labor Day, with fifteen states already committed to the idea, Governor John Bartlett risked a special session. The tally demonstrated he was right to hesitate – the once controversial idea of women voting still had plenty of critics in the "Live Free or Die" state. The vote was 212–143 in the House, 14–10 in the Senate. It was the squeakiest victory to date.

The campaign grew more perilous when, in September, Alabama became the first state to reject ratification. After the Senate vote, critics had formed a Woman's Anti-Ratification League of Alabama. "The

Southern ladies will never endorse the movement, preferring as they do to preside as queens in the hearts and homes of the men they love," the Huntsville *Mercury* had explained in 1895 after Susan B. Anthony campaigned there with a charismatic 35-year-old Carrie Chapman Catt. "Their duties to God, their families and society sufficiently employ the minds of true Southern women, without entering the political arena." As the Nineteenth Amendment neared Montgomery, one Alabama judge warned that any lawmaker who voted to enfranchise women risked impeachment.

Next came easy wins in states that had already enfranchised women. In Utah on October 2, Senate Joint Resolution No. 1 passed after being introduced by Senator Elizabeth Hayward, a Salt Lake City Democrat. In November, California, whose enfranchisement of women in 1911 had served as an early pivot point, became the eighteenth state to ratify. The vote was easily won – 73–2 in the Assembly, unanimous in the Senate, and the greatest controversy was the governor's refusal to include anti-Japanese legislation in his call for the special session. The two issues were not unrelated. As Assemblyman Carlton Green of St. Luis Obispo explained, "The negro problem in the South is as serious to the Southern states as is the Japanese problem to us here in California. If we expect sympathy from the East and South on our Japanese issue we must show the same sympathy for their racial problems."

On November 5, in a nail biter, Maine joined the suffrage states, the House voting 72–68 to ratify. "We are proud to have our State fall into line with the progressive states of the Union on this important matter," said Katharine Reed Balentine, legislative chair of the Maine Woman Suffrage Association. The victory was slim, acknowledged her colleague Helen Bates, but "it sufficed." Maine's ratification also meant suffrage had cleared the halfway point. Now, nineteen states of the thirty-six needed had validated the claims of woman on the vote. By the end of the year three more capitols, all in suffrage states, had ratified – North Dakota on December 1, South Dakota on December 4, and Colorado on December 15. The role of the states in spearheading change meant there were already female politicians practiced in the art of politics. Colorado sent its ratification to Washington with the names of three women in the legislature – Senator Agnes Riddle and House members Mabel Baker and May Bigelow.

When new sessions convened in January, five states quickly ratified the amendment. On January 6, Kentucky's House voted 75–25 to ratify. The Senate voted 30–8, after first defeating an amendment to submit the measure to a statewide voter referendum. The same day, Rhode Island ratified the amendment – with one dissenting vote in the Senate and a vote of 89–3 in the House. The federal amendment had now been ratified by twenty-four states, with twelve to go. Three more came in during January. In Oregon, where women's suffrage was rejected in 1884, sentiment was so overwhelmingly positive that the Senate and House conducted a race to see which chamber could ratify the amendment first – the Senate winning by six minutes. The vote in both chambers was unanimous and the governor signed the ratification on January 13. In Indiana, opponents, encouraged by the Indiana *Daily Times*, argued that the state constitution prohibited both houses from passing the same bill on the same day. But Governor James Goodrich praised state lawmakers for their efforts to "free the women of America from the last vestige of political disability." The House ratified the measure within 15 minutes of the Senate vote. Officials began making plans, in anticipation of a large female turnout, to change precinct borders to prevent overcrowding at the polls. The drumroll of state actions was much covered in world press, and soon women in the Philippines launched a campaign for suffrage, appealing to lawmakers in Washington, DC to hold public hearings on their claims to citizenship.

Wyoming, the first state in the nation to grant women the right to vote, first as a territory in 1867 and then when it was admitted to the union in 1890, was like a coda on a month that demonstrated the tide of public opinion had long since shifted. In a special session that began January 27, the Senate ratified the measure 37 minutes after the Judiciary Committee brought it to the floor, without a dissenting vote, and then the House voted unanimously to enfranchise women. The day after Wyoming's ringing endorsement, South Carolina served notice on suffrage leaders that the battle might yet be lost. Rejecting a resolution to ratify, lawmakers instead proactively rejected the measure. In the House the vote was 93–21. In the Senate, sentiment was even more overwhelming, the rejection resolution passed by 31–4, without debate and in 10 minutes. Later that year, when the state Democratic Convention convened in Columbia, suffragists asked for an endorsement of female voting in primaries, only to be rebuffed. "The determination to keep women out of the primaries," observed Senator Neils Christensen, was "strong and uncompromising." South Carolina had spoken, and though its rejection of the amendment was not unexpected, its verdict was chilling.

Six more states approved in February. Nevada ratified on February 7, unanimously in the Senate and with but one dissent in the Assembly, from an assemblyman named Ferguson, who said he had expected to stand alone but would "stand supreme" among taxpayers. New Jersey ratified on February 9, where the Senate vote was 18–2 and the Assembly's 34–24. A delaying ploy by opponents, what the Camden *Courier-Post* called "exasperating parliamentary tactics," found opponents conducting a four-hour filibuster to press for a referendum, which was defeated 33–25. The *Trenton Times* called the vote "a rebuke to the vacillating Republican leaders who shifted their position from last year, and to the bolting Democrats who repudiated the declaration made in their party platform." New Jersey, the first in the nation to grant women and blacks of property the right to vote, in 1776, and then the first to revoke that right in 1908, became the 29th state to ratify the amendment.

On February 11, Dr. Emma Drake of Payette County, the only female legislator in attendance, rose to introduce a resolution in the Idaho House ratifying the amendment. A temperance advocate, she made what one commentator called "a strong and logical speech," pointing out that ratification was in keeping with Idaho's history as a suffrage state of twenty-three years standing. Six hours later, the amendment was part of Idaho lore – approved unanimously by the House and by a 29–6 vote in the Senate. The next day, Arizona likewise gave its approval to the amendment, unanimously, in both houses of the legislature.

Next up was New Mexico, where opponent Pan Padilla claimed to have the votes to defeat the measure in the House. In the end, the vote in the House was 36–10, in the Senate 17–5. In Oklahoma, anti-suffrage forces again tried the gambit of calling for a referendum, but Governor J. B. A. Robertson declared the motion out of order. Three days later, the Senate passed the resolution 25–13, and the House followed with a 76–4 vote.

But rejections had piled up too – Virginia on February 12, Maryland on February 24. Just after rejecting the amendment, a delegation of anti-suffrage lawmakers from Maryland arrived in Charleston, West Virginia, in hopes of swaying opinion there. As the *Washington Star* put it, they were "received with open arms by the party opposed to ratification and given a taste of that hospitality for which Charleston is famous." But leaders of the national ratification effort issued a statement expressing "our unswerving confidence in the West Virginia legislature as being perfectly qualified and competent to act upon the federal suffrage amendment without the aid of members of the Maryland legislature."

The Baltimore contingent had been right to sense trouble brewing in West Virginia. The House of Delegates quickly ratified the amendment, 47–40, but the Senate was wrenched by dissension. After an initial defeat, pro-suffrage forces arranged for a second vote. This time, State Sen. Jesse Bloch made "a sensational cross-country" California vacation "to break a deadlock in favor of ratification," reported the *New York Times*. A special train, "which cost $5,000, enabled him to clip two hours from the regular express time and to catch the NY train over the C&O Railroad," and that got him to Charleston early the next morning. Asked about his vote, Bloch explained that he was "not a suffragist and I have no personal axe to grind," but argued that "Election Day comes but once a year and if it will add to the peace of mind of the women and aid the United States to cast a ballot with the men, I'll do my bit." His vote made the difference. Four years after a ballot initiative for women's suffrage went down to an ignoble defeat – failing by a more than two-to-one margin – and despite lobbying by Maryland lawmakers, West Virginia became the 34th state to ratify the amendment. The state of Washington, which had enfranchised women in 1910, ratified unanimously in both chambers, and became the 35th state out of the thirty-six required.

And then, the process stalled. Through the summer, all that was heard from the remaining states was no. On June 2, Delaware rejected the amendment despite telegrams from Wilson to three legislators, all Democrats, thought to be on the fence. Despite the fact that no direct vote had been taken, the Delaware Equal Suffrage Association vowed to defeat men against suffrage and appeal to voters in new ballot initiatives. Mary Wilson Thompson, leader of the Delaware Anti-Suffrage Association, credited "the splendid character and steadfastness of our Delaware men." Noting that both parties and "the entire strength of the suffrage forces" had brought "every known form of pressure," she said, "They withstood all tests and remained true to their convictions and the wishes of their constituents." In the end, she added, "The death knell of suffrage has been sounded." Suffragists worried she might be right. Alice Paul marshaled two hundred picketers to the Republican Convention in Chicago. Noting that it was Republicans who defeated suffrage in Delaware, they urged Republicans to pressure governors in Vermont and Connecticut to call special elections. Equally chagrined, NAWSA strategists looked at the remaining states and saw their worst nightmare: final ratification would have to come from the South, a region so hostile that male anti-suffragists were recruiting women to lead the charge in anti-ratification leagues.

And still the rejections came. Louisiana rejected the measure on July 1, when the House defeated the resolution, 52–46, and then adjourned the legislature. Georgia, where the Senate had weeks earlier killed a ratification proposal, 19–15, now recorded its "no" vote. Carrie Chapman Catt's promise of ratification before the November 2 elections looked increasingly unlikely. Anti-suffrage forces were guardedly confident, feeling momentum swinging their way. The Southern Women's League for Rejection of the Susan B. Anthony Amendment sought a meeting with Ohio Governor James Cox, the Democratic nominee for president. "The home-loving women of the South, who do not picket, card-index or blackmail candidates, appeal to you as the leader of the Democratic Party to grant us a hearing," said the group's statement. They did not want to talk about suffrage but about "two fundamental democratic principles, states rights and party honor." The press was devoting much coverage to the foreign policy views of Cox and his opponent, Republican Senator Warren G. Harding, also from Ohio. After all, the election was widely seen as a referendum on Woodrow Wilson's failure to win Senate approval for the Versailles Treaty. But behind the scenes, as the nation debated Europe, suffragists and their opponents were focusing their efforts on a goal closer to home. The battle for women's suffrage – born with the founding of the republic, launched as a mass movement at the improbable 1848 Seneca Falls convention, site of unseemly tensions between white and black suffragists, subject of fifty-two years of campaigning in the states – would come down to one more campaign, in one more state, in search of the 36th state. The showdown was set for August, in Nashville.

The Fight for Tennessee

Anita Pollitzer was confident. The legislative secretary for the NWP, she spoke to reporters after interviewing Harding and Cox. Both candidates had endorsed the amendment. The previous year, Tennessee had granted women the right to vote in municipal and presidential elections. "If Republicans who control one-fourth of the legislature are true to their party platform, and if Governor Cox does all he has assured us he will do, Tennessee will be the 36th state without doubt," she said. "It is the acid test of their sincerity." The *Chattanooga Times* did not agree. On the eve of the vote, one headline writer proclaimed, "Many Believe Ratification is Now Doomed." All sides agreed that it had been a fight to the death like no other in the long history of women's suffrage. "The Battle of Nashville in 1864 was a five o'clock tea in comparison with this one," observed journalist Edwin Mims.

Anti-suffragists, called "antis," were clever, well funded, and willing to go to almost any length to stop the march of women toward the polls. The president of the Southern Women's League for Rejection of the Susan B. Anthony Amendment was Josephine Pearson – college-educated, world-traveled, and driven to oppose suffrage by a deathbed promise she made to her mother. If Pearson was the public face of the opposition, its godfather was John Vertrees, a Nashville lawyer who had once issued a manifesto against the female vote. In "An Address to the Men of Tennessee on Female Suffrage," he argued that most citizens, male and female, did not want women to have the vote. Anyway, he said, "It's not a question of what women *want* but what they *ought* to have." Aside from women being too physically weak to bear the ordeal of politics, and unqualified because they could not serve in the military or law enforcement, the real danger, he suggested, was that enfranchisement of African American women would threaten white supremacy in the southern states.

Vertrees telephoned the 52-year-old Pearson at her home in Monteagle and invited her to his home for dinner in Nashville. There he explained, in her telling, that he wanted her to head the effort because she had "outstanding ability," and mostly because "you are too brainy – as well as tactful – to want to direct the strong alliance of men constituents." In short, she was willing to do the work but let men run the show. With help from Anne Pleasant, president of Louisiana Women's Rejection League, she perfected the art of appealing to prejudice – conflating women's suffrage with intermarriage, free love, socialism, and racial equality.

In one pamphlet, called "That Deadly Parallel," she quoted the Fifteenth Amendment and the proposed Nineteenth Amendment to show how similar their language was. ("The right of citizens of the United States to vote shall not be denied or abridged by the United States or by any State on account of race, color, or previous condition of servitude" had changed to "on account of sex.") In another, called "Beware," she tried to frighten Tennessee lawmakers by invoking haunting memories of Reconstruction passed down from one generation of southerners to another. "Remember that *woman suffrage* means a reopening of the entire *Negro suffrage* question, loss of State rights, and another period of reconstruction horrors." The pamphlet went on to quote the *Messenger*, a black newspaper, as advocating intermarriage, free love, socialism, and "social equality in every sense of the Phrase." The implication was clear – a vote for the women was a vote for African American equality. And finally "The Dark and Dangerous Side of Woman Suffrage," forecasting the death of the American family by quoting Anna Howard Shaw as saying she believed in women's enfranchisement "whether women will love their husbands after they vote or forsake them, whether they will neglect their children or never have any children."

Against this backdrop of rhetorical hysteria, suffrage supporters organized. On July 12, Catt had written a colleague, "I don't believe there's a ghost of a chance of ratification in … Tennessee." The state, she wrote, "has always been torn by factions in all men's and women's work, and it was these factions which defeated us in Delaware." But later in the month she arrived in Nashville after a speaking tour of major cities in the state. She surrounded herself with local activists who would become the face of the effort – Anne Dallas Dudley of Nashville and Abby Crawford Milton of Chattanooga. She installed herself in Room 309 of the Hermitage Hotel, Nashville's first million-dollar hotel, a magnet for world leaders and dignitaries of all kinds. Soon the Hermitage became a site for suffrage. Pearson moved her headquarters there, to Room 708, as did the anti-suffrage liquor interests, who set up a hospitality suite on the eighth floor. The so-called Jack Daniels Suite offered illegal booze, and what critics alleged was a back-deal room for bribes. Two suffragists, Sue Shelton White, a Tennessean who had gone to jail with Alice Paul's Silent Sentinels, and Anita Pollitzer, a South Carolinian who later served as chair of the NWP, were caught eavesdropping on conversations in the Jack Daniels Suite, and escorted off site. After witnessing a 48-hour drinking binge in the hallways, Catt despaired of locating a sober politician in Nashville. She was assured that this was just "the Tennessee way."

At first, opposition forces had objected over legal issues. Article II Section 32 of the state constitution prohibited approval of any proposed amendment to the U.S. Constitution unless the "General Assembly shall have been elected after such amendment is submitted." For much of the year, critics had argued that only a state legislature elected in 1920 could consider the amendment, when it convened in 1921. But in June 1920, the U.S. Supreme Court handed down a decision widely interpreted as nullifying the Tennessee barrier. In *Hawke v. Smith*, the court declared that a similar Ohio constitutional provision – requiring a vote of the public before a vote of the legislature – was void. The reason: it violated the federal amending process as outlined in the U.S. Constitution.

Governor Albert Roberts had been under enormous pressure all year – from local suffragists as well as the White House – to call a special session. He was not an avid supporter of suffrage – one activist claimed he had signed a bill granting Tennessee women municipal and presidential suffrage in 1919 only because he assumed it would be ruled unconstitutional. Two days after he defeated a Democratic primary opponent in his re-election bid, calculating that he needed women's votes to offset anger from farmers for hiking tax assessments, the 52-year-old Roberts called a special session. The showdown would begin August 9.

By August 13, the Senate, with thirty-three members, began debate. Opponent H. M. Candler of Athens predicted that if the amendment were ratified, "Tennessee would have negroes down here to represent her in the Legislature." He accused Catt of being an anarchist who favored interracial marriage, which would "drag the womanhood of Tennessee down to the level of the negro woman." Catt, ignoring the slur to African American women, issued a statement calling intermarriage "an absolute crime against nature." Senator Albert E. Hill of Nashville was among those who defended ratification, saying, "With equal suffrage we will have a better country and better government." John C. Houk of Knoxville likewise called the amendment a matter of "right and justice." After the debate, the Senate adopted the measure 25–4. Catt wrote a friend, "We now have 35½ states. We are up to our last half of a state."

The opposition, she noted, would now mount a campaign without scruples. She believed they were appealing to "Negro phobia and every other cave man's prejudice.... We believe they are buying votes ... We are terribly worried and so is the other side. I've been here a month. It's hot, muggy, nasty, and this last battle is desperate. We are low in our minds – even if we win we who have been here will never remember it with anything but a shudder."

Pearson tried to discredit Catt, often issuing statements about the 61-year-old suffrage veteran as an outside agitator who was aligned with radical views. She accused Catt of contributing to Stanton's controversial 1895 book, *The Woman's Bible*, which accused church leaders of misogyny. Catt resisted any instinct she might have had to respond. Later, however, she unloaded. "In the short time I spent in Tennessee's capital, I have been called more names, been more maligned, more lied about than in the thirty previous years I worked for suffrage," she said, decrying their "vulgar, ignorant, insane" letters. She and her team had been forced to battle against lobbyists from the railroads, the steel lobby, the aluminum interests, and the Manufacturers' Association. Until Wilson called them off, she said they had also been harassed by Internal Revenue Service agents who "appropriated our telegrams, tapped our telephones, listened outside our windows."

On August 17, four days after the Senate vote, debate began in the House. By every account, it was historic, and lasted for hours. House Speaker Seth Walker, who only in July had served on the Men's Ratification Committee, opened debate with an impassioned speech explaining why he had changed his position. He denied it was because of pressure from "a certain railroad." Instead, he urged lawmakers to reject the amendment to defend states' rights. Representative Robert Bratton of Davidson County had signed a pledge to vote for ratification but said during the debate critics' arguments had persuaded him to switch sides.

The next day, August 18, the House would vote, and everyone expected a cliffhanger. The vote would turn on three or four lawmakers, predicted the *Chattanooga News*, who "will make Tennessee the thirty-sixth state or they will keep 20,000,000 women from voting this November." Activists stood outside the chamber, antis handing out red rose boutonnieres for lawmakers to wear in their lapels, signaling their positions, suffragists distributing others in yellow. "The hour has come," shouted Walker. And the roll call began.

Walker tried to maneuver the measure to defeat by a procedural gambit of moving to table the resolution. Each time he tried, the vote was 48–48. One of those who sided with Walker to delay the vote was Harry Burn (Fig. 10.2), a 24-year-old Republican from McGinn County in East Tennessee. Later he said that though he favored women's suffrage as a "moral right" he had planned to vote against it in deference to his constituents, who had let him know in no uncertain terms that they opposed the measure. Now he stood to vote, a red rose in his lapel. Stunning everyone in earshot, he voted yes. He later explained he had received a note from his mother, which he was carrying in his pocket. In it, Phoebe Ensminger Burn said she had been following the debate, including Senator Chandler's "very bitter" speech. "Hurrah and vote for Suffrage and don't keep them in doubt," she wrote. "Be a good boy and

Figure 10.2 Harry Burn, a 24-year-old Republican from McGinn County in Tennessee, was the last hope, in the last state, at the final hour, in the battle for ratification of the Nineteenth Amendment. Stunning everyone in earshot, he defied expectations and voted yes. He later explained he had received a note from his mother, Phoebe Ensminger Burn, who urged him to "vote for Suffrage and don't keep them in doubt." She signed her letter "Lots of love, Mama." Critics castigated him as "a traitor to manhood's honor." Anti-suffrage newspapers spread rumors he had taken a bribe. Conflicted though he may have been, Burn, seen here shaking hands with suffrage and anti-suffrage activists outside the legislature, marveled that "a Republican from the mountains of East Tennessee … made national woman suffrage possible at this time not for any personal glory, but for the glory of his party." *Source:* Public Domain. Courtesy of the Tennessee State Library and Archives.

help" Carrie Chapman Catt "put the rat in ratification." She signed her letter "Lots of love, Mama." Conflicted though he may have been, Burn also took a certain pride in the act, marveling that "a Republican from the mountains of East Tennessee ... made national woman suffrage possible at this time not for any personal glory, but for the glory of his party."

It took a moment for the victory to sink in. The Nineteenth Amendment had cleared its last hurdle, 49–47, in the Tennessee House. When it did, said the Bristol *Herald Courier,* activists watching the proceedings "launched an uproarious demonstration," as their allies on the floor took off the "yellow flowers they had been wearing and threw them upward to meet a similar shower from the galleries." The vote had not turned on party allegiance – thirty-three Democrats voted for it with thirty-six against. Among Republicans, the tally was sixteen in favor and eleven against. Suffrage had divided the parties as it had the nation. Now it was passed.

Anti-suffragists were not finished. Josephine Pearson castigated Harry Burn as "a traitor to manhood's honor," and anti-suffrage newspapers spread rumors that he had taken a bribe. In response, Burn issued a personal statement that he inserted into the *House Journal,* saying that he was glad of an opportunity to free women from "political slavery," and thought his mother's advice sound. Walker filed a motion to reconsider the vote, and a posse of anti-suffragists, who called themselves the Red Rose Brigade, left Nashville in the middle of the night August 20, decamping for Decatur, Alabama, some 114 miles away, to prevent a quorum, to prevent final action on the amendment. On August 30, the House reconvened, two members short of a quorum. Walker ordered the sergeant at arms to round up absentees. Burn fled to his hotel, trailed by two officers, eluding them. Lawyers won an injunction from Judge E. F. Langford prohibiting state officials from certifying the results to Washington. And antis staged a mass rally "to save the South." Many whites in the South were bereft. Martin Lee Calhoun, of Selma, Alabama, likened Tennessee legislators to "assassins of the night who have stabbed the heart of the South and its traditions to the core."

On August 23, the Tennessee Supreme Court overturned Judge Langford's injunction, and Governor Roberts sent certification of the ratification to officials in Washington, DC. There, Secretary of State Bainbridge Colby had left orders that he was to be notified the moment the certification arrived. Solicitor General William Frierson had stayed up all night waiting. He wakened Colby in the middle of the night and at 3:45 a.m. on August 26, 1920, Colby signed a proclamation announcing that the Nineteenth Amendment had become part of the U.S. Constitution. Some speculate that the Secretary of State, mindful of the last-minute procedural attempts in Tennessee to revoke the state's ratification, wanted to effect the change as quickly as possible. Others argue that he was loath to negotiate a signing ceremony between the rival suffrage organizers. The Alice Paul and Carrie Chapman Catt forces had been at odds on how to stage the event, and perhaps Colby wanted to avoid entanglement by not inviting either side. When Paul asked Colby to recreate the historic event for movie cameras, he refused, but he did agree to pose for photographs later that afternoon.

Catt (Fig. 10.3) arrived in Washington, en route back from Nashville, at 8 a.m. that morning. On calling the Secretary of State's office, she

Figure 10.3 Carrie Chapman Catt, president of the National American Woman Suffrage Association, returned from Tennessee at 8 a.m. on August 26, 1920 to find the Secretary of State had already signed the Nineteenth Amendment. Years later she would look back at the costs of the campaign. "To get the word male in effect out of the Constitution cost the women of the country fifty-two years of pauseless campaigning," she wrote. "During that time they were forced to conduct fifty-six campaigns of referenda to male voters; 480 campaigns to urge Legislatures to submit suffrage amendments to voters; 47 campaigns to induce State constitutional conventions to include woman suffrage planks; 30 campaigns to urge presidential party conventions to adopt woman suffrage planks in party platforms; and 19 campaigns with 19 successive Congresses.... Young suffragists who helped forge the last links of that chain were not born when it began. Old suffragists who forged the first links were dead when it ended." *Source:* Library of Congress Prints and Photographs Division.

learned that the work of many generations was now complete, that women could vote in the November elections, and all elections to come. The next day Catt continued to New York, where a mass of suffrage activists met her train at Penn Station. As a band played "Hail the Conquering Hero," Governor Alfred E. Smith congratulated the state's "distinguished citizen." Admirers gave her a huge bouquet of blue delphiniums and yellow chrysanthemums with a blue ribbon inscribed by Tiffany's, "To Mrs. Carrie Chapman Catt from the enfranchised women of the United States." She responded, "This is a glorious and wonderful day. Now that we have the vote let us remember we are no longer petitioners. We are not wards of the nation but free and equal citizens." Years later she would look back in astonishment at the breadth of this remarkable campaign. "To get the word male in effect out of the Constitution cost the women of the country fifty-two years of pauseless campaigning," she wrote. "During that time they were forced to conduct fifty-six campaigns of referenda to male voters; 480 campaigns to urge Legislatures to submit suffrage amendments to voters; 47 campaigns to induce State constitutional conventions to include woman suffrage planks; 30 campaigns to urge presidential party conventions to adopt woman suffrage planks in party platforms; and 19 campaigns with 19 successive Congresses." Beyond the halls of power, "millions of dollars were raised, mainly in small sums, and expended with economic care. Hundreds of women gave the accumulated possibilities of an entire lifetime, thousands gave years of their lives, hundreds of thousands gave constant interest and such aid as they could. It was a continuous, seemingly endless, chain of activity. Young suffragists who helped forge the last links of that chain were not born when it began. Old suffragists who forged the first links were dead when it ended."

And yet it was not over. Like the Fifteenth Amendment after the Civil War, which had removed race as a barrier to the ballot, the Nineteenth Amendment eliminated gender as an obstacle to women voting. But as it became clear that male resistance was tenacious, and often backed by law, some women realized that they would have to fight again. Especially in the South, where Jim Crow laws prevented both black men and women from exercising their legal rights to vote, the campaign continued, for the next forty years, and beyond.

11

The Voting Rights Act of 1965 and Beyond

In January 1926, a 24-year-old schoolteacher named Indiana Little led "as many as one thousand Black women and a few men" into the Jefferson County Courthouse in Birmingham, Alabama to register to vote. Told she would have to take a literacy test, she protested that it was discriminatory to give intelligence tests to blacks but not to whites. She was arrested for vagrancy, a charge later reduced to disorderly conduct. In an affidavit given to the U.S. Justice Department, she accused her jailer of beating her "over the head unmercifully" and forcibly raping her, "forced upon the officer's demand to yield to him in an unbecoming manner." The Ex-Soldiers Cooperation Association, the group funding the black registration drive, paid her fine and court costs. It would be another thirty-one years – amid a new push for black votes in 1957 – before Indiana Little, at the age of 55, cast her first vote.

Soon after the Nineteenth Amendment's ratification, many African American women went to county courthouses throughout the country to register, often turned away, sometimes in humiliating fashion. Susie W. Fountain, a 51-year-old college-educated resident of Phoebus, in Virginia's Tidewater region, was handed a blank page, then told she had failed the literacy test. In Birmingham, Alabama, Lula Murry was so furious at being denied that she wrote the president, in letters unearthed by historian Liette Gidlow. "Here I stand," she wrote Calvin Coolidge, "denied the constitutional rights" of the Fourteenth and Fifteenth Amendments, and "being a woman," the Nineteenth Amendment. As if this catalog of

And Yet They Persisted: How American Women Won the Right to Vote, First Edition. Johanna Neuman.
© 2020 John Wiley & Sons, Inc. Published 2020 by John Wiley & Sons, Inc.
Companion website: www.wiley.com/go/Neuman

qualifications was not enough, she added, "I am a sister of a deceased Ex-Soldier." In Richland County, South Carolina, dozens of black women sought to register on September 8, the first day of new voter enrollment. Taken aback by this surge of interest, registrars neglected to subject them to the literacy tests and poll taxes required of black men. The sight of these women, grasping the significance of their new constitutional right to vote, was too much for one white segregationist who asked at day's end, "Who stirred up all these colored women to come up here and register?"

What "stirred them up" was a profound understanding of the vote's import. Since passage of the Fourteenth Amendment guaranteeing black men the right to vote after the Civil War, black women had been proactive in guarding the franchise, treating it as a community asset. According to a northern white missionary serving as an observer, in Yazoo County, Mississippi in 1868, black women "formed a line of one hundred or more." At one polling place in Macon, Georgia in 1872, they explained their presence as "part of their religion to keep their husbands and brothers straight in politics." And in South Carolina in 1876, witnesses said black women went to the polls with sticks to mete out punishment for those who veered toward the Democratic party of slavery, threatening to withhold sex from husbands who failed to vote Republican, the party of Lincoln, or evict them altogether.

During the fourteen years of Reconstruction after the Civil War, black political life had flourished. In Mississippi, black men registered in large numbers, and elected the state's first – and to date only – black members of the U.S. Senate – Blanche K. Bruce and Hiram Revels. Black male voters in the states of the former Confederacy elected fourteen African Americans to the U.S. House of Representatives, six black men as state lieutenant governors, and so many black men to state houses that two of them were elected by their colleagues as speakers. But by century's end, southern states were rewriting their constitutions to strip away black male voting rights. Poll taxes, literacy tests, physical violence – all served as an effective barrier to the ballot. In both North and South, African Americans also faced discrimination in education, housing, employment, and accommodations. The U.S. Supreme Court gave official blessing to these Jim Crow laws in 1896, in *Plessy v. Ferguson*, enunciating a "separate but equal" theory of law that guided American life for more than half a century. Even after most women won the right to vote with ratification of the Nineteenth Amendment, African American women in the South were systematically denied the ballot.

In 1964, two years after Fannie Lou Hamer, a 44-year-old Mississippi sharecropper in poor health and with little education, had declared her intention to register to vote, three thousand northern college students, white and black, came south to help black Mississippians overcome the obstacles that had been erected by a white establishment to prevent their political empowerment. Called Freedom Summer, this movement intended to challenge white male supremacy peacefully, even when it required staring down guns in the face. Herbert Lee, a black farmer who was a founding member of the NAACP in the small town of Amite, was assassinated for working with them on the registration drive. They would confront violence and intimidation at county courthouses, teach rural Mississippians the tools of constitutional literacy, and force the federal government to defend black voting rights. They would force a national spotlight on the injustices of the country's poorest state.

Journalists also descended on the scene, with notebooks, cameras, and new television equipment that captured brutal police reaction to students and civil rights leaders whose only crime was to attempt to register to vote. In 1965, after the campaign moved to Alabama, cameras again revealed police response to protest in the streets of Selma and Montgomery. These photographs and accounts – of water hoses, snarling dogs, and savage beatings – stirred public outrage. As the Reverend Martin Luther King Jr. and President Lyndon Johnson pushed – King bringing pressure from the streets, Johnson from the White House – Congress passed the Voting Rights Act. Some have called it the most far-reaching legislation enacted in U.S. history, as it reversed the grand compromise at the Constitutional Convention of 1787, putting the federal government, rather than the states, in charge of black suffrage in the South. But for all the contributions of the nation's male political figures, black and white, the fire under their feet was a legion of women who served as the movement's most dedicated soldiers. Beauty salon owners and schoolteachers, college students and high school dropouts, members of women's clubs and church choirs, they were the glue that cemented the aspirations of movement leaders to the community. In the 1950s, they stirred.

Women Organize

The greatest vehicle for their activism was the National Association for the Advancement of Colored People (NAACP). Formed as a biracial organization seeking justice for black Americans, national membership skyrocketed after World War II, increasing from 50,000 in 1940 to 450,000 by 1946. After graduating from Alcorn A & M College with a degree in business, Medgar Evers, who had served in World War II fighting Germans in France, took a job traveling the state, selling insurance to African Americans. "All we wanted to be was ordinary citizens," he said of himself and his brother Charles. "We fought during the war for

America and Mississippi was included. Now after the Germans and the Japanese hadn't killed us, it looked as though the white Mississippians would." By 1952, he was traveling the state for the NAACP, recruiting African Americans to register to vote. And when whites in Mississippi killed Emmett Till, he investigated the murder for the NAACP.

Nothing galvanized black activism more than the lynching of Emmett Till, a 14-year-old black teenager visiting the small town of Money, Mississippi in 1955. Perhaps for looking or whistling at a white clerk at Bryant's Grocery and Meat Market – it is hard to know for sure as the clerk later recanted her story – Till was beaten to a pulp, shot in the head, tied with barbed wire to a metal cotton gin fan, and then thrown into the Tallahatchie River. His father, Luis Till, had served in World War II. His mother, Mamie Till, had been the first black student to make the honor roll at suburban Chicago's white Argo Community High School. After conferring with Evers, Mamie Till decided to hold an open-casket funeral when the body returned to Chicago. Asked about it later, all she would say is, "I wanted the world to see what they did to my baby." For five days, thousands of mourners, witnesses all, came to Roberts Temple Church of God to see this child brutalized by hatred. Chicago activist Jesse Jackson, once a part of Martin Luther King's inner circle, would call this public display of mourning "the largest single civil rights demonstration in American history." Mamie Till Bradley also allowed *JET Magazine*, a bible of black community life, to take photos of Emmett's face, so disfigured that it was difficult not to look away.

To many black youngsters, this hate crime was the great traumatic event of their growing up years, the spur to activism. "Ours was the Emmett Till generation," said Joyce Ladner, who was 12 years old when Emmett Till was murdered. "No other single incident had a more profound impact on so many people," said Ladner, who in the 1960s would help organize voter registration drives in Mississippi and later still serve as interim president of Howard University. "We had seen the *JET Magazine* cover of Emmett Till's disfigured and bloated face with one eye missing. It was just an awful picture.… We were his age and could identify with him. I felt that if they had killed a 14 year old they could also kill me, or my brothers. We knew that men were lynched but we'd never known of a *child* being lynched before. On a profound, personal level, this reality had a strong, galvanizing effect on all of us."

The next event that galvanized their activism took place far from the backwaters of Mississippi's bayous. On May 17, 1954, the U.S. Supreme Court handed down a landmark decision. In a unanimous ruling, the court held that separate public schools for blacks and whites were "inherently unequal," and violated the Equal Protection Clause of the Fourteenth Amendment. Argued by a young lawyer named Thurgood

Marshall, who thirteen years later would become the first African American named a Supreme Court justice, *Brown v. Board of Education of Topeka* effectively overturned the "separate but equal" doctrine enunciated in *Plessy v. Ferguson* nearly sixty years before. White school boards and state governments across the South reacted with anger, resistance, and violence. In the Sea Islands off the coast of South Carolina and Georgia, Septima Poinsette Clark reacted with determination.

Clark (Fig. 11.1) had been teaching in the schools for over thirty years, imbued by her father, a former slave, with the importance of education. A graduate of Benedict College, with a masters' degree from Hampton University in Virginia, Clark was barred, as a black woman, from teaching in Charleston's public schools. Instead she had found a position in a rural school district on Johns Island. After the *Brown v. Board* decision, white officials throughout the South tried to minimize the effectiveness of the NAACP, which had brought the case. Founded in 1909 in response to a wave of lynching against black men, the NAACP was dedicated to overcoming racial discrimination in every arena, including the vote. In Greenville, Mississippi, the White Citizens' Council demanded that local school boards dismiss African American teachers whose names appeared on voting rolls. And in South Carolina, the legislature passed a law banning any city or state employee from belonging to the NAACP, viewed as a subversive organization harboring Communist sympathizers. After a failed attempt to organize a protest, Clark and forty-two others who admitted to their affiliation were fired. To Clark this was absurd, part of the instinct by whites to view any black movement as inspired by Communists. "The KKK is an organization and the White Citizens' Council is an organization and they can belong to those," she said. "Why can't I belong to the NAACP?"

Newly fired from her job, Clark decided to start a school for black adults. With Esau Jenkins, a bus driver who had coached some passengers to pass voter registration tests, they built a stealth front, a grocery store where local Johns Island farmers could sell goods to residents, with profits earmarked for hiring a teacher. It was a façade to hide classrooms in the back, where they would teach blacks to read and write, without detection by whites. Clark hired Bernice Robinson, a beautician, to teach. When Robinson protested that she had no training, Clark said, "We need a community worker ... who cares for the people." They scheduled classes around the farm calendar – mostly in off-season months of December, January, and February. When students stumbled over their words, Robinson would use the words in her next spelling lesson. When they asked her how to fill out a money order, she got one from the post office to demonstrate. And when they could read, she coached them on election laws and parts of the state constitution a

Figure 11.1 Septima Poinsette Clark (center) organized the first citizenship schools for black adults in the Sea Islands, South Carolina. In 1954, Septima Clark was fired from her job as a teacher after the Supreme Court ruled in *Brown v. Board of Education* against separate but unequal education. Instead, she began citizenship schools to teach black adults how to pass literacy tests. Martin Luther King later hired Clark to expand the program throughout the South. In 1955, Rosa Parks (left) refused to give up her seat to a white passenger, sparking a 381-day boycott in which the 50,000 black residents of Montgomery, Alabama, most women, walked to work. "I'll never forget the pictures of old black women walking in the sun," recalled activist Charles Jones. "When you see an old black woman in her 70s walking with her shoes in her hand, you know that there is something very profound about that." Also pictured (right) is Parks' mother Leona McCauley and civil rights leader Rosa Parks (left). *Source:* Library of Congress Prints and Photographs.

registrar would likely require them to recite. As the number of blacks registered to vote on Johns Island increased, so did excitement about the promise of citizenship schools, which spread throughout the islands. Eventually they would become a staple of civil rights activism.

Resistance was also stirring elsewhere in the South. On December 1, 1955, a 42-year-old seamstress named Rosa Parks refused to give up her seat to a white passenger at the front of a public bus in Montgomery, Alabama. In fact, Parks was of mixed race – three of her four grandparents were white – but the discrimination against her stemmed from her black ancestry. Like many women drawn to the movement, she had first organized resistance to sexual violence against black women. On meeting Recy Taylor in 1945, a young woman from Abbeville, Alabama who had been raped by a gang of white men, Parks helped found the Committee for Equal Justice. Now, Parks' political defiance set off a year-old boycott of Montgomery's businesses that saw many women playing singular roles in the drama.

Jo An Robinson risked her job at Alabama State College to organize the boycott under the Women's Political Council, distributing more than 50,000 flyers on the evening of Parks' arrest. As the Rev. Martin Luther King Jr. debated whether to join the fight, black women forced his hand. For 381 days, the 50,000 black residents of Montgomery, most women, walked to work. Sometimes they were showered with rotten eggs or water balloons. Some were fired from their jobs. Others had crosses burned on their lawns. Still they marched. "I'll never forget the pictures of old black women walking in the sun," marveled activist Charles Jones. "When you see an old black woman in her 70s walking with her shoes in her hand, you know that there is something very profound about that." It was, said one observer, as if "leaders were trapped by the effectiveness of the grassroots." Throughout the boycott, the black population was divided – between those who wanted to end the conflict and take the issue to the courts, and those who wanted to keep fighting. Afterward, male civil rights leaders posed for photos on Montgomery's newly integrated buses. Rosa Parks was at home, taking care of her mother. As no one hired her in Montgomery, she later moved to Detroit.

Inspired by Rosa Parks and the Montgomery bus boycott, New York activist Ella Baker, who had been raised in Raleigh, North Carolina, co-founded a new organization called In Friendship. In the 1940s, Baker had risked her life traveling through the South to recruit new members and open new chapters for the NAACP. Now she wanted to fight against Jim Crow laws in the South. In her years of travel, she had come to feel the NAACP was too bureaucratic to spark social change. She was delighted by the idea that Montgomery, the Confederacy's former capital, might launch a new civil rights movement, where grassroots activism and mass resistance would finally topple the web of laws meant to keep blacks from their rights of citizenship, including the vote. A beyond-the-scenes organizer, she eschewed what she called "charismatic leadership," preferring the "participatory democracy" of action in the street. It was up to the oppressed to decide on the avenue of their liberation. "You didn't see me on television, you didn't see news stories about me," she later reflected. "The kind of role that I tried to play was to pick up pieces or put together pieces out of which I hoped organization might come. My theory is, strong people don't need strong leaders."

One who answered the call was Vera Mae Pigee (Fig. 11.2), whose beauty salon at 407 Ashton Street in the heart of Clarksdale's black business district had long been a gathering place for activists. A business-woman whose profession allowed her to talk to clients while doing their hair about the importance of the vote or of education, Pigee was also head of the Coahoma County NAACP Youth Council. Under her leadership, young activists one summer went door to door for the NAACP's Crusade for Voters. Announcing the drive at churches and schools, they managed to sign up new voters.

On Thanksgiving Day in 1961, Clarksdale Mayor W. S. Kincaide announced that bands from two black institutions – the High School and Coahoma County Junior College – would be banned from the annual Christmas Parade, long a city tradition. By then, Pigee's beauty shop had become a center of the female economy, a site of "activist

Figure 11.2   Vera Mae Pigee (center) was a hairdresser whose beauty salon at 407 Ashton Street in the heart of Clarksdale's black business district in Mississippi had long been a gathering place for activists. A businesswoman whose profession allowed her to talk to clients while doing their hair about the importance of the vote or of education, Pigee led a boycott against white businesses after local officials banned black student bands from participating in the annual Christmas Parade, with the slogan, "No Parade, No Trade." Like many African American women involved in the civil rights movement, she organized from the grassroots. Here she uses a back room at her salon to teach black adults in citizenship classes, what historians call a site of "activist mothering." In 1965 alone, one hundred of her graduates registered to vote. *Source:* Getty Images. Charles Moore.

mothering" and a safe space for civil rights work. Meeting at Pigee's shop, students debated options. A few nights later their parents joined them for a mass meeting at the Metropolitan Baptist Church. She suggested a boycott of downtown businesses with the phrase, "No Parade, No Trade."

The boycott, endorsed by Aaron Henry, a pharmacist and drug store owner in Clarksdale who was chairman of the state's NAACP, lasted two years. On December 7, Coahoma County officials began prosecuting Aaron Henry and Vera Pigee and others, charging them with conducting an illegal boycott and sentencing them to fines, and jail sentences for the men. There were also retaliations. Henry's wife Noelle was fired from her teaching job. Vera Pigee's husband Paul managed to retain his job at a local plant despite pressure from the White Citizens' Council. When Police Chief Ben Collins entered her home, he called her Vera, the vernacular whites used to disparage blacks. Describing herself as "a wife, mother, political prisoner, business and professional woman," she corrected him. "Even if I am brought in handcuffs," she said, "my name is still *Mrs.* Vera Pigee." On December 18, so many African Americans came to the courthouse for the trial that officials moved the proceedings to a room in the jail, where spectators were not permitted.

Tapped by Septima Clark, by 1961 Pigee was running four citizenship schools in Clarksdale, offering night classes at her shop. Once, under her tutelage, black citizens attempting to register at the courthouse arrived in their Sunday best to find a witness – Curtis Wilkie, a reporter for the *Clarksdale Press Register* and later the *New York Times*. Wilkie observed that only a handful of citizens were allowed to register that day, as county officials wanted to ensure "a solid white majority." Within four years, Pigee was supervising twenty citizenship schools. In 1965 alone, some one hundred of her graduates had registered to vote.

In September 1957, nine black students enrolled at the all white Central High School in Little Rock, Arkansas. Governor Orval Faubus called in the Arkansas National Guard to block their entry. In response, President Eisenhower sent in federal troops to escort them into the school. The nine students – Minnijean Brown, Elizabeth Eckford, Ernest Green, Thelma Mothershed, Melba Patillo, Gloria Ray, Terrence Roberts, Jefferson Thomas, and Carlotta Walls – had been recruited by Daisy Gatson Bates, president of the Arkansas NAACP and with her husband publisher of the African American newspaper, the Arkansas *State Press.* During the tense three-month desegregation fight at Central High, a rock crashed the window of her newspaper with a note that read, "Stone This Time, Dynamite Next." Soon the paper would be closed because of boycotts from white advertisers and threats from white vigilantes. Every morning during the crisis, the nine students would gather at the Bates home, and arrive at school together. And every afternoon, they met in the Bates' basement to talk about the day's experiences. Harry Ashmore, the white liberal editor of the Arkansas *Gazette*, said he doubted they would have withstood the pressures of "that disoriented school year" without her "undaunted presence." When the NAACP announced in 1958 it was giving the prestigious Spingarn Award to the nine students, outraged friends insisted that Bates be included. The NAACP capitulated, and she was honored with them.

The Movement Rises

On February 1, 1960, four black college students from North Carolina A & T University sat down at a "whites-only" Woolworth counter in Greensboro, asking for a cup of coffee. They were ignored, but stayed until the store closed. The next day several dozen protesters arrived, including female students from nearby Bennett College. By the third day, when sixty African American protesters asked for service, television cameras were also on hand. By the fourth day, so many black college students appeared – by one estimate 300 – that they spread out to integrate other businesses in the city. Within three months, the idea had spread to fifty-five cities in thirteen U.S. states. In Nashville, protesters led by an influential Fisk student named Diane Nash successfully integrated downtown lunch counters. Meeting at Shaw University to organize this nascent movement, students elected a president – Marion Barry Jr., later mayor of Washington, DC – who hadn't even been present for demonstrations. "Diane was a devoted, beautiful leader but she was the wrong sex," explained activist John Lewis. "There was a desire to emphasize and showcase black manhood." Prathia Hall, a leading Student Non-Violent Coordinating Committee organizer, argued that black women had no problem with men being out front, because "it was important to our community that black males be seen as competent, standing up and giving strong leadership." The sit-in tactic was born, and so were Freedom Rides aimed at desegregating public buses and accommodations.

Though the protesters practiced non-violence, taking training in how to curl up to avoid the blows of angry white crowds, law enforcement did not. Often the students on the Freedom Rides, leaving northern cities on interstate buses, arrived in the South to be bloodied, injured, and in some cases maimed for life. In the 1960s, there were only three television stations, ABC, CBS, and NBC, that offered news, and now they sent their video cameras into the scenes of conflict. Rather than reading about the events in the newspapers, viewers could experience the shock of seeing images of beefy white police officers beating young, appealing college students to keep them from integrating the American South. The effect was explosive, and enraged public opinion in the United States and around the world.

U.S. Attorney General Robert F. Kennedy urged a "cooling off period" in attempts to integrate the interstate transportation system, saying images of Freedom Riders enduring beatings and imprisonment were undermining U.S. credibility abroad. To this James Farmer, director of the Congress of Racial Equality (CORE), replied, "We have been cooling off for 350 years. If we cool off any longer we will be in a deep freeze." Tactics divided the movement in emotional debates, pitting those who wanted to battle discrimination against those who wanted to fight for the vote. Baker, the only civil rights leader to organize for all three of the principal organizations of the day – the NAACP, the Southern Christian Leadership Conference (SCLC), and the Student Non-Violent Coordinating Committee (SNCC) – finally quieted internal conflict by suggesting that each side work for its own goal, in tandem.

To Robert Kennedy and his allies, the fight for the right to vote seemed far more attainable, a goal whose justice even southern politicians might eventually acknowledge, at least in private. In addition, key civil rights supporters – including black singer and actor Harry Belafonte – argued that African Americans, especially in the rural South, did not need integration at expensive lunch counters. What they needed was political power, to make social change from the ballot box. To steer the process, in the spring of 1961, civil rights activists and Justice Department officials met with philanthropists in Washington, DC to coordinate funding for a voting registration drive in the South. This campaign for electoral equality would reach its apogee during the Mississippi Freedom Summer of 1964, with its call for an end to whites-only primaries, and the famous "Bloody Sunday" protest walk from Selma to Montgomery in 1965, which led directly to the Voting Rights Act. All would test the mettle of the Justice Department and the backbone of civil rights leaders, and demonstrate the power of grassroots activism – and television – to inspire political action.

During the drive, King, Abernathy, Hosea Williams, Jesse Jackson Jr., Julian Bond, John Lewis, Aaron Henry, James Farmer, Robert Moses, Amzie Moore, and other men often set the agenda for voting rights advocacy, nationally and at the local level. Often they skillfully parried protests in the South with one eye on press coverage in the North. Sometimes they clashed with one another, about tactics, optics, and effect. And occasionally they stood toe-to-toe with white officials from the White House, Congress, Justice Department, and Supreme Court. But it was the African American women, attuned to the wounds and temperature of the community, who often mustered the shock troops for social change. One historian noted that women represented the majority at mass meetings, did most of the voter registration work, led registration marches to county courthouses, and served time in prison. Women, said one activist, were "the real movers of the people."

When SNCC came looking for volunteers to recruit voters in Mississippi towns, women offered leadership. Fannie Lou Hamer in Ruleville and Laura McGhee in Greenwood answered the call. Like the Montgomery bus boycott inspired by Rosa Parks and organized by Jo Ann Robinson, the voter registration drive engineered by Vera Mae Pigee in Clarksdale, the integration of Little Rock High School staged by Daisy Bates, women led in place.

Winning the Vote in Mississippi and Alabama

Medgar Evers had been gaining visibility and reputation for attempting to awaken this new generation to the task of reclaiming their rights. As he pulled into the driveway of the home he shared with his wife Myrlie and their three young children in Jackson on June 12, 1963, he was shot in the back. White supremacist Byron De La Beckwith, whose fingerprints were found on a nearby gun, was charged with the murder. Two trials in 1964 ended in hung juries, with witnesses testifying he had been elsewhere. A third jury, in 1994, convicted De La Beckwith of murder. Sentenced to life in prison, he died in jail seven years later, at 80. Evers was buried, at 37, with full military honors, at Arlington National Cemetery.

As if history was repeating this vicious trail of blood, one day before Mississippi Freedom Summer officially began in 1964, three volunteers – James Chaney from Meridian, Mississippi, and Andrew Goodman and Michael "Mickey" Schwerner from New York – went missing in Neshoba County. By August their bodies were found in an earthen dam, red clay in Goodman's lungs and fists, suggesting he had been buried alive. Like Emmett Till, they had been murdered for defying the South's code of white supremacy, of fraternizing and working together to empower black women and men.

The day after their bodies were found, a delegation of blacks and whites, mostly women, including Fannie Lou Hamer, went to the Democratic National Convention in Atlantic City. They left by bus to challenge the all-white delegation elected by Mississippi's white electorate. As Hamer began to describe her travails in seeking the vote to a televised hearing by the credentials committee, Lyndon Johnson was watching from the White House. Eager to win a term of his own after inheriting the presidency of the slain John F. Kennedy, LBJ was fearful this display of democracy would jeopardize his chances. So he scheduled a news conference that made no news, only drew the television cameras away from the convention. Instead, the networks broadcast Hamer's entire testimony that evening, to a larger audience.

In the face of intimidation, assassination, and political opposition, the young students of the Mississippi Freedom Summer – along with interfaith and interracial clergymen, and the reformers of Wednesdays in Mississippi – descended from the North to join the effort. To many in Mississippi, the infusion of new energy into a voter registration drive was an invasion. In Jackson, the police force beefed up its arsenal with shotguns, tear gas, and a tank. Newspapers predicted a coming occupation by protesters. Governor Paul Johnson Jr. warned that "law and order" would be "maintained, and maintained Mississippi style." During the summer, at least eighty civil rights volunteers were beaten, 1,000 arrested, and thirty-seven churches bombed or burned to the ground. For the governor and his supporters, the line against expanding the voting rolls to include black men and women was sacrosanct, a line not to be crossed, at whatever price. For activists, black and white, the racism, sexism, and hostility they encountered and the community support they received were life changing.

Before she came to Mississippi Gwendolyn Zoharah Simmons had been arrested for trying to desegregate a local restaurant in Atlanta. The president of Spelman University, where she was a sophomore, threatened to revoke her scholarship and asked her if she was a Communist or a paid agitator. Her grandmother told her she had disgraced her relatives by becoming the first person in the family ever to be arrested. Told by her family never to come back if she persisted, she left for Mississippi to work in Freedom Summer. Before summer's end, she was supervising twenty-three volunteers in Laurel, running a Freedom School, a day care center and a library, which she created, boasting 1,500 volumes. As the Laurel Public Library was closed to the black community, it was a first for many adults in the city ever to set foot in a library to borrow books. Over the summer white supremacists firebombed the SNCC offices and its library, burned crosses on supporters' lawns, and harassed them with undeserved arrests and beatings. When summer ended she waived a full scholarship from Antioch College in Ohio, electing to stay in Mississippi to finish the work. Like other female activists, Simmons adhered to what she saw later as "a feminist style of leadership," democratic to a fault, a contrast to the authoritarian, top-down style of many male leaders. Still she gained a reputation as an Amazon, a no-nonsense administrator.

Like Simmons, many young women were determined not to accept the harsh cruelties and limitations imposed by a century of segregation.

And like Hamer, many older women had been hardened by poverty and survived bigotry, and they were tired of waiting. Together, these generations of women changed the face of the movement. Fred Powledge covered civil rights protests for the *Atlanta Journal* and later the *New York Times*. A young man, he was struck by the toughness of these women. It was as if they were rising up and saying, "I'm not going to take any more of this shit. Send me to jail, shoot me, but no more." He called them the movement's "fiercest, most courageous, heaviest battering ram against segregation."

As the SNCC muscled up its presence in Mississippi in 1962, Charles McLaurin arrived in Ruleville, going door to door, seeking blacks willing to risk economic hardship and police brutality to register to vote. By mid-August the SNCC volunteer had recruited only three women willing to drive with him to the Indianola Courthouse. As they approached the courthouse, he recalls his knees shaking. But the three women just got out of the car and headed toward the courthouse, "as if this was the long walk that [led] to the Gold Gate of Heaven, their heads held high." The county clerk had locked the door. No matter. They would return. "This was the day I learned that numbers were not important," he said, "that a faithful few was better than an uncertain ten."

Later that month, at Williams Chapel Church in Ruleville, SCLC's James Bevel preached. Then SNCC's James Forman spoke. It was the first meeting Hamer had attended. "He told us we could vote out people – hateful policemen – and how if we had a chance to vote, you know, that we wouldn't allow these people to be in office … It made so much sense to me because right then, you see, the man that was our night policeman here in Ruleville was a brother to J. W. Milam." Milam, acquitted by a white jury, confessed to *Look Magazine* later that he helped lynch 14-year-old Emmett Till when he visited Mississippi from Chicago. The open casket of his deformed face was so horrific it had seared itself into the memory of many activists, including Fannie Lou Hamer. Now Forman was offering her a tool, the beginning of a remedy to centuries of abuse, violence, discrimination, and segregation.

Two weeks later McLaurin returned to the courthouse – this time with seventeen black Mississippians willing to take the risk. When their bus pulled up in front of the Indianola Courthouse, many hesitated. Here was the citadel of white dominion, the arsenal of police power. There was a collective doubt of will, a shared fear. "Then this one little stocky lady just stepped off the bus and went right on up to the courthouse and into the circuit clerk's office," McLaurin recalled. Fannie Lou Hamer (Fig. 11.3), a sharecropper who had picked cotton on the Marlow plantation since the age of 6, announced that they were there to register. The clerk asked her to interpret section 16 of the state constitution,

Figure 11.3 From the age of 6, Fannie Lou Hamer picked cotton in the fields of Mississippi. A childhood case of polio left her with a battered leg and a lifelong limp. Still, by the age of 13, she could pick 300 pounds of cotton a day. After marrying Perry Hamer, a 32-year-old tractor driver, the two lived on the W. D. Marlow plantation outside Ruleville. But when she marched to the registrar's office in Indianola to register to vote, Marlow told her, "We're not ready for that in Mississippi now." To which Fannie Lou Hamer replied, "Mr. Marlow, I didn't go down there to register for you. I went down to register for myself." Losing her house and her job, fired on by vigilantes trying to kill her, she joined the civil rights movement. And after she was beaten in a sexualized attack, she told the nation about it in a televised speech before the Democratic National Convention in 1964, where she and others had gone to challenge the credentials of the all-white Mississippi delegation. As she once said, "Nobody's free until everybody's free." *Source:* Library of Congress Prints and Photographs.

on de facto laws. "I knew about as much about a facto law as a horse knows about Christmas Day," she said. Her application rejected, she and the others returned to their bus for the ride home. On the road, a policeman stopped them and arrested the driver because, he said, the color of their bus was too similar to school bus yellow. They pooled their funds to bail the driver out of jail. Hamer, with "her huge sad eyes and a voice that rolled like thunder," led them in song.

On returning to her home, her two daughters warned her that Marlow had been around, that he planned to evict her from their home. She moved into town with her friend Mary Tucker. Vigilantes fired shots into the bedroom where Hamer slept, and into two other homes, wounding two young girls. Intimidation was the weapon of choice for white supremacists intent on squashing this nascent claim on black electoral power. For their participation in the movement, a black city worker was fired, two black dry cleaning firms were closed, and the Williams Chapel Baptist Church lost its tax exemption. At one point, after the Hamers moved to a rickety house on Lafayette Street, the city sent them a water bill for $9,000. Fannie Lou Hamer protested – pointing out to officials the house had no running water.

Robert Parris Moses, a Harvard-trained philosopher and math teacher who first came to Mississippi in 1961, wanted Fannie Lou Hamer to come to Nashville with him for a SNCC rally. He understood, as he reflected later, that Hamer "had Mississippi in her bones. Martin Luther King or the SNCC field secretaries, they couldn't do what Fannie Lou Hamer did. They couldn't be a sharecropper." So McLaurin was asked to locate the woman who had been evicted from her home and fired from her job for registering to vote, the one who had kept a busload of frightened people calm with her booming voice, singing Freedom Songs. McLaurin worked local sources to locate her. Once he arrived at her front door, it was as if Fannie Lou Hamer had been waiting all her life. "I'll be ready in a minute," she said. As he stood there waiting, "alone, in a strange place and an unknown land," McLaurin marveled that "although these old ladies knew the risk involved … they were willing to try."

Soon Fannie Lou Hamer became a public persona, touring the country, raising money, shocking audiences with her tales of discrimination. While on the road, she asked SNCC workers to help her study the Mississippi state constitution so she could register to vote. On December 4 she again appeared at the county courthouse in Indianola. This time she passed the test. But the next day she and three other women – Irene Johnson, Hattie Sisson, and Ruby Davis – went to Ruleville City Hall to secure their names in the roll of voters. They were told they could not, as they had not paid their poll taxes for two years.

And later, after she and seven others had gone to Charleston to get training at Septima Clark's citizenship school, they stopped in Winona, Mississippi on the way home. The date was June 9, 1963 and the air was thick with hostility. Some got off the Continental Bus to use rest rooms, others sought service at a lunch counter. The waitress refused and called the police. They were jailed. Most were beaten, including 15-year-old June Johnson. Annelle Ponder was pummeled, for refusing to say "yes, sir," to the officer beating her. For Hamer, the beating was a trauma whose story she would retell all her life, a reminder that the white political establishment would sink to any means to keep exclusive hold on political power.

"It wasn't too long before three white men came to my cell. One of these men was a State Highway Patrolman ... And he said, 'We're going to make you wish you was dead,'" she said. They carried her to a cell where a black prisoner was ordered to take up the blackjack and beat her. "I was beat by the first Negro until he was exhausted." Then a second black prisoner beat her as she screamed and a white State Highway Patrolman lifted her dress above her shoulders, sexualizing the encounter. "I began to scream and one white man got up and began to beat me in my head.... All of this is on account of we want to register."

In nearby Greenwood, early movement efforts had led to fewer than thirty registrations, many followed by shootings, bombings, and arrests. Sam Block, a Mississippi native, recalled the work. "I canvassed every day and every night until I found about seven or eight people to carry up to register." The first time they went to the courthouse in Greenwood, the sheriff told him, "Where you from? I know you ain't from here, cuz I know every nigger and his mammy." Block replied, "Well, you know all the niggers, do you know any colored people?" The sheriff spat in his face and warned him to get out of town. To which Block, in a reply of remarkable audacity, told the sheriff that he was the one who should pack up and leave: "I'm here to stay, I came here to do a job and this is my intention, I'm going to do this job."

One of Block's earliest supporters was Laura McGhee, who owned a small farm outside of the city, and had raised her six sons to be fearless in fighting for racial justice. She was drawn to the cause in 1955, after her brother, an NAACP official named Gus Courts, was shot by assailants in retaliation for the *Brown v. Board* decision and fled his home. "She had this feeling that if it's worthwhile, it's worth fighting for," said her youngest son, Silas, "and if you don't want to fight for it, you don't need it." In the 1950s, white neighbors coveting her land and livestock often harassed her. Once she saw a neighbor cutting a ditch across her land. She climbed up on his bulldozer and shook him. When the sheriff arrived, she told him they had ten minutes to get that bulldozer off her land or she would burn it.

When SNCC came to town, she made her farm available for citizenship schools and put her property up as bail for jailed activists so frequently authorities eventually prohibited it. Perhaps her greatest feat was to confront police officers at a jail where her son Jake was imprisoned for trying to integrate a public theater. When a cop said she couldn't go through a door to see her son, she replied, "The hell I can't. I come down here to get my son Jake." Then, according to SNCC lawyer Bob Zellner, she slugged the policeman in the face.

Zellner was SNCC's first white field secretary, an Alabama-born southerner who had parted from his family history – his father and grandfather had both been Klan members. He recalled the scene with a mixture of awe and fear, sure there would be reprisal. "She kept jabbing the policeman like a prizefighter and every time she hit him, his head banged into the door," he recounted. Finally Zellner told her, "Mrs. McGhee, I think you've hit him enough here. You've got him pretty well subdued." She seemed little perturbed. "Here's this policeman, and he's got this huge black eye and Mrs. McGhee is totally unrepentant," Zellner recalled. Though police arrested Laura McGhee, they never pressed charges. To Zellner, who understood white southerners perhaps more than most civil rights workers, it would have been too embarrassing to explain that a black woman had pounded one of Mississippi's finest. In any event, the story only gilded her reputation for fearlessness, and in coming registration drives, many in the town of Browning, just outside Greenwood, refused to go to the county courthouse to attempt to register unless she was with them. She accompanied every caravan, standing across the street while they went inside to the clerk's office. It was a form of shared community, of standing together instead of alone.

By 1965, King was leading a series of efforts to win the vote for blacks in Alabama. Activists had chosen Selma, because Dallas County Sheriff Jim Clark was known as a staunch white segregationist whose violent tactics against peaceful protesters might finally engage the nation's ire. Eventually, in a Bloody Sunday crackdown Sunday March 7, those predictions came true. Clark unleashed his deputies to batter, assault, bloody, and gas peaceful protesters who were seeking the vote. The *Washington Post* editorial was blistering. "The news from Selma, Alabama, where police beat and mauled and gassed unarmed, helpless and unoffending citizens, will shock and alarm the whole nation," editors wrote. Calling the attack a "brutality" of a state government "without conscience or morals," the *Post* called for legislation to make the federal government a protector of electoral rights. ABC, which had been broadcasting a primetime debut of *Judgment at Nuremberg*, about the trial of Nazi officials for war crimes, interrupted the program for fifteen minutes to show video from Selma. Some confused viewers thought the scenes from Selma were actual footage of Third Reich criminals assaulting the innocent. One of those beaten was Annie Cooper.

A few years earlier, Annie Lee Wilkerson Cooper had returned to Alabama from the North to care for her mother. She was dumbfounded to discover that she could not vote in Alabama, though she had previously voted in Kentucky and Ohio. She tried to register in Montgomery in 1963, only to be fired from her job as a nurse at the Dunn Rest Home. So on January 25, 1965, when the voting rights crusade came to Alabama, she stood for hours at the Dallas County courthouse. Clark prodded her with a club, ordering her to leave. A lifetime of frustration and anger welled up. She wheeled and gave him a hard right hook in the jaw, knocking him backward. Deputies pinned her arms to the ground as Clark reared up. After deputies threw her to the ground, Annie Lee Cooper yelled at the sheriff, "I wish you would hit me, you scum." At which point Clark "brought his Billy club down on her head with a whack that was heard throughout the crowd gathered on the street." The photo of the white sheriff striking a middle-aged black woman – which the *New York Times* ran on its front page, the *Washington Post* on page two – roused white sympathy around the country.

Women of Color and the Vote

On paper, the Nineteenth Amendment empowered women throughout the country to vote. In truth, state and local ordinances used intimidation and legal obstacles to prevent that right, especially for women of color. For African American women in the South, and other women of color, it would take decades more. The coloring of the electorate – begun in the 1890s when the United States acquired imperial territories – then moved to the ballot box.

For Native Americans, disenfranchisement has a long history, including Andrew Jackson's Indian Removal Policy that robbed them, without consent, of their land and heritage. Even later, when they had been sequestered on reservations, the vote proved elusive. In 1871, when still a territory, Montana refused to open voter precincts on Indian reservations, claiming they were not residents, and thus not eligible to vote. The federal Dawes Act of 1887 offered the promise of the vote to Native Americans who agreed to leave their tribes and pay taxes on their land as individuals. As the bill's author, Senator Henry Dawes of Massachusetts, explained, until Native Americans "will consent to give up their lands, and divide them among their citizens so that each can own the land he cultivates, they will not make much progress." Few Native Americans accepted the terms. After the Dawes bill was enacted, Congress admitted Montana to the union with a state constitution that extended voting to all male citizens, black or white, but not to Indians, on grounds that they paid no taxes on their land. Often, even Indians who paid taxes were discouraged from exercising their rights by voter identification laws that required them to travel great distances to register and, once arrived, to withstand abject discrimination from white officials. Even after Congress passed the Indian Citizenship Act in 1924, various states with large Native American populations, including Montana, passed local laws to thwart Indian voting.

In June 1986 – more than sixty years after Indians won the right to vote – a federal judge in Montana declared that "official acts of discrimination" had "interfered with the rights of Indian citizens to register and vote" in Big Horn County, Montana. At-large elections for county and school board effectively denied them participation. Indians constituted 46 percent of the population, but plaintiffs, represented by the American Civil Liberties Union (ACLU), argued that white voters routinely blocked their candidates for seats on the board of commissioners and school districts. No further evidence of the merit of their claim was needed than the reaction of a local rancher, Big Horn County Commissioner Ed Miller. He said he longed "for the good old days" when Indians stayed on the reservation. Threatening to challenge the ruling, based on protections of the Voting Rights Act, to the Supreme Court, Miller said, "The Voting Rights Act is a bad thing" and insisted, "Things were fine around here" until the law. "Now they want to vote. What next?" What happened next is that abandonment of at-large districts allowed Native Americans in District 2 to elect John Doyle Jr. as Big Horn County's first Indian county commissioner. What also happened is that white opponents organized. Ranchers formed a Secret Concerned Citizens Committee to look for evidence against Janine Windy Boy and other plaintiffs. And in 2004, Native American voters were prevented from voting in South Dakota's primary after they failed to show photo IDs, not required under state law.

Chinese Americans were granted citizenship, and the right to vote, in 1943. Other Asian Americans were not entitled to vote until 1952, when the McCarran-Walter Act declared them citizens, overturning the Asian Exclusion Act of 1924. Ten years after passage of the Voting Rights Act of 1965, Congress added Section 203, requiring special language ballots in communities with 5 percent or more than 10,000 citizens of Hispanic, Asian, Native or Alaskan Native heritage and poor English skills. By 2018, states were printing ballots in dozens of languages, and Arizona offered oral help for Apache, Navajo, and Pueblo voters. So pervasive has the practice become that in Los Angeles County alone, language minority ballots are printed in Spanish, Filipino, Japanese, Korean, and Vietnamese. Participation rates have risen, and with them victories at the polls for minority candidates. Before the twenty-first century, for instance, no Asian American had been elected in New York City, despite the fact that nearly a million Asian Americans called the city home, more than their combined totals in San Francisco and Los Angeles. In 2001, thirteen ran for the city council and one was elected. In 2004, Texas elected its first Vietnamese American to the legislature. But Asian American voters supporting a Vietnamese candidate in an Alabama primary election that same year were challenged at the polls. The losing candidate, an incumbent, justified the challenge by reportedly saying, "We figured if they couldn't speak good English, they possibly weren't American citizens."

For Hispanic Americans, the struggle to achieve voting rights began in 1848, with the Guadalupe Hidalgo Treaty that ended the Mexican–American War and ceded to the United States 525,000 additional square miles, including lands in what are now Arizona, California, Colorado, New Mexico, Utah, and Wyoming. Under the treaty, Mexico gave up all claims to Texas, recognizing the Rio Grande as the new boundary between the two countries. Finally, the treaty declared that Mexicans who opted to stay in the new American territories were U.S. citizens, with the same rights of life, liberty, and property as other citizens. For men, this included the right to vote, but as happened with other minorities, Mexican American rights were soon nullified by local laws that required English proficiency tests and property requirements. More, as would happen later in the South against black men, local vigilantes in the Southwest threatened Mexican American men who attempted to exercise their right to vote. More than a century later, Congress renewed the Voting Rights Act in 1975, lawmakers added Section 203, requiring minority language ballots in locations where non-English-speaking citizens were prevented from voting. Only then did the promise of Guadalupe Hidalgo come full circle. By 2018, Census Bureau data suggested that more than 29 million Latino Americans were eligible to vote, representing 12.8 percent of the eligible electorate.

In 1952, Congress enacted the Immigration and Nationality Act, which established a quota system for immigration, and extended citizenship to residents who lived in the U.S. territories of Puerto Rico, the Virgin Islands, and Guam. Under the law, they were not entitled to vote in national elections but could send delegations to the national party conventions every four years and they would have non-voting representatives in Congress. In 2000, Puerto Rican Gregorio Igartúa filed a new court case, claiming a constitutional right to vote for President and Vice President of the United States. "Panels of this court have rejected such claims on all three occasions," said an appellate court. "We now do so again." The court also rejected Igartúa's claim that "the failure of the Constitution to grant this vote should be declared a violation of U.S. treaty obligations." Bowing to the essential compromises made during the nation's founding, the court said it was the states, not the federal government, that extended voting privileges. Those in the territories, already citizens, could vote if they resided in one of the nation's states.

The history of female activism to win the vote is a story of how women of all races convinced men in power that it was in their interests to relinquish exclusive hold over the nation's political system. From the country's revolutionary roots, in which mothers were assigned and embraced the political purpose of educating the next generation in the nation's republican ideals, women have been political actors alongside men. And for African American and other women of color, the achievement of the Voting Rights Act of 1965 and its extension ten years later was the capstone of an ideal, that every voter should be equal in importance to any other. This new value of "one person, one vote" – hardly the Founders' intent – was codified in the 1964 Supreme Court decision, *Reynolds v. Sims.* In that case, an 8–1 majority invoked Equal Protection Clause of the Fourteenth Amendment to rule that state legislators had to apportion their districts not on land mass geography but on "one person, one vote." As Chief Justice Earl Warren wrote, "Legislators represent people, not trees or acres. Legislators are elected by voters, not farms or cities or economic interests."

The principle of "one person, one vote" enunciated by the Supreme Court in 1964 also opened the door to a series of challenges that are still roiling the nation's politics. They are the unfinished business of suffrage, from Voter ID laws to Electoral College reform. Like the women's suffrage movement, these campaigns to change American election laws will likely spring up from the local level. Giving states power over elections was one of the compromises the Founders made in writing the U.S. constitution in 1787 to knit the new republic together. It remains for a new generation of reformers to drive the campaign from the grassroots, much as their ancestors did in winning the vote for women, from the revolutionary fervor of the American colonies to the brave resistance to discrimination in the American South. May this history of suffrage activism inform the journey.

Bibliography

Chapter 1

Adams, Catherine, and Elizabeth H. Pleck. *Love of Freedom: Black Women in Colonial and Revolutionary New England.* New York: Oxford University Press, 2010.

Dunbar, Erica Armstrong. *Never Caught: The Washingtons' Relentless Pursuit of Their Runaway Slave, Ona Judge.* New York: Simon and Schuster, 2017.

Jones, Martha S. *All Bound Up Together: The Woman Question in African American Public Culture, 1830–1900.* Chapel Hill: University of North Carolina Press, 2009.

Kelley, Mary. *Learning to Stand & Speak: Women, Education, and Public Life in America's Republic.* Chapel Hill: University of North Carolina Press, 2006.

Kerber, Linda K. *Women of the Republic: Intellect and Ideology in Revolutionary America.* Chapel Hill: University of North Carolina Press, 1980.

Klinghoffer, Judith Apter, and Lois Elkis. "'The Petticoat Electors': Women's Suffrage in New Jersey, 1776–1807." *Journal of the Early Republic* 12, no. 2 (July 1, 1992): 159–193.

Nash, Margaret A. "Rethinking Republican Motherhood: Benjamin Rush and the Young Ladies' Academy of Philadelphia." *Journal of the Early Republic* 17, no. 2 (Summer 1997): 171–191.

Norton, Mary Beth. *Liberty's Daughters: The Revolutionary Experience of American Women, 1750–1800 : With a New Preface.* Ithaca: Cornell University Press, 1996.

Solomon, Barbara Miller. *In the Company of Educated Women: A History of Women and Higher Education in America.* New Haven: Yale University Press, 1985.

Zagarri, Rosemarie. *Revolutionary Backlash: Women and Politics in the Early American Republic.* Philadelphia: University of Pennsylvania Press, 2011.

And Yet They Persisted: How American Women Won the Right to Vote, First Edition. Johanna Neuman.
© 2020 John Wiley & Sons, Inc. Published 2020 by John Wiley & Sons, Inc.
Companion website: www.wiley.com/go/Neuman

Chapter 2

Beecher, Catharine. "Circular Addressed to the Benevolent Ladies of the U. States," Dec. 25, 1829, in Theda Purdue and Michael D. Green, eds., *The Cherokee Removal: A Brief History with Documents*. Boston: Bedford/St. Martin's, 2005.

Camp, Stephanie M. H. *Closer to Freedom: Enslaved Women and Everyday Resistance in the Plantation South*. Chapel Hill: University of North Carolina Press, 2009.

Faulkner, Carol. *Lucretia Mott's Heresy: Abolition and Women's Rights in Nineteenth-Century America*. Philadelphia: University of Pennsylvania Press, 2011.

Hansen, Debra Gold. *Strained Sisterhood: Gender and Class in the Boston Female Anti-Slavery Society*. Amherst: University of Massachusetts Press, 2009.

Jeffrey, Julie Roy. *The Great Silent Army of Abolitionism: Ordinary Women in the Antislavery Movement*. Chapel Hill: University of North Carolina Press, 1998.

Jones, Martha S. *All Bound Up Together: The Woman Question in African American Public Culture, 1830–1900*. Chapel Hill: University of North Carolina Press, 2009.

Kidd, Sue Monk. *The Invention of Wings*. New York: Penguin, 2014.

Portnoy, Alisse. *Their Right to Speak: Women's Activism in the Indian and Slave Debates*. Cambridge, MA: Harvard University Press, 2005.

Sterling, Dorothy. *Ahead of Her Time: Abby Kelley and the Politics of Antislavery*. New York: W. W. Norton & Company, 1994.

Wallace, Anthony. *The Long, Bitter Trail: Andrew Jackson and the Indians*. New York: Farrar, Straus and Giroux, 2011.

Chapter 3

Buhle, Paul, and Mari Jo Buhle. *The Concise History of Woman Suffrage: Selections from History of Woman Suffrage, Edited by* Elizabeth Cady Stanton, Susan B. Anthony, Matilda Joslyn Gage, and the National American Woman Suffrage Association. Urbana: University of Illinois Press, 2005.

DuBois, Ellen Carol. *Woman Suffrage and Women's Rights*. New York: NYU Press, 1998.

Dunbar, Erica Armstrong. *A Fragile Freedom: African American Women and Emancipation in the Antebellum City*. New Haven: Yale University Press, 2008.

Ginzberg, Lori D. *Elizabeth Cady Stanton: An American Life*. New York: Macmillan, 2010.

Inazu, John D. *Liberty's Refuge: The Forgotten Freedom of Assembly*. New Haven: Yale University Press, 2012.

Kennon, Donald R. "'An Apple of Discord': The Woman Question at the World's Anti-Slavery Convention of 1840." *Slavery & Abolition* 5, no. 3 (1984): 244–266.

McMillen, Sally G. *Seneca Falls and the Origins of the Women's Rights Movement*. Oxford: Oxford University Press, 2008.

Roybal, Karen R. *Archives of Dispossession: Recovering the Testimonios of Mexican American Herederas, 1848–1960*. Chapel Hill: University of North Carolina Press, 2017.

Stanton, Elizabeth Cady, Susan Brownell Anthony, and Matilda Joslyn Gage, eds. New York: *History of Woman Suffrage Vol. 1: 1848–1861.* Susan B. Anthony, 1881.

Tetrault, Lisa. *The Myth of Seneca Falls: Memory and the Women's Suffrage Movement, 1848–1898.* Chapel Hill: University of North Carolina Press, 2014.

Chapter 4

Douglass, Frederick. *Frederick Douglass on Women's Rights.* Edited by Philip Sheldon Foner. Cambridge, MA: Da Capo Press, 1992.

Dudden, Faye E. *Fighting Chance: The Struggle Over Woman Suffrage and Black Suffrage in Reconstruction America.* New York: Oxford University Press, 2011.

Gillette, William. *The Right to Vote: Politics and the Passage of the Fifteenth Amendment.* Baltimore: Johns Hopkins University Press, 1969.

Gornick, Vivian. *The Solitude of Self: Thinking About Elizabeth Cady Stanton.* New York: Macmillan, 2006.

Havelin, Kate. *Victoria Woodhull: Fearless Feminist.* New York: Twenty-First Century Books, 2006.

Lasser, Carol, *and Merrill, Marlene Deahl, eds. Friends and Sisters: Letters between Lucy Stone and Antoinette Brown Blackwell, 1846–93.* Champaign: University of Illinois Press, 1987.

McMillen, Sally G. *Lucy Stone: A Life.* New York: Oxford University Press, 2014.

Naparsteck, Martin. *The Trial of Susan B. Anthony: An Illegal Vote, a Courtroom Conviction and a Step Toward Women's Suffrage.* Jefferson, NC: McFarland, 2014.

Rhodes, Jane. *Mary Ann Shadd Cary: The Black Press and Protest in the Nineteenth Century.* Bloomington: Indiana University Press, 1999.

Chapter 5

Ault, Nelson A. "The Earnest Ladies: The Walla Walla Women's Club and the Equal Suffrage League of 1886–1889." *Pacific Northwest Quarterly* 42 (April 1951): 123–137.

Buechler, Steven M. *The Transformation of the Woman Suffrage Movement: The Case of Illinois, 1850–1920.* New Brunswick: Rutgers University Press, 1986.

Gullett, Gayle. *Becoming Citizens: The Emergence and Development of the California Women's Movement, 1880–1911.* Champaign: University of Illinois Press, 2000.

Hendricks, Wanda A. *Gender, Race, and Politics in the Midwest: Black Club Women in Illinois.* Bloomington: Indiana University Press, 1998.

Kerber, Linda. *No Constitutional Right to Be Ladies.* New York: Hill and Wang, 1998.

Madsen, Carol Cornwall, ed. *Battle for the Ballot: Essays on Woman Suffrage in Utah, 1870–1896.* Logan: Utah State University Press, 1997.

Marilley, Suzanne M. *Woman Suffrage and the Origins of Liberal Feminism in the United States, 1820–1920.* Cambridge, MA: Harvard University Press, 1996.

McCammon, Holly J., and Karen E. Campbell. "Winning the Vote in the West: The Political Successes of the Women's Suffrage Movements, 1866–1919." *Gender and Society* 15, no. 1 (February 1, 2001): 55–82.

Mead, Rebecca. *How the Vote Was Won: Woman Suffrage in the Western United States,* 1868–1914. New York: New York University Press, 2006.
Smith, Julia E. *Abby Smith and Her Cows.* New York: Arno Press, 1972.

Chapter 6

Cooper, Brittney C. *Beyond Respectability: The Intellectual Thought of Race Women.* Champaign: University of Illinois Press, 2017.
Giddings, Paula J. *When and Where I Enter: The Impact of Black Women on Race and Sex in America.* New York: William Morrow & Company, 1984.
Gilmore, Glenda Elizabeth. *Gender and Jim Crow: Women and the Politics of White Supremacy in North Carolina, 1896–1920.* Chapel Hill: University of North Carolina Press, 2013.
Hamlin, Kimberly A. *From Eve to Evolution: Darwin, Science, and Women's Rights in Gilded Age America.* Chicago: University of Chicago Press, 2014.
Kinzer, Stephen. *The True Flag: Theodore Roosevelt, Mark Twain, and the Birth of American Empire.* New York: Henry Holt and Company, 2017.
Materson, Lisa G. *For the Freedom of Her Race: Black Women and Electoral Politics in Illinois,* 1877–1932. Chapel Hill: University of North Carolina Press, 2009.
Newman, Louise Michele. *White Women's Rights: The Racial Origins of Feminism in the United States.* New York: Oxford University Press, 1999.
Silva, Noenoe K. *Aloha Betrayed: Native Hawaiian Resistance to American Colonialism.* Durham, NC: Duke University Press, 2004.
Sneider, Allison L. *Suffragists in an Imperial Age: U.S. Expansion and the Woman Question, 1870–1929.* Oxford: Oxford University Press, 2008.
Welch, Richard. *Response to Imperialism: The United States and the Philippine-American War, 1899–1902.* Chapel Hill: University of North Carolina Press, 1979.

Chapter 7

Barber, Lucy G. *Marching on Washington: The Forging of an American Political Tradition.* Berkeley: University of California Press, 2004.
DuBois, Ellen Carol. *Harriot Stanton Blatch and the Winning of Woman Suffrage.* New Haven: Yale University Press, 1997.
Finnegan, Margaret Mary. *Selling Suffrage: Consumer Culture and Votes for Women.* New York: Columbia University Press, 1999.
Goodier, Susan, and Karen Pastorello. *Women Will Vote: Winning Suffrage in New York State.* Ithaca: Cornell University Press, 2017.
Kraditor, Aileen S. *The Ideas of the Women's Suffrage Movement 1890–1920.* New York: W. W. Norton & Company, 1965.
Lindsey, Treva B. *Colored No More: Reinventing Black Womanhood in Washington.* Champaign: University of Illinois Press, 2017.
Mukherjee, Sumita. *Indian Suffragettes: Female Identities and Transnational Networks.* Oxford: Oxford University Press, 2018.

Neuman, Johanna. *Gilded Suffragists: The New York Socialites Who Fought for Women's Right to Vote.* New York: NYU Press, 2017.

Tickner, Lisa. *The Spectacle of Women: Imagery of the Suffrage Campaign 1907–14.* Chicago: University of Chicago Press, 1988.

Zahniser, Jill Diane, and Amelia R. Fry. *Alice Paul: Claiming Power.* New York: Oxford University Press, 2014.

Chapter 8

Bederman, Gail. *Manliness and Civilization: A Cultural History of Gender and Race in the United States, 1880–1917.* Chicago: University of Chicago Press, 2008.

Biel, Steven. *Down with the Old Canoe: A Cultural History of the Titanic Disaster.* New York: W. W. Norton & Company, 2012.

Cooney, Robert. *Winning the Vote: The Triumph of the American Woman Suffrage Movement.* Santa Cruz, CA: American Graphic Press, 2005.

Dyer, Thomas G. *Theodore Roosevelt and the Idea of Race.* Baton Rouge: Louisiana State University Press, 1992.

Graham, Sara Hunter. *Woman Suffrage and the New Democracy.* New Haven: Yale University Press, 1996.

Hoganson, Kristin L. *Fighting for American Manhood: How Gender Politics Provoked the Spanish-American and Philippine-American Wars.* New Haven: Yale University Press, 2000.

Keyssar, Alexander. *The Right to Vote: The Contested History of Democracy in the United States.* New York: Basic Books, 2009.

Kimmel, Michael S., and Thomas E. Mosmiller. *Against the Tide: "Pro-Feminist Men" in the United States: 1776– 1990, a Documentary History.* Boston: Beacon Press, 1992.

Kroeger, Brooke. *The Suffragents: How Women Used Men to Get the Vote.* New York: SUNY Press, 2017.

McCurry, Stephanie. *Confederate Reckoning: Power and Politics in the Civil War South.* Cambridge, MA: Harvard University Press, 2010.

Chapter 9

Adams, Katherine H., and Michael L. Keene. *Alice Paul and the American Suffrage Campaign.* Urbana: University of Illinois Press, 2008.

Capozzola, Christopher. *Uncle Sam Wants You: World War I and the Making of the Modern American Citizen.* Oxford: Oxford University Press, 2010.

Dumenil, Lynn. *The Second Line of Defense: American Women and World War I.* Chapel Hill: University of North Carolina Press, 2017.

Halcy, Sarah. *No Mercy Here: Gender, Punishment, and the Making of Jim Crow Modernity.* Chapel Hill: University of North Carolina Press, 2016.

Irwin, Inez Haynes. *The Story of Alice Paul and the National Women's Party.* Fairfax, VA: Denlingers Publishers, 1977.

Mayhall, Laura E. Nym. *The Militant Suffrage Movement: Citizenship and Resistance in Britain, 1860–1930.* Oxford and New York: Oxford University Press, 2003.

Morgan, Francesca. *Women and Patriotism in Jim Crow America.* Chapel Hill: University of North Carolina Press, 2005.

Pugh, Martin. *The March of the Women: A Revisionist Analysis of the Campaign for Women's Suffrage,* 1866–1914. Oxford: Oxford University Press, 2000.

Stevens, Doris. *Jailed for Freedom.* New York: Boni and Liveright, 1920.

Chapter 10

Brown, Nikki. *Private Politics and Public Voices: Black Women's Activism from World War I to the New Deal.* Urbana: Indiana University Press, 2006.

Catt, Carrie Chapman, and Nettie Rogers Shuler. *Woman Suffrage and Politics: The Inner Story of the Suffrage Movement.* New York: Charles Scribner's Sons, 1923.

Gidlow, Liette. "Resistance after Ratification: The Nineteenth Amendment, African American Women, and the Problem of Female Disfranchisement After 1920." *Women and Social Movements,* 2016.

Lentz-Smith, and Adriane Danette. *Freedom Struggles.* Cambridge, MA: Harvard University Press, 2010.

Park, Maud Wood. *Front Door Lobby.* Boston: Beacon Press, 1960.

Van Voris, Jacqueline. *Carrie Chapman Catt: A Public Life.* New York: Feminist Press, 1996.

Weiss, Elaine. *The Woman's Hour: The Great Fight to Win the Vote.* New York: Penguin, 2019.

Wheeler, Marjorie Spruill, ed. *Votes for Women! The Woman Suffrage Movement in Tennessee, the South, and the Nation.* Knoxville: University of Tennessee Press, 1995.

Yellin, Carol Lynn, and Janann Sherman. *The Perfect 36: Tennessee Delivers Woman Suffrage.* Vote 70 Press, 2013.

Chapter 11

Anderson, Carol. *One Person, No Vote: How Voter Suppression Is Destroying Our Democracy.* New York: Bloomsbury, 2018.

Blackwell, Unita, and JoAnne Prichard Morris. *Barefootin': Life Lessons from the Road to Freedom.* New York: Crown, 2006.

Dittmer, John. *Local People: The Struggle for Civil Rights in Mississippi.* Urbana: University of Illinois Press, 1995.

Garrow, David J. *Protest at Selma: Martin Luther King, Jr., and the Voting Rights Act of 1965.* New Haven: Yale University Press, 1978.

Gill, Tiffany M. *Beauty Shop Politics: African American Women's Activism in the Beauty Industry.* Champaign: University of Illinois Press, 2010.

Gordon, Ann Dexter, Bettye Collier-Thomas, et al. *African American Women and the Vote,* 1837–1965. Amherst: University of Massachusetts Press, 1997.

Hamlin, Françoise N. *Crossroads at Clarksdale: The Black Freedom Struggle in the Mississippi Delta after World War II*. Chapel Hill: University of North Carolina Press, 2012.

Payne, Charles M. *I've Got the Light of Freedom*. Berkeley: University of California Press, 1995.

Terborg-Penn, Rosalyn. *African American Women in the Struggle for the Vote, 1850–1920*. Bloomington: Indiana University Press, 1998.

Tyson, Timothy B. *The Blood of Emmett Till*. New York: Simon and Schuster, 2017.

White, Deborah Gray. *Too Heavy a Load: Black Women in Defense of Themselves, 1894–1994*. New York: W. W. Norton & Company, 1999.

For suggestions on additional primary source materials and a reader's guide, please visit: www.wiley.com/go/urltbd

Index

And Yet They Persisted: How American Women Won the Right to Vote, First Edition. Johanna Neuman.
© 2020 John Wiley & Sons, Inc. Published 2020 by John Wiley & Sons, Inc.
Companion website: www.wiley.com/go/Neuman